GREAT BRITAIN
AND THE UNITED STATES
1895–1903

Great Britain
and the United States
1895–1903

A. E. CAMPBELL

Fellow of Keble College, Oxford

LONGMANS

LONGMANS, GREEN AND CO LTD
6 & 7 CLIFFORD STREET, LONDON WI
605–611 LONSDALE STREET, MELBOURNE CI
443 LOCKHART ROAD, HONG KONG
ACCRA, AUCKLAND, IBADAN
KINGSTON (JAMAICA), KUALA LUMPUR
LAHORE, NAIROBI, SALISBURY (RHODESIA)
LONGMANS, SOUTHERN AFRICA (PTY) LTD
THIBAULT HOUSE, THIBAULT SQUARE, CAPE TOWN
LONGMANS, GREEN AND CO INC
119 WEST 40TH STREET, NEW YORK 18
LONGMANS, GREEN AND CO
137 BOND STREET, TORONTO 2
ORIENT LONGMANS PRIVATE LTD
CALCUTTA, BOMBAY, MADRAS
DELHI, HYDERABAD, DACCA

We are indebted to Miss Anne Wolfe for
permission to quote four lines from *The
Uncelestial City* by Humbert Wolfe, published by Messrs. Victor Gollancz Ltd.

*Printed in Great Britain by Robert MacLehose and Co. Ltd
The University Press, Glasgow*

CONTENTS

FOR
J. Y. C. AND E. C.

ACKNOWLEDGMENTS

Most of the materials on which this work is based are in public archives. To their custodians I owe the common debt of students. I must, however, acknowledge more particularly the generosity of the Marquess of Salisbury and of Earl St Aldwyn in allowing me to use their family papers, still in their hands. I am grateful to the Dean and Students of Christ Church, Oxford, for access to the Salisbury papers, presently in their keeping.

Chapter 6 first appeared, with only minor amendments, in the pages of *The Historical Journal*. I am grateful to the editor of the *Journal*, Mr J. P. T. Bury, for permission to reprint it.

It is one of the pleasures of publication to be enabled to acknowledge debts to teachers and colleagues. Among mine, two must stand out. The first is to Mr F. H. Hinsley, Fellow of St John's College, Cambridge, who supervised the doctoral thesis out of which this book has grown, and to whom I owe many and continuing kindnesses. The second is to Professor Dame Lillian Penson of Bedford College, London, who, ever since I had the good fortune to attend her graduate seminar, has been lavish of interest and criticism and encouragement.

Professor W. L. Langer of Harvard University generously advised on the early stages of the work. Mr Frank Thistlethwaite, Fellow of St John's College, Cambridge, stimulated a fuller study of American policy than I at first intended. He, Mr J. F. Lively of University College, Swansea, and Dr M. M. Robson, have all at various stages read parts of the manuscript and made such improvements as the obduracy of the author would allow. I thank them all; and with them I thank my wife, whose inability to understand the needlessly obscure did much to improve the manuscript she typed. The remaining imperfections are my own.

Finally, I am grateful to two Cambridge colleges, St John's College where, as a research student, I began this study, and King's College where, as a Fellow, I finished it. The contribution of such communities to the work of their members is more than material.

A. E. C.

Mental interests, hypotheses, postulates, so far as they are bases for human action — action which to a great extent transforms the world — help to *make* the truth which they declare. In other words, there belongs to mind, from its birth upward, a spontaneity, a vote. It is in the game, and not a mere looker-on; and its judgments of the *should-be*, its ideals, cannot be peeled off from the body of the cogitandum as if they were excrescences, or meant, at most, survival.

WILLIAM JAMES

The good qualities of this so-called Anglo-Saxon are many, and I am certainly not disposed to question them, but I here pass them over without apology, for he devotes practically the whole of his literature and fully a half of his oral discourse to celebrating them himself, and so there is no danger that they will ever be disregarded.

H. L. MENCKEN

CHAPTER ONE

Introduction

IT is generally agreed that Anglo-American relations are in some sense more than merely diplomatic, and that the two countries are connected by social, economic, cultural and historic links. That these links exist, and are more important than those between most countries, need not be questioned; but they are seldom dispassionately observed. The insistence on their reality and strength is evidence of a desire that they should be diplomatically important, influential in world politics. The desire may not be surprising; what is surprising is the readiness with which it is assumed to be fulfilled. It runs counter to a tradition of historiography long-established and still dominant, that diplomatic history can be studied as a thing apart, and that the relations of nation states proceed with little reference to, and sometimes at variance with, the emotions and the private interests of the people who live in them.

For that tradition diplomatic archives and the way in which they are used are partly responsible. Because nation states are clearly defined and rigidly separated, their relations can be studied by the historian when they are still almost contemporary. Then, however, they must be studied from partial evidence, and within the framework of the assumptions of the statesmen and diplomats concerned. These assumptions the historian necessarily largely shares even while he may be concerned to challenge some of them. When in due course additional evidence becomes available, the importance which is attached to the new sources reveals the characteristic limitations of diplomatic historiography. Not merely the nature of the materials, but the questions which historians have been trying to answer and the tradition which earlier study established, inhibit criticism and the integration of diplomatic with other history. The opening of diplomatic archives and private collections provides valuable information on the details of policy, on the opinions and motives of the men who made it, and sometimes on the disagreements which preceded its formulation. It throws no light, except in rare instances, on the fundamentals of policy, the ideas so generally shared as to pass without criticism or discussion. It is, after all, only rarely that there is a revolution in policy. Much more often fundamental changes come about as a result of slow development, almost without the notice of those engaged in the detailed work of diplomacy. It has long been a commonplace of historians that what men do not say may be as important as what they debate most seriously, but this knowledge has been little regarded by diplomatic historians.

The study of diplomacy within the limits set by its practitioners has, however, much justification. It is not merely a convention of historians. Often, perhaps always, a change in policy follows only at a distance a change in the facts of politics. Moreover, the relationship between foreign policy and other national activities varies from time to time and from place to place, both in kind and in degree. The relations between nation states have changed much less in the past centuries than has society within them. These states, which are the actors in diplomacy, have in the modern western world acquired a rigidity, a vigour and a mystique of their own so powerful as to override all other associations, and to render insignificant, where they act, all other commitments. It is this fact that is recognized by diplomatic historians and that enables them to personify nations and speak of them as if they were single-minded agents. It is simpler to treat foreign policy as a thing apart, but the treatment has the merit that sometimes it accords with the facts.

If, then, students of Anglo-American relations are to reject this convention of diplomatic history, they must justify their doing so. If there do exist links between the two countries, links extra-diplomatic but strong enough to affect the conduct of diplomacy, the fact is of the first importance. The existence of such links must be demonstrated; it cannot be assumed. Still less can it be assumed that the links are constant and permanent, and change only in the sense that certain misunderstandings which have weakened them are progressively cleared away. It need not even be assumed that any relationship is mutual—in international affairs it is not true that to every action there is an equal and opposite reaction. These points call for examination, yet the special relationship between Britain and the United States is of the kind that is assumed when it is invoked at all. Clearly, if it cannot be assumed it is hardly likely to be useful, but though the publicist has good reason for wanting to make use of it, the historian is more fortunate. He need only try to understand it.

This essay is an examination of Anglo-American relations during a period at the end of the nineteenth century which, although short, was important both in American and in world diplomacy, and was a period of marked characteristics, the zenith of political imperialism. During the years 1895 to 1903 there were three important clashes between the United States and Great Britain. In 1895 the United States asserted her right to intervene in a quarrel in which she had no direct concern between Britain and a South American state. Between 1898 and 1902 the United States wholly altered the balance of power in the Caribbean by gaining complete control over a canal which under an earlier agreement would have been international and neutral. Between 1898 and 1903 the United States forced Britain to accept at the expense of Canada her own interpretation of an earlier Anglo-Russian treaty, and did so in a way peculiarly offensive to British *amour-propre*. These were not the only matters in dispute between Britain — often representing Canada — and the United States. They *were* the most important, and they were, moreover, the most important disputes in which the United States then engaged with any major Power — from which rank one may exclude Spain. Yet to none of these aggressions did either British opinion or those responsible for British policy react with any vigour.

This, surely, is a phenomenon worth examination. These three conflicts were at least as great measured on any objective scale as those between Britain and any other Power. It is no sufficient explanation to say that none of the regions affected was an area of vital importance to Great Britain. That is true, but by what standards was importance judged? China, for example, was given a place in British policy greater than the size of the China trade warranted; nor is British policy there understandable in terms of trade and investment alone. The importance of the Far East was differently assessed by different British statesmen — Salisbury perhaps valued it as little as any — but Britain watched the activity of Russia and other Powers there closely and jealously. Though the selection was not, of course, entirely arbitrary, an area was important to Britain when British opinion chose to make it so. The British chose to regard their exclusion from the Caribbean as of no great moment. They failed to see in the rise of the United States to the status and to the pretensions of a world Power any threat to their own position, to be countered by new *ententes* or changes of policy. They appealed to the United States in defence of their position in China (and were disappointed); it never occurred to them to appeal to any of the European Powers in defence of their position in the western hemisphere. The Monroe Doctrine was enlarged against them and they hardly noticed. They continued to accept the old prohibition in the new circumstances.

This ready acquiescence of the British public in the American policy of their statesmen is the crux of the question. It may be that the policy pursued was in fact the only possible one. But if it had been unwelcome it would, even though accepted, have caused more stir. The historian could then attribute it to the statesmen responsible, the men who rode out the storms of public opinion for their country's greater good. Salisbury and Lansdowne in fact conducted their American diplomacy with skill and restraint; but it is legitimate to ask why wisdom adequate to American relations should have been less effective in European affairs. The extent to which their policy went unchallenged has allowed two different answers. The historian working in the diplomatic tradition has been apt, largely because his attention has been focused on the origins of the First World War, to treat Anglo-American relations as unimportant. In this he gets support from the diplomatic archives, which treat their problems formally and necessarily deal with points of detail. Their volume is less and their intensity lower than those of archives covering British relations with some other Powers.

This conclusion, however, is not accepted by the historian whose interests are chiefly social or cultural. The historian of the Atlantic community must regard Anglo-American relations as of

the first importance. Just at present, many who are not historians, mindful of the enormous power of the United States and her
role in two world wars, share his view. Their readiness to assume
the diplomatic consequences of extra-diplomatic links is suspect.
It usually involves the still more questionable assumption that
what happened was necessary; it smacks of Whig history. But the
diplomatic archives themselves may bear an interpretation con-
sonant with this view — that Anglo-American relations were
taken for granted. On this interpretation, it was fundamental to
politicians and diplomats that good relations with the United
States must be preserved. The principle that the United States
was the one Power Britain could not afford to cross occasioned no
argument. It was an axiom of British policy, and it is a measure of
its general acceptance that Anglo-American relations could be
handled so economically and caused so little debate. This possibility must at least be considered. For that the archives alone are
clearly not adequate, though they must be closely examined.
They are necessary, but not sufficient, evidence.

If an attempt is to be made to extend the terms of reference of
diplomatic history, where is the evidence to be found? One obvious answer must be in the intelligent (or even the unintelli-
gent) Press of the day, the writing in which partly moulds and
partly reflects informed public opinion. Newspapers and periodicals have long been standard sources for the historian, but they
have been neglected or underestimated by the diplomatic historian. They have usually been regarded either as necessary but
unsatisfactory sources of information when the archives are not
available; or as presenting such information about a negotiation
as a government has been willing to divulge, and so providing
indirect evidence on *government* policy. The first of these views
says nothing of the historian's attitude to the Press. It is determined merely by the limits of the problem in which he is interested. But the second usually implies, though it may not logically
require, the belief either that the Press is deprived of information,
or that its statements are controlled, by the government.

Often enough there is a considerable contrast between what the
Press thought was going on and what the historian, deep in the
archives, knows to have been going on, and the demonstration of
this has its intellectual satisfaction. But the study of the Press

has other uses. The results, if not the stages, of nearly all diplomatic negotiations ultimately come before the public, and there
follows a crucial period when the issues are made known and
when government policy is expounded, and challenged or accepted. It should then be revealing to study the points thought
important, the arguments used and the arguments neglected —
to study the contrast, in short, between policy as analysed by the
historian and policy as it appeared to contemporaries. Sometimes
Press accounts suffer from lack of detailed knowledge; but allowance can be made for that. Comment in the Press is usually
biased to some extent; but the bias can often be easily detected.
Even when a writer has no axe to grind there is apt to be a large
measure of rationalization in his comment. (To a lesser extent
that is true of private sources as well.) This presents a more difficult problem, but the connection between the facts and their
rationalization is important. The rationalizations of today make
the foreign policy of tomorrow.

This is to say no more than that not even in the heyday of
secret diplomacy was the Press of any country so rigorously controlled that it transmits *only* the information supplied by the
government; but the information it does give can be very various.
If one may assume that any periodical has a certain identity with
at least a section of public opinion — a fair assumption in most
European states in the late nineteenth century — the relationship between government and public opinion is nevertheless itself
a variable. Sometimes the pressure of opinion forces a change
even in foreign policy, traditionally an affair for experts and so
the area in which criticism of government is apt to be least effective. More often, a government tries to direct public opinion by
means of a bought or controlled Press; and these are only the
extremes. Before citing evidence from newspapers and periodicals,
it is important to have some idea of their connection with the
government.

In Britain at the end of the nineteenth century the connection
between Press and politics was particularly close. The standard of
the Press has probably never been higher. Those newspapers
stigmatized by Lord Salisbury as for those who could read but not
think and those who could see but not read, were only beginning,
and had as yet no great effect. Public opinion on politics was

influenced (and reflected) by the 'reputable' papers, led by *The Times*, and by the serious weeklies and monthlies. These reported and commented on foreign affairs at length, responsibly, and from excellent information. It was a British boast that unlike most continental countries Britain had a free Press. The boast caused some resentment abroad because, while foreign diplomats who took exception to the tone of the Press were apt to be reminded that it *was* free, it was perfectly well known that several papers, notably *The Times*, were something like official government organs. There was at that time, in fact, an intimacy between government and Press which made bribery or pressure needless.[1] It did not necessarily take the form of giving confidential information to the Press, still less any hand in the conduct of policy, though on occasion journalists got both. It sprang rather from the fact that in England, as in no other country, politicians and the leaders of journalism were of the same class, knew each other at school and university, met in clubs and country houses, shared the same background, prejudices and habits of thought. Britain could do without a managed Press because most of the Press was naturally identified with the activity of the ruling class.

The last sentence suggests that there was very general agreement on the main lines of British policy. There was, and this unity of opinion is a fact of the first importance. That is not to say that there was no criticism of government policy, but there was remarkably little and that little was on the means rather than on the ends of policy, or on points of detail. Above all, criticism did not take a party line. It has often been pointed out that since parties are usually defined by their attitude on home affairs, debate on foreign policy tends to cut across party lines. That was true in the 1890s. The immense confidence and equally immense prestige of Lord Salisbury were largely responsible. There was as yet little fundamental questioning of British foreign policy, little suggestion that any major alteration was necessary, and none sufficiently widespread or well-defined to make a party issue. Although it still contained a few formidable old-timers like Sir

---

[1] You cannot hope to bribe or twist
(Thank God) the British journalist;
But seeing what the man will do
Unbribed, there's no occasion to. — *Humbert Wolfe*

William Harcourt, the Liberal party had become almost indistinguishable from the Conservative. Rosebery with his Liberal imperialism had split the party, and had accepted for himself the principles on which Salisbury's policy was based. Responsible Parliamentary spokesmen were hard put to it to be both consistent and critical of their opponents; and the pedlars of foreign policy nostrums — who were not few — spoke only for themselves.

It can be forcibly argued that imperialism, with its competition among nations for limited prizes, places an undue premium on national unity and inhibits legitimate debate on foreign policy on the specious ground that debate gives an impression of weakness.[1] At any rate the general agreement on foreign policy did not, as it sometimes may, indicate that no choice was open. The country was by no means convinced that, as some maintained, isolation was now a source of danger, but those who thought it was had a variety of solutions to propose, ranging from a return to the virtue of 'little Englandism' to any of several alliances. Isolationists got a new lease of confidence from the Boer War, and when the plunge into alliance was taken the country selected for the new departure was, significantly, Japan. Alliance with Japan had the most limited effect and left Britain's European position almost unchanged.

Since Britain had, or the British thought she had, considerable room for diplomatic manoeuvre, public opinion became of importance. It would be a mistake to regard 'public opinion' as a force which governments must try to control from without. At the end of the century the ideas and emotions which affected the public also affected the members of the government. Since foreign policy was competently handled there was never, in fact, occasion for public opinion to revolt; but since there was no dominant pressure to dictate policy and silence debate, it had to be taken into account. Public opinion was the ostensible reason, and in part at least the real one, for the refusal of Salisbury and Chamberlain to conclude a canal treaty in 1899. The British were in no mood, and felt there was no need, to swallow unpalatable policies

---

[1] See especially J. A. Hobson, *Imperialism, A Study* (3rd ed., London, 1938), still the shrewdest critique, pp. 145–52.

or to select from among disagreeable alternatives. No doubt they would have done so had their desires outrun the means to gratify them; but on the whole they were satisfied with their position and their ability to maintain it, without having any great desire to extend it. They were therefore very ready to react violently to an affront. The Kruger telegram incident, when all allowance has been made for those special elements in Anglo-German relations and for British sensitivity to pressure in Africa which can be called on to explain it, shows how strongly they could resent a challenge. The absence of a similar reaction to Cleveland's Venezuela message at the same time is not to be explained by any realization that it would be unwise to oppose the United States.[1]

In these circumstances what we get from the journals of the day is not effective criticism of government policy, not evidence of governmental attempts to influence the Press through such mediums as *The Times*, but an expression of those general considerations of policy which were also accepted by members of the government and of the Foreign Office but which got no space in official documents and little in private letters. It is against this background of British politics that the evidence of the Press must be evaluated. The serious journals were freed from the need or the temptation to follow the party line, and they were notably independent. Since a large part of their stock in trade is generalization, they provide invaluable evidence of a contrast between events as they were and events as they were seen, a contrast which greatly helped the development of good Anglo-American relations.

In Anglo-American relations opinion probably played a larger part than in most diplomacy. To analyse it further here would be premature; but it is worth emphasizing that no less than in other relations the important attitude was that of the middle class. By the 1890s America was losing its value for the radical mythology. Conservatives were no less pro-American than Liberals, and it was the Labour movement, not yet effective in foreign affairs, which viewed the United States with hostility. The development

---

[1] For an admirable analysis of British opinion on the Kruger telegram, see W. L. Langer, *The Diplomacy of Imperialism, 1890–1902* (2nd ed., New York, 1951), pp. 240 ff.

of finance capitalism and the difficult position of trade unions in America were the main reasons for Labour antagonism. The liberal American political structure, long admired, was now thought inadequate. That was rational enough, but it had no direct bearing on international relations. Middle-class approval of the United States was less closely reasoned. It was not essentially the converse of the Labour attitude. It owed more to a very different concept, a concept which will be a recurring theme throughout these pages and one which, as was plain long before the First World War, was hardly consistent with class analysis — that of race.[1]

This study, then, is not primarily an account of Anglo-American diplomatic relations between 1895 and 1903. There would be small point in merely rehearsing the detail of negotiations whose outlines have long been known; many minor disputes have deliberately been given no space, and some matters not exclusively Anglo-American discussed.[2] But neither is it a study of non-diplomatic relations, an attempt to invade a small corner of the field Professor H. C. Allen has made his own in *The Anglo-American Relationship since 1783*. It does not consider exhaustively even the British end of the relationship. Rather it attempts a task which if lesser is also neglected: that of establishing, from diplomatic evidence and the comment upon it, which of these various interests, ideas and emotions — if any — affected significantly the conduct of diplomacy. Its subject, in short, is the international function and effectiveness, rather than the origin or the nature, of what has recently been called 'the Anglo-American connection'.[3] Perhaps the strength of a link may be held as important a quality as its substance.

---

[1] See Frank Thistlethwaite, 'America and Two Nations of Englishmen' in *The Virginia Quarterly Review*, XXXI, Autumn 1955; and Henry Pelling, 'The American Economy and the Foundation of the British Labour Party' in *The Economic History Review* (2nd Series), VIII, August 1955.

[2] For the most recent and thorough survey of the diplomacy of part of the period, see C. S. Campbell, Jr., *Anglo-American Understanding, 1898–1903* (Baltimore, 1957).

[3] Frank Thistlethwaite, *The Anglo-American Connection in the Early Nineteenth Century* (Philadelphia, 1959).

CHAPTER TWO

The Venezuela Crisis, 1895–1896

T H E crisis in Anglo-American relations over Venezuela arose at a time when there was much to cause Great Britain anxiety in other parts of the world. The difficulties she was facing in the Near and Far East were overshadowed towards the end of 1895 by the Jameson Raid and its results. But before that raid focused attention on South Africa, Richard Olney, then American Secretary of State, had intervened dramatically in the long-drawn-out boundary dispute between Venezuela and British Guiana, a dispute of such long standing that it had ceased to engage public attention.

Olney's despatch, dated 20 July, 1895, marked a change in American policy from the patient effort to persuade Venezuela and Great Britain to agree, to the determination to see the matter settled, by the direct action of the United States if need be. It asserted the right of the United States to intervene, invoking in support of that right the Monroe Doctrine, and maintaining that British activity in South America might, if it could be shown that she was extending her territory at the expense and against the opposition of Venezuela, be contravening that doctrine. From this it followed, said Olney, that it was the right and duty of the United States to determine the facts, and to judge whether the Monroe Doctrine was relevant. Lord Salisbury's reply, sent four months later in two despatches dated 26 November and couched in coolly superior language, was essentially a denial of the right of the United States to intervene, and of the extended interpretation which, he claimed, Olney had put on the Monroe Doctrine.[1]

---

[1] These despatches are printed in *Parliamentary Papers*, 1896, XCVII, State Papers, United States. No. 1 (1896), (C–7926), nos. 11, 15, 16.

In this diplomatic exchange Salisbury undoubtedly came off better, for much of Olney's analysis of the situation was indefensible;[1] and the final settlement of the boundary by arbitration substantially admitted Britain's territorial claims. One American scholar describes the settlement as 'a diplomatic victory for Great Britain, and . . . a severe reflection upon the unfortunate policy pursued by President Cleveland and Secretary Olney in the whole matter of the boundary controversy'.[2]

This is less than just to Olney. Plainly the boundary itself was not of great importance, and British official opinion never maintained that it was. By the time Olney entered the dispute, the only obstacle to a rapid settlement was the absurd extent of the Venezuelan claim.[3] A good deal was made at the time of British reluctance to face arbitration as being evidence of wrong-doing.[4] That reluctance had some reality, and sprang from the fear that arbitrators might be tempted to split the difference between the British and Venezuelan claims, motivated by hostility to Britain, or sympathy for the smaller nation, or the natural tendency of arbitrators to compromise. In the last resort, however, the very absurdity of the Venezuelan claim meant that any reasonable tribunal must, as that eventually set up did, concede most of the British boundary. It was claimed, too, and may well have been true, that the area of British colonization was expanding, so that if the controversy were allowed to drift Britain could only gain;[5]

---

[1] See Dexter Perkins, *The Monroe Doctrine, 1867–1907* (Baltimore, 1937), ch. iii. For contemporary American criticism, see J. B. Moore, 'The Monroe Doctrine: Its Origin and Meaning' in *The Collected Papers of John Bassett Moore* (New Haven, 1944), Vol. I, p. 334; and 'The Monroe Doctrine', ibid., Vol. II, p. 1.

[2] Charles C. Tansill, *The Foreign Policy of Thomas F. Bayard, 1885–1897* (New York, 1940), p. 776.

[3] For an immense amount of material on the historical and geographical background of the dispute, see the *Report and Accompanying Papers of the Commission Appointed by the President of the United States* (Washington, D.C., 1896–7); and *British Guiana Boundary. Arbitration with the United States of Venezuela. The Case on behalf of the Government of Her Britannic Majesty* (London, 1898).

[4] See, for example, Oscar S. Straus, 'Lord Salisbury and the Monroe Doctrine' in *Forum*, XX, February 1896, pp. 718–19; and Andrew Carnegie, 'The Venezuelan Question' in the *North American Review*, CLXII, February 1896.

[5] G. H. D. Gossip, 'England in Nicaragua and Venezuela from an American Point of View' in the *Fortnightly Review*, LXIV, December 1895.

but it is a long step to the conclusion that Britain was deliberately declining a settlement while her grip on the disputed lands grew ever stronger. The possible gains were not important, and against them must be set the endless tedious work which the dispute involved for the Foreign and Colonial Offices alike. Neither singly nor together can arguments like these bear more than the conclusion that while Britain would have been glad to end the dispute, it was intolerable to concede to Venezuela the arbitration of a claim so exorbitant. It was a matter not of interest, but of pride.

Yet Britain made precisely this concession to American demand in 1896. The land was unimportant, but the concession was not. And it was made at a time when Britain, if the strain of maintaining her international position was increasing, was nevertheless still maintaining it as firmly as ever. The year that saw Olney's despatch saw not only a swift and furious reaction to the Kruger telegram, but, a little earlier, Sir Edward Grey's famous and emphatic statement of the British position in the Nile Valley.

The development of the crisis had two main phases. The first was that during which Britain insisted on the Schomburgk line[1] as the basis for any arbitration, the second that during which, having admitted the right of America to intervene, her only stipulation was for the retention of bona fide British settlements. The change from the first to the second is the fundamental change in British policy.

Four months elapsed between Olney's 'ultimatum' of 20 July and Salisbury's reply, which was plainly intended from its tone and content to end the discussion. The first of the two despatches in which it was sent dealt only with the standing of the Monroe Doctrine in international law and with its applicability to the present dispute. The second gave Salisbury's version of the history of the boundary dispute itself, in opposition to that offered by Olney, which he, Olney, had rashly believed could not be challenged.[2] Of these two despatches the second was certainly the less important. Not that the historical debate was unimportant. The widespread American feeling that Britain was encroaching on

---

[1] A boundary line surveyed in the years 1841–3 by Sir Robert Schomburgk, surveyor and geographer, at the instance of the British government. See the *Dictionary of National Biography*, L, p. 437*b*.

[2] *Parliamentary Papers*, loc. cit., no. 11, p. 13.

Venezuela, a feeling certainly shared by both Cleveland and Olney, was principally responsible for American intervention. As Sir Michael Hicks Beach, Chancellor of the Exchequer, remarked,

> though Olney says that 'the United States may not, under existing circumstances at least, take upon itself to say which of the two parties is right and which is wrong', the whole basis on which his argument for the application of the Monroe doctrine to this case rests, is the assumption that *we* are wrong; and that we have appropriated and are appropriating Venezuelan territory.[1]

In fact, had Olney come to the conclusion that Venezuela was making unwarranted inroads on the territory of British Guiana, he would have seen no reason to intervene, holding that as against Venezuela Great Britain could well protect her own interests. The difference in power between the two protagonists and the *assumption* that Britain was wrong, provided the motive for American intervention and at the same time made that intervention far from impartial.

This did not pass unnoticed in the United States. E. L. Godkin, of the *Nation* and the *Evening Post*, with his usual vigour, pointed it out.

> The first intimation we got of what was brewing was the announcement, in the President's message, that we were opposed to 'the forcible increase by any European power of its territory on this continent'; that Great Britain was actually guilty of this offence, as it was trying 'to enlarge the area of British Guiana in derogation of the rights and against the will of Venezuela'. This positive pronouncement on the merits of the controversy had two consequences. It made it impossible for us to act as arbitrators if arbitration there should be, and it left, in our judgment, nothing to arbitrate. Great Britain was wrong and Venezuela was right.[2]

In the event Salisbury did challenge Olney's history, and argued that even were the validity of the Monroe Doctrine admitted in certain circumstances it was not relevant to this issue;

---

[1] Hicks Beach to Salisbury, 4 November, 1895: Coln St Aldwyn, St Aldwyn (Hicks Beach) Papers, PCC/33.

[2] The *Nation*, LXI, 26 December, 1895, p. 458. All this, though written of Cleveland's message, would have been equally applicable to Olney's despatch.

but that was secondary. His main retort was to minimize the importance of the doctrine itself, and to insist that while it might be a reasonable principle of American policy it could not be cited in international justification of that policy. Up to this point, in short, the British position was a complete denial of any American right to intervene, a refutation of Olney's history and international law and a blunt indication that the United States should mind her own business.[1] The subsequent history of the controversy is that of British retreat from that position.

Salisbury may well have expected that his reply to Olney would end the exchange. Every line of that reply suggests that he knew he had a cast-iron case, as indeed, by the ordinary standards of diplomacy, he had. It has been suggested, too, that he deliberately delayed his reply until it should be too late for President Cleveland to make any reference to it in his annual message to Congress on 2 December.[2] If so, he made a mistake. He was dealing not with an Old World diplomat, but with a man of exceptionally firm character and one who embodied that curious American phenomenon of moral self-righteousness to an extraordinary degree. Cleveland had no intention of letting the matter drop.

The magnitude of Salisbury's error was made clear on 17 December, when Cleveland sent a special message to Congress. Briefly, Cleveland claimed that the American government had made repeated attempts to persuade Great Britain and Venezuela to reach agreement, by arbitration or otherwise, and that these efforts had failed through British obduracy. It was now time for the United States to determine the correct boundary and to impose that line, if need be by force, against — presumably — Great Britain. As a start, he proposed to appoint an American

---

[1] *Parliamentary Papers*, loc. cit., no. 15, pp. 23–4. See the note at the end of this chapter.

[2] The long delay before Salisbury replied is certainly suspicious. Formal apology was of course made, and accepted by the American Ambassador at its face value. But Francis Bertie, the Foreign Office official concerned, offered two excuses which are, as the American reports give them, difficult to reconcile. (See Tansill, op. cit., pp. 714–15.) Lady Gwendolen Cecil, in the draft of her unpublished fifth volume (Salisbury Papers), lends the weight of her name to the suggestion that the delay may have been deliberate, in an attempt to prevent public discussion.

commission to investigate the boundary dispute, and he asked Congress to appropriate the necessary funds.[1]

With this message the Venezuela crisis became public property, and the immediate reaction in the United States was overwhelmingly in favour of Cleveland's stand. As Sir Julian Pauncefote, the British Ambassador in Washington, and always a moderate observer, wrote to Salisbury, 'The Venezuelan crisis which is raging here makes all other questions appear ancient history. Even "Behring Sea" is forgotten for awhile and nothing is heard but the voice of the Jingo bellowing out defiance to England. We must wait until the noise has subsided to judge of the real attitude of the country.'[2] No one in the United States misunderstood the import of the President's message, or doubted that it implied war unless Britain gave way. Whether they approved or disapproved of Cleveland's action, all knew what it meant. The very knowledge produced a reaction. Financiers were not anxious to face the risks of a war, especially a war with the financial centre of the world. Churchmen all over the country looked at the prospect and recoiled. Some publicists did not wait for the reaction. Godkin, normally a supporter of Cleveland, regarded his stand on Venezuela as a betrayal, a vote-catching surrender to the jingoes, and leapt into action. And Godkin was a power in the Press, a man whose views his fellow editors were eager to get before committing themselves.[3] Perhaps most important of all, the atmosphere of tension could not be maintained. Cleveland's message provided for a commission of investigation, and postponed other action till the results of its work were known. While the commission gathered evidence, the crisis faded away.[4]

---

[1] Printed in *Papers Relating to the Foreign Relations of the United States* (Washington, D.C., annual), 1895, Part I, pp. 542–5. Congress voted the money.

[2] Pauncefote to Salisbury (private), 20 December, 1895: Christ Church, Oxford, Salisbury Papers, Bound Volume, Private — America (from) 1895–8.

[3] For an excellent summary of the development of American opinion during the week following Cleveland's message, see Pauncefote to Salisbury, no. 280 (confidential), 24 December, 1895: Public Record Office, Foreign Office 80/364.

[4] This would seem to be a strong argument against those who thought that Cleveland, in part at least, engineered the crisis as an election manoeuvre. If he did, he timed it very badly.

Salisbury, who regarded the whole intervention of the United States as artificial and unnecessary, did his best to ensure that the crisis should fade. He took the view that Cleveland's message was not addressed to him and required no reply. He had answered Olney's note of July, and the next move was with Olney. The message to Congress he officially ignored. On 7 February he could write coolly to Pauncefote, 'I did not hear from the American Govt. after the delivery of our despatches till three days ago . . .';[1] and from the first he held that haste in reaching a settlement was unnecessary. Haste was repugnant to Salisbury and he avoided it when he could. In a minute of 6 January he wrote,

> . . . I do not quite agree with those who think great haste necessary. When time is given material interests tend to outweigh sentiment especially sentiment superficially held. So that the situation in U.S. ought to . . . [two words illegible]. The chances that Venezuela will commit a blunder are considerable. At present I am inclined to the view that we should play the game regularly — and wait for U.S. to answer our letters. I am speaking of official diplomatic action. There is no reason that amateur diplomacy should not have a free field.[2]

And again, on a proposal urged by Sir Thomas Sanderson, Permanent Under-Secretary at the Foreign Office, on the 9th he noted, 'Not yet, I think. I almost should be inclined to say that we should let Parliament have its say first.'[3]

Amateur diplomacy did have a free field. Between Cleveland's message to Congress of 17 December and 4 February, when Salisbury received a formal invitation from T. F. Bayard, American Ambassador in London, to supply the American commission with information,[4] several channels of communication were employed. As Salisbury wrote, 'though no open negotiation has been going on, there have been several efforts on the part of amateur diplomatists. Lord Playfair has been in communication with Mr Bayard; Mr Smalley with Mr Olney; and Mr Norman also of the

---

[1] Salisbury Papers, Bound Volume, Private — America (from and to) 1899 and 1900. [This volume in fact contains correspondence *to* the United States from 1896.]

[2] Foreign Office Library, Sanderson Papers, Vol. 1.

[3] Sanderson Papers, Vol. 1.

[4] Printed in *Parliamentary Papers*, loc. cit., no. 18.

"Daily Chronicle" has been in communication with Mr Olney.'[1]
All these efforts Salisbury regarded as unlikely to lead to anything
very much, but incapable of doing much harm; and they prevented any immediate and drastic action by the United States.
Time was of the essence in Salisbury's policy; and in this negotiation delay was helpful.

At any rate it did no harm. Possibly Cleveland's special message
gained in force from the conviction produced in his mind that
Salisbury's delay in answering Olney's despatch showed a disposition to treat the United States with contempt. Olney, who
wrote the first draft of the message, certainly had this idea. Much
later he wrote that 'in English eyes the United States was then so
completely a negligible quantity that it was believed only words
the equivalent of blows would be really effective', and as Cleveland accepted Olney's draft with only a few minor alterations, he
presumably took the same view.[2] But when the immediate furore
produced by that message had subsided, neither party showed any
disposition to move in haste. One other suspicion haunted the
American official mind — that Salisbury was stalling in the hope
that the next administration (already widely recognized as almost

---

[1] Salisbury to Pauncefote (private), 7 February, 1896. Salisbury
Papers, Bound Volume, Private — America (from and to) 1899 and
1900.

Playfair's negotiations with Bayard led to nothing but misunder-
standing. See Henry James, *Richard Olney and his Public Service*
(Boston, 1923), pp. 124–7; Tansill, op. cit., pp. 740–64; J. L. Garvin,
The Life of Joseph Chamberlain, Vol. III (London, 1934), pp. 161–3.
Since the negotiations on the American side were conducted by Bayard,
the correspondence is to be found in the National Archives, State
Department, from London, Vols. 182–3 *passim*; and Post Records,
London, Notes to the British Government, C8.5/47.

Smalley was the Washington correspondent of *The Times*. For his
activities see James, op. cit., pp. 127–9; Tansill, op. cit., pp. 746–52.
Smalley's letters to Olney are in the Library of Congress, Olney Papers,
Vols. 40–7. His offers reached Salisbury through Buckle, editor of *The
Times*. Some letters from Buckle to Salisbury are to be found in the
Salisbury Papers, unbound, Chronological series 1896, Foreign —
America; and some Cabinet memoranda based on this correspondence in
the Salisbury Papers, Bound Volume, Private — Cabinet Memoranda,
1895–1900.

Some letters from Norman to Olney, of no great interest, are in the
Olney Papers, Vols. 42–5.

[2] James, op. cit., pp. 118–19; Olney to Secretary Knox, 29 January,
1912: Olney Papers, Vol. 117.

certainly Republican) would be more reasonable than Cleveland's. This is hardly credible. Certainly if Salisbury — or Chamberlain — had any such idea it was not for lack of information to dispel it. The jingo thunder which Cleveland was accused of trying to steal was, after all, chiefly Republican.[1]

Salisbury, in fact, held that in the manner of their intervention Cleveland and Olney had put the United States in a false position, and that he need take no very active part in extricating them. Olney, on the other hand, after his despatch of July was eager to show some result, and was irritated by the delay and his feeling that it was somehow intentional. This feeling was aggravated by his increasing lack of sympathy with and distrust of Bayard, a man whom he regarded as so pro-British as to be un-American, and who was not, he thought, representing the American case with vigour or even accuracy.[2] Because of this fact, and because Venezuela had an able representative in Washington and none at all in London, Olney was anxious that negotiations should be carried on in Washington.[3] No one doubted the advantages of this arrangement, but it proved difficult to make. Bayard, who was aware of Olney's distrust and found the negotiations distasteful, announced himself as quite willing to acquiesce in having them removed from his hands, but was not prepared to suggest the

[1] Nevertheless, John Hay, some months later, when on a visit to England, was still concerned to disabuse British statesmen of this idea. On 5 August he wrote to Henry White, 'I had a long and serious talk with Sir Wm. Harcourt, by his own appointment, the day before I left, in which he referred, as you do, to the idea the Government seem to have, of the advisability of delay. I assured him, almost in your very words, that it was a great mistake; that McKinley could not yield an inch of the position taken by Cleveland. He was anxious I should let Chamberlain and Curzon know this, which opportunity aiding, I did.' (Library of Congress, Henry White Papers, Correspondence [miscellaneous] 1896.) That Salisbury saw no need for haste we have already shown; and probably Harcourt's nagging did more harm than good by merely irritating him. There is, however, no need to seek any such large reason for British delay as the hope of great advantage from it. Salisbury's habits and the pressure of business at the Foreign Office are quite enough.
[2] Bayard strongly disapproved of Olney's policy. For a highly detailed, though not unbiased, account of the differences between the two men see Tansill, op. cit., ch. xix, *passim*.
[3] James, *Richard Olney*, p. 129; and see Olney's correspondence with J. R. Roosevelt: Olney Papers, Vols. 43–7.

change formally to the British government.[1] In this his attitude was correct according to diplomatic usage. The negotiations should be carried on in London while the initiative lay with the United States; and Salisbury was determined that it should stay there. Finally, however, on 21 February, Olney suggested transferring the negotiations to Washington, and on the 27th Salisbury agreed.[2]

From this point onward the right of the United States to intervene had been fully conceded. Moreover, the Schomburgk line had been quietly dropped. As *The Times* had already remarked,

> . . . it is well known that Great Britain will not insist upon that line as a limit, having only suggested it with a view to securing, as Lord Salisbury pointed out, the retention under British rule of districts settled by British subjects and protected by the British flag for a number of years and never in any way occupied or ruled by the Venezuelans. This country is now perfectly willing to refer to arbitration the title to all unsettled territory, discarding the Schomburgk line, but excluding the settled districts. This is a large, a generous concession. . . .[3]

Only such relatively minor questions remained to be settled as whether one of the arbitrators might properly be a Venezuelan and how much territory should be arbitrated.[4] The details, of course, proved difficult to arrange, and occupied the attention of Olney and Pauncefote till July, when Pauncefote came home to England on leave and for consultation with his government.[5] While Pauncefote was in England, Chamberlain visited the United States, but though he had an interview and an exchange

---

[1] J. R. Roosevelt to Olney, 7 February, 1896: Olney Papers, Vol. 44.

[2] See below, p. 26. Olney to Sir J. Pauncefote (private and confidential), 28 February, 1896: Olney Papers, printed in James, op. cit., pp. 238–9.

[3] 6 February, 1896, p. 9, col. *d*.

[4] Pauncefote to Olney, 5 June, 1896, reporting the substance of a telegram from Salisbury: Olney Papers, Vol. 54; and see below, pp. 27–29.

[5] R. B. Mowat, *The Life of Lord Pauncefote* (London, 1929), pp. 196–7. Pauncefote also consulted the views of the Opposition. For the part played by Harcourt in an interview with Pauncefote, see A. G. Gardiner, *The Life of Sir William Harcourt* (London, 1923), Vol. II, pp. 401–2.

of correspondence with Olney (and was threatened with assassination by Irish nationalists) he did not materially affect the course
of the negotiation.[1]

On Pauncefote's return to Washington at the end of October
the final details of the terms of arbitration were settled, and
Salisbury was able to announce agreement in a speech at the Guildhall on 9 November.[2] No territory was excluded from the scope
of arbitration, but settled districts were dealt with by agreeing
that 'exclusive political control of a district, as well as actual
settlement thereof' for fifty years should make a good title.[3]
Though the award of the arbitration tribunal was not made for
more than two years, this virtually ended the case, and since the
treaty of arbitration was, in its final form, technically between
Great Britain and Venezuela, it fell safely outside the cognizance
of the United States Senate.

During the Venezuela crisis, Salisbury was dealing with two
remarkable men. Those ideas and prejudices which Olney and
Cleveland shared with their countrymen will be considered later
when public opinion is analysed, but their personal qualities were
of some importance.

Cleveland was a man the essence of whose whole character was
the most rigid honesty and the highest sense of public duty, no
man to swim with the current of his time against his own conscience.[4] As a practical politician he was certainly aware of the
political advantages of gaining credit for the administration, and
distracting attention from the 'silver war', by a vigorous 'American' foreign policy. He was the more sensitive because of the
damage done by his failure to modify British action at Corinto
earlier in the year, action which, although within the bounds of

---

[1] Garvin, *Joseph Chamberlain*, III, pp. 163–8. His correspondence
with Olney (and the reports of the Pinkerton men detailed to guard him)
are in the Olney Papers. Garvin thinks more highly of Chamberlain's
efforts; but here, as on many other points, his judgment is at fault. The
verdict of James, *Richard Olney*, pp. 132–3, must be accepted.
[2] *The Times*, 10 November, 1896, p. 4*e*.
[3] Treaty between Great Britain and Venezuela, Article IV, rule (a).
Printed in *Parliamentary Papers*, 1897, CII, State Papers, Treaty
Series. No. 5 (1897), (C–8439).
[4] The most satisfactory study of Cleveland is Allan Nevins, *Grover
Cleveland: A Study in Courage* (New York, 1932).

international law, had disturbed Cleveland and alarmed American opinion.[1] But motives like this never dominated Cleveland's policy. He had himself shown the highest standards of political morality, if not of political judgment, in his handling of Hawaii in 1893 (when he had gone firmly against the general feeling of the country); and he now felt it his duty to ensure for a small neighbouring republic treatment according to the same high standards. Moreover, to Cleveland readiness to arbitrate was almost a test of the desire for peace, and persistent British rejection of arbitration increased his suspicion of British motives and objectives, aroused by the Corinto incident and by British behaviour in Samoa. Cleveland's attitude was not typical. His stand on Venezuela was taken for reasons different from those of most of his supporters, and the fact that his policy was popular was coincidental. He genuinely thought that the Monroe Doctrine in its narrowest interpretation was infringed by the claims and practices of the British Foreign Office. He was, moreover, a man who liked action, to get a problem cleared up and off his hands, and he was irritated by delay in London and by the tone of British replies to earlier American notes. Violent action with no warning given was a political habit of Cleveland's. Long before July he was ready for some decided move.

His opinions were shared by Olney, a man of similar blunt honesty and 'dogmatic common sense',[2] a shrewd lawyer but a man tough to the point of brutality in handling a political situation, as his action in the Pullman strike had already shown. Finesse, tact, ability to compromise gracefully — the diplomatic virtues — were alien to Olney's character, and his influence on Cleveland was to drive him to more extreme courses than the President would have chosen for himself.

These were the men Salisbury faced; and their character intensified difficulties which originated in a more general American attitude. Salisbury in conducting British policy had to deal with a problem quite unlike any he faced in Europe. Neither Cleveland nor Olney was anti-British. Both of them had a high regard for

---

[1] Nevins, op. cit., p. 632. See also J. A. Sloan, 'Anglo-American Relations and the Venezuelan Boundary Dispute' in *The Hispanic American Historical Review*, XVIII, November 1938.

[2] Nevins, op. cit., p. 618.

Anglo-American friendship. On the other hand, they were not careless of American interests. Both regarded themselves as taking a wholly 'American' line (and were applauded for doing so).[1] But they were certainly interpreting national interests in a manner alien to the statesmen of Europe, introducing into their analysis of those interests a moral tone (above that of ordinary commercial morality), a conviction of being not only sensible and patriotic but 'right' that made it impossible for them to compromise, and very difficult for anyone else to negotiate. Cleveland and Olney were not manoeuvring for advantage against a rival Power. They were not merely negotiating interests, they were upholding the right. Of course, American interests marched with the dictates of justice — that was one of the rewards of virtue; but no hypocrisy was involved in their position. This approach had all sorts of awkward consequences throughout the period under consideration. It made American statesmen extremely sensitive to their own public opinion, and equally insensitive to the embarrassing force of that of other nations; and it led them greatly to overestimate the value of very small concessions, since they regarded these as compromises with the right made not as a *quid pro quo* but out of sheer goodwill. To their opponents things were apt to look very different.

The evidence for this must necessarily be a matter of tone rather than of statement, but a letter from Olney to Chamberlain shows the tone clearly enough. After disclaiming, with justice, any very strong general hostility towards Britain in America and inveighing against Bayard (though not by name) Olney continues,

> the seeming if not intentional, contumely with which the statement of our position on the Venezuelan boundary question was received by the British Foreign Office, stirred the American heart as it has not been since the Civil War. It was thus stirred because the British position seemed to be explicable only on the theory that we had no policy such as we claimed to have, or, if we had, that we had no

---

[1] See Cleveland's letter to Bayard as abstracted in Nevins, op. cit., p. 643; also Olney to Chamberlain, 28 September, 1896: Olney Papers, Vol. 62. A large number of letters of commendation for Olney (many of which, of course, give Cleveland equal credit) are in the Olney Papers, Vols. 37–9.

right to it, or, if we had, that we had neither the spirit nor the ability to stand up and defend it.[1]

This is not a politician phrase-making, not even a statesman unburdening himself to a friend in an unguarded moment; it is a private but not unconsidered letter to a member of the British government. Yet the line taken is that if the United States adopts a position she somehow has a 'right' to it; and the determination to maintain it, at any cost in offence to other powers, becomes admirable on principles which any Briton — since 'nothing could be more un-English or more contemned of Englishmen than an appearance of fawning or toadyism'[2] — must be presumed to share. Olney naturally thought his policy sound and reasonable, but there is no room in his statement for criticism of any policy, no matter how foolish or indefensible. It is excluded by the nature of the argument. The conviction that the United States was maintaining the right gave to Olney's negotiation the quality of rock. No wonder Chamberlain replied, '. . . we have been . . . mistaken in the interpretation we have placed on your despatches and on the President's message.'[3]

Though Cleveland's message, by the appointment of a commission of investigation, gave a breathing space, this attitude left no real opportunity for compromise, in spite of Pauncefote's first hopeful opinion.[4] That being so, it was as well that Great Britain showed great eagerness to reach an accommodation.[5] This eagerness was for reasons almost unconnected with the temper of the United States government. There is no evidence that Salisbury was adequately aware of the feelings of Cleveland and Olney. Even Pauncefote, shrewd and experienced, very much *persona grata* in American political and government circles, and

---

[1] Olney to Chamberlain, 28 September, 1896: Olney Papers, Vol. 62.
[2] ibid
[3] Chamberlain to Olney, 28 September, 1896: Olney Papers, Vol. 62.
[4] Pauncefote to Eric Barrington [Salisbury's private secretary] (private), 17 December, 1895: Salisbury Papers, Bound Volume, Private — America (from) 1895–8.
[5] For two typical articles on the subject, written from very different points of view, see James Bryce, 'British Feeling on the Venezuelan Question' in the *North American Review*, CLXII, February 1896; and Edward Dicey, 'Common Sense and Venezuela' in the *Nineteenth Century*, XXXIX, January 1896.

intimate enough with Olney to have an excellent basis for judgment, underestimated the moral content of the American stand,
and attributed more of the crisis to a jingo outburst than the facts
warranted. He spoke of the roar of the jingoes when the President's message was published, apparently feeling that time would
modify Cleveland's position; and in the same despatch he described an interview with Olney, overestimating the Secretary's
willingness to compromise.[1] H. O. Bax-Ironside, on the other
hand, writing on the background of the President's message,
described Olney as a jingo 'appearances notwithstanding', and by
implication likely to withdraw under pressure.[2] Even if these two
accounts of Olney were not easy to reconcile, they both suggested
a policy of reason and firmness. Either Olney would see reason, or
he would retreat before a firm stand.

Salisbury was probably more influenced by the second idea than
by the first. Not only was the tone of his November despatches
such as to indicate that he regarded the argument as closed; not
only did he probably delay the sending of those despatches of set
purpose; not only was his policy of delay based on the idea that,
given time, material interests would outweigh 'sentiment super-
ficially held', so that he made little attempt to argue the case; but
he was strongly concerned that nothing should be done or said
which might indicate a rift in Parliament or country. As a result
he was particularly worried by the activity of Sir William Harcourt, still a power in Parliament and the Liberal party though
already at odds with his colleagues over (among other things) his
adherence to a line of foreign policy which had been generally
abandoned with the retirement of Gladstone. On 7 February
Salisbury expressed this anxiety to Pauncefote, writing that
'there will probably be a recrudescence in the war feeling in
America in answer to the speeches which the Opposition will
make here. Harcourt is likely to be very vehement'.[3] This danger

---

[1] Pauncefote to Salisbury (private), 20 December, 1895: Salisbury
Papers, Bound Volume, Private — America (from) 1895–8.

[2] Bax-Ironside was Second Secretary of the British Embassy in Washington. His memorandum (very confidential) was forwarded by Pauncefote in another letter to Salisbury of 20 December, 1895: Salisbury
Papers, loc. cit.

[3] Salisbury Papers, Bound Volume, Private — America (from and to)
1899 and 1900.

was avoided, at least for a time, by getting Asquith to warn Harcourt that Rosebery and others

> think that it is very important to avoid saying anything that can stiffen the backs of the American jingoes — as, e.g. anything that would seem to admit that a case had actually arisen in Venezuela affecting the interests of the U.S. and so coming within the Monroe doctrine; or anything that would exclude the question of the character and extent of the actual occupation on both sides from the proposed arbitration.[1]

It is plain from all this that in Salisbury's eyes the action of Cleveland and Olney was indefensible. It was no part of British policy to make things more uncomfortable than they need be, and if the jingo hue and cry were given a chance to die down all would yet be well. From the logic of this position as well as from Salisbury's temperament sprang his disinclination to haste, already noted; but this was strengthened by his desire that the lead in negotiation should be taken by the United States. It was not merely Bayard's tiresome sense of protocol which prevented Olney from moving the negotiations to Washington. Salisbury was not anxious to help. When J. R. Roosevelt, the First Secretary of the American Embassy, finally asked Bertie '*avec intention*' why the British government did not work through Pauncefote, and this question was passed on to Salisbury, he minuted in reply, 'Obviously because then we should have to make the proposals — and it is much better to receive them.'[2]

That, however, is the tactics of policy — delay, play a waiting game, give American jingoes no encouragement. This Salisbury could do very well indeed; but the strategy was already determined, and it was solidly one of concession to the United States. There was no longer any question of rejecting American intervention and denying the relevance of the Monroe Doctrine. That had been the tone of Salisbury's reply to Olney, but from the moment of Cleveland's message, American intervention was accepted. On 20 December, Pauncefote was reporting to Salis-

---

[1] Quoted in Gardiner, *Life of Harcourt*, II, p. 400.
[2] Minute by Salisbury on a memorandum by Barrington, 11 February, 1896: Salisbury Papers, Bound Volume, Private — Private Secretary and Memoranda 1895–1900.

bury, 'Mr Olney seemed very anxious when I read Your Lord-
ship's despatches to him, and he asked me whether I viewed them
as an absolute refusal to refer the whole controversy to arbitration.
That, I said, was quite apparent from the despatches . . .'; but
he added that he went on to suggest to Olney that the United
States might reasonably advise Venezuela to accept restricted
arbitration, which would probably settle the whole dispute, and
would at worst do no harm.[1] Already this seems to involve a *de
facto* acceptance of American standing in the dispute. And in
February Salisbury himself wrote '. . . though we would not bind
ourselves not to arbitrate the *unsettled* districts within the Schomburgk line, we certainly could not see our way to arbitrate districts that had been long settled. This point the U.S. have never
been willing to concede . . .'.[2] Setting aside the question of
whether the emphasis on settled districts rather than insistence on
the Schomburgk line itself represents a change in British policy
(though it does), it is evident that the United States had been
accepted as an interested party, indeed as *the* interested party.
From now on Venezuela became almost unimportant. The question now was how much territory Britain could save from arbitration and on what grounds. The difference between this reaction
and that to the German effort to support the Transvaal government has been often enough noted, but can hardly be over-
emphasized. It illumines British policy in the Americas as nothing
else does.

In the negotiations that followed, Great Britain made almost
all the concessions, and all the important ones. The initial British
position was that expressed by Salisbury in the quotation above.
They were willing to submit to arbitration a good deal of land to
which they believed they had as much right 'as the United States
have to the State of Maine',[3] but insisted that the rights and property of British subjects who had settled in good faith on land in
the boundary area must be protected by removing these 'settled

---

[1] Pauncefote to Salisbury (private), 20 December, 1895: Salisbury
Papers, Bound Volume, Private — America (from) 1895–8.
[2] Salisbury to Pauncefote (private), 7 February, 1896: Salisbury
Papers, Bound Volume, Private — America (from and to) 1899 and
1900.
[3] Chamberlain to Olney, 9 September, 1896: Olney Papers, Vol. 61.

districts' from the scope of the arbitration. The American reply was that settled districts could not be removed from arbitration without a preliminary enquiry to decide what constituted settlement. This, they said, would prolong the proceedings indefinitely; and further, any rule agreed for the guidance of a preliminary investigating body could equally be made binding on the court of arbitration itself. A more fundamental argument was that the mere fact that British subjects had settled on disputed ground in good faith did not give them a valid title to it. If it were found that the land belonged to Venezuela (which had consistently been laying claim to it), dispossessed Britons might have a claim against their own government for compensation, but none against Venezuela. This point Great Britain conceded. In the final instrument of arbitration none of the disputed territory was excluded from the scope of the court's enquiry.

Some rules for the guidance of the court were, however, laid down; and about these the next struggle took place. If Britain could obtain that the court should give weight to occupation or political control of any area in making its decision as to ownership, the interests for which Great Britain was contending — 'men not land' in Chamberlain's phrase — might yet be safeguarded. The question then was, how long should it be before occupation or control gave any prescriptive right? The British began by suggesting ten years. Olney countered with sixty. The British moved up to thirty. Storrow, counsel for Venezuela, and by this time Olney's chief adviser in the affair, came down to forty. But there was a difficulty. A *modus vivendi* had been reached in 1850; and Salisbury had committed himself to the position (legally sound) that no possession by Venezuela since then could have any validity.[1] 'Lord Salisbury would not be willing to depart from it; nor should we', wrote Storrow.[2] The date 1850 finally dictated the length of time required for prescriptive right, and fifty years was agreed. This concession was certainly inherent in the position taken by Salisbury in his first despatch, but nevertheless fifty

---

[1] Salisbury to Pauncefote, 26 November, 1895. Printed in *Parliamentary Papers*, 1896, XCVII, State Papers, United States. No. 1 (1896), (C–7926), no. 16.

[2] Storrow to Olney, no date (early October 1896): Olney Papers, Vol. 63.

years is much longer than ten, and in admitting so long a time as necessary to establish ownership, Britain was giving up the major part of what had been her contention ever since the tacit abandonment of the Schomburgk line itself. With this concession it is fair to say that the United States won a complete diplomatic victory. The United States had no interest in the position of the boundary finally fixed, which was substantially that of the British claim.

The details of the negotiation are entirely secondary in importance to the admission of the right of the United States to intervene, and have therefore been dealt with in summary fashion. Only two points need be emphasized: the completeness of the British retreat, and the extreme legalism of the terms in which the debate was conducted. The second of these points must be postponed; but the first calls for some examination here.

The British position was to all appearances a reasonably strong one. In population and industrial potential the United States was already ahead, but in military and especially, of course, in naval power, there was as yet no comparison between the two countries. Canada could not be adequately defended; but against that, the cities of the Atlantic coast were exceptionally vulnerable to naval bombardment. Some aggressive naval opinion in Britain favoured this kind of use of sea power, and America realized with some shock that she had become involved with the only Great Power against which the Atlantic was no adequate defence. In 1895–6 the United States possessed only three first-class battleships, though three others were building. The agitation for a larger American navy, and the endorsement of the battle-fleet theory of naval strategy which sprang from the work of Mahan, had been set back by the financial panic and depression of 1893, and although they had been revived the results did not yet show.[1] As John Bassett Moore, the distinguished international lawyer, remarked, 'Our own demagogues . . . are professing to court a conflict with the power which can do us the most harm, but which

---

[1] *Report of the Secretary of the Navy* (Washington, D.C., annual), 1895; H. and M. Sprout, *The Rise of American Naval Power, 1776–1918* (Princeton, 1946), pp. 219–20.

. . . is of all powers in the world at least as desirous as any to keep the peace with us.'[1]

Britain's position was not so strong as it looked. The weakness of the United States became less important in face of the fact that Britain was unable to strengthen her squadrons in American waters. At that time her margin of superiority over the Dual Alliance alone was too slender to enable her to spare ships, even had the international situation in Europe been less tense. The United States, in fact, was benefiting from the growing naval rivalry of Europe, but also from a more fundamental strategic advantage. Britain's undisputed command of the sea had sprung, more than from any other single factor, from her position in the narrow seas, enabling her to oppose the main naval strength of any European rival with all the advantages given her by that position. A victory over their battle-fleets would make the continued existence of French, or even of Russian, squadrons on outlying stations unimportant.

The United States navy created, as did the Japanese navy, an entirely different problem. Here, a British overseas squadron would have to match a home fleet, fighting in its own waters and with all the advantages of bases, supplies and reserves. This was a strategic disadvantage that could not have been met for long, even had the European balance of power allowed Britain greater freedom of choice. The United States may have been fortunate in that the Venezuelan crisis arose at a time when Britain was particularly hard pressed; but the rise of America and Japan, more even than that of Germany, marked the end of the old order of British sea power. The claim of the United States to hegemony in the Western hemisphere was not one which Britain, or any other single European Power, could have disputed for long.

In 1895 the end of British sea power was not yet. It was still possible to maintain that British moderation over the Cleveland message sprang from consciousness of strength, not weakness.[2] The Venezuela crisis did not produce a naval scare. The policy of abandonment of naval control of the Caribbean was, neverthe-

[1] J. B. Moore to Bayard, 26 November, 1895. Quoted in Tansill, *Foreign Policy of Bayard*, p. 715, note 216.
[2] See 'Mr Goschen on the Naval Estimates', in *The Spectator*, LXXVI, 14 March, 1896, p. 365.

less, already well under way. An Admiralty memorandum for the Cabinet of December 1899 recites the relative decline in strength of the British North America and West Indies Squadron, and concludes, 'Our squadron, which in 1889 was superior to that of the United States, is now in 1899 completely outclassed by them.'[1] This is not to imply that this was so in 1895–6, but does indicate that no attempt was made to match the growth of American naval power. The important point is that no attempt seems to have been made in 1895 to consider the naval implications of resisting the United States.

One letter of Salisbury's might suggest otherwise. On 2 January, 1896, he wrote to Hicks Beach,

> I was preparing to indite to you an indignant letter, on the hollowness of the Admiralty reasons for their vast expenditures. I do not believe that the junction of Russia and France in a maritime war is at all a probable contingency. . . . But recent events have introduced a new element into the calculation. A war with America — not this year but in the not distant future — has become something more than a possibility. . . .

Hicks Beach replied, 'I agree — With present feeling in U.S., and the Emperor telegraphing to Kruger, we have to think of other matters besides a Franco-Russian alliance against us.'[2] In the light of later events, however, it seems possible that Salisbury was overstating an argument he thought likely to weigh with Hicks Beach, a Chancellor whose tenacious refusal to spend money was notorious and often a trial to his colleagues.

The discussion so far has suggested that the Venezuela dispute concerned only Great Britain and the United States, and that the major European Powers were affected only in so far as they might seize an opportunity to aggrandize themselves if these two countries became involved. This assumption is an obvious one to make after reading the course of the dispute, for neither country made any effort to enlarge the terms of reference or to introduce European Powers into the controversy. Yet to conduct the dispute in a vacuum, so to speak, was not so obvious a decision as it later appeared. The results of the negotiation, after all, were not

---

[1] St Aldwyn Papers, PC/PP/74.
[2] St Aldwyn Papers, PCC/69 and PCC/33.

without interest to several other Powers, and European opinion
was generally favourable to Britain. Even while the Press, both
directed and independent, of Austria and Germany was displaying hostility towards British policy in other fields, it supported
the British stand on Venezuela.[1] Indeed, all European Powers
with the exception of Russia were solidly hostile to American
pretensions.

Russia was hardly a reliable supporter of the United States.
The possibility of Russian advance in Asia if Britain became
seriously involved elsewhere gave Salisbury's Cabinet some concern; but Breckenridge, American Ambassador at St Petersburg,
reporting home on Russian intentions, argued that while Russia
was certainly friendly to the United States and not unwilling to
see Britain weakened, she would not be prepared to do anything
herself, since her internal situation was not good. Her use to the
United States would at best be confined to opposing a European
combination against that country.[2]

On the other side there was the possibility of German support
for Britain. It probably disappeared after the Kruger telegram,
when the violence of public reaction meant that no government
could have considered a German alliance against the United
States; but the very violence of that public reaction was due at
least in part to disappointment in the conduct of Germany,
generally regarded as a friendly state. To view the same phenomenon from the German angle, it is probable that the Kruger
telegram was not evidence of German hostility to Britain but an
attempt at 'kicking Britain into friendship'.[3] Of all European
Powers Germany was most widely suspected of harbouring de-

---

[1] Sir F. Lascelles (in Berlin) to Salisbury, no. 318, 24 December, 1895;
Sir E. Monson (in Vienna) to Salisbury, no. 393 (confidential), 27
December, 1895: P.R.O., FO 80/364.

[2] Breckenridge to Olney, 14 and 16 January, 1896: Olney Papers,
Vol. 43. Russia had a tradition of friendship for the United States, and
no interest in the Western hemisphere.

[3] 'The German Emperor's Policy' in *The Spectator*, LXXVI, 11
January, 1896, p. 41. For a general appreciation of the Kruger telegram
in German policy, see Langer, *Diplomacy of Imperialism*, pp. 232–47;
and A. J. P. Taylor, *The Struggle for Mastery in Europe, 1848–1918*
(Oxford, 1954), pp. 363–6. The Germans apparently grossly miscalcu-
lated the importance of South Africa in British imperial policy, and selected
it for their gesture because they thought it relatively unimportant.

signs on South America as a field for that colonialism which it was too late for her to exercise elsewhere. Not merely because the Cleveland message was outrageous by the standards of diplomatic protocol, but because it was to Germany's interest to see the United States rebuffed, Germany might well have been expected to support Britain.

The French Press, too, was hostile to American pretensions, and it is at least arguable that the Jameson Raid and its results played a dual role, not merely distracting British attention from the Cleveland message, but distracting European attention from what was widely interpreted as an act of effrontery on the part of the United States to 'deliberate brigandage'[1] on that of Britain. In general, there is at least enough evidence to suggest that the possibility of Continental pressure on the United States was one that could not be ignored, not merely because informed Continental opinion held that the United States was stretching the Monroe Doctrine very far indeed, but because the rise of a new world Power was, as later events were to make clear, inimical to the interests of all major Powers except Britain. The abortive attempts to organize Europe against the United States at the time of the Spanish-American War suggest that something of the kind might equally well have developed two years earlier.

The United States, of course, ignored this possibility — that follows from the very logic of the position taken by Cleveland and Olney. When one acts for reasons of self-interest, calculation is in order; but when he acts in the genuine belief that the action is for the furtherance of justice, it is not — that was then implicit in the *naïveté* of American thinking on foreign policy. There is nothing in Olney's papers to lead one to suppose that a consideration of the possible European repercussions of Cleveland's message played any part in affecting his actions.

As the event proved, his calculation, or lack of it, was quite correct. Britain showed no disposition to extend the terms of the conflict or to try to gain European backing for her position. In part, this may have been because the Kruger telegram and its violent repercussions made the acceptance of support from

---

[1] *Le Temps* (Paris), 2 January, 1896. Quoted by Langer, op. cit., p. 247.

Germany impossible. Cleveland's message came with a shock of surprise even to Salisbury, and before anyone had any time to consider how best to deal with it the Kruger telegram had distracted attention. After that the alternatives were to settle with Germany or to settle with the United States, and they were hardly real alternatives. British interests lay in Africa, not in British Guiana.

But Salisbury, after all, spent four months meditating his reply to Olney; and if he hoped to end the controversy at a blow, he must have considered what might happen if he failed to do so. Yet nowhere in Salisbury's papers is there any hint that he considered extending the scope of the argument. Salisbury was a reticent man, but it is difficult to believe that this silence was that of mere reticence.

Salisbury's determination to treat the quarrel as a purely Anglo-American one was shared by his colleagues. And this for several reasons. Britain was at this time a satiated Power. She had no expansive intentions anywhere in the western hemisphere. Senator Lodge's idea that she was steadily turning the Caribbean into a British lake and was about to encircle the United States from north and south is no more than another example of the grotesque errors of political judgment of which Lodge was capable.[1] Therefore South America was, unlike South Africa, an area in which Britain was willing to abdicate, so far as that could be done without loss of prestige. The most important immediate consideration preventing a settlement was to avoid giving the Canadians and other interested parties to suspect Britain of weighing their interests lightly against the friendship of the United States. This consideration weighed most heavily with Chamberlain, responsible as Colonial Secretary for defending the interests of British Guiana, and the man with the largest concept of empire. Harcourt, who held exactly the opposite view on that point though they had a good deal in common, thought that he was the member of the government standing in the way of agreement;[2] and Chamberlain certainly made an intensive effort to wring concessions from Olney. At the same time, his policy was modified, as Salisbury's was not, by a genuine if not very know-

---

[1] H. C. Lodge, 'England, Venezuela, and the Monroe Doctrine' in the *North American Review*, CLX, June 1895.

[2] Gardiner, *Life of Harcourt*, II, pp. 397, 401.

ledgeable sympathy with America and Americans. His second
wife was an American; and, his background that not of aristo-
cracy but of the tough radical politics of Birmingham, he found
America congenial as Salisbury never did. His various remarks,
often indiscreet, of the 'blood is thicker than water' kind are too
well known to need quoting here;[1] and, himself liable to shock
the delicate balance of public opinion with utterances from the
heart rather than from the head, he was not to be put off by
breaches of diplomatic etiquette.

To Salisbury the ideas which affected Chamberlain were of
small importance. His imperialism was of an older kind, owing
little to ideas of race expansion or the white man's burden, always
tested against a clearly defined concept of national interest, and
secondary to the maintenance of the balance of power. The preconceptions and habits of mind he carried over from the earlier
years in which he had got his diplomatic training led him to
minimize the importance of questions not intimately connected
with the European balance, and to regard events outside Europe
and the Near East as not very momentous. Salisbury therefore
regarded the Venezuela crisis as unimportant.

He might have considered another policy. It was already a
widely held theory in Britain that Germany, eager to embark on
an imperial career, regarded Britain with jealous rivalry as the
Power that stood in the way, and that the success of German
policy could only be achieved at the expense of Britain. It was
further pointed out, however, that South America, and especially
Brazil, where Germans were already settling in large numbers,
was the only area in which Germany could establish an empire
without directly conflicting with Britain. The Power immediately
concerned in keeping Germany out of the Americas was the
United States; and from this it was a small step to the conclusion
that Britain's rivalry with Germany really originated in British
support of the Monroe Doctrine, or could be eased by abandonment of that support. The Venezuela crisis — if one may
ignore for the moment the Kruger telegram and its unfortunate

---

[1] See Alexander Mackintosh, *Joseph Chamberlain, an Honest Bio-
graphy* (London, 1906), ch. xxix, *passim*; also L. M. Gelber, *The Rise of
Anglo-American Friendship, a Study of World Politics 1898–1906*
(London, 1938), chs. i and ii, *passim*.

consequences — offered an opportunity for Germany and Britain to work together. If British friendship for America offended Germany and gained nothing, an alternative line-up of Britain and Germany might be preferable.

What prevented Salisbury from following out this line of reasoning, apart from that aversion to change and action which even friendly critics noticed[1] was his concentration on the European balance of power, and more particularly his conviction that Germany and Britain were in competition to hold that balance. As the United States began to extend her interests and her pretensions beyond her own borders, it was with Great Britain that she came into contact and conflict; and a series of diplomatic incidents was the result. On the other hand, if Salisbury was right, the emergence of the United States as a great Power was in a large sense likely to be advantageous to Britain, with no great interest in further expansion and beginning to feel the pressure of French, German, and Russian imperialism. If the United States were not provoked into active hostility, it was a fair British calculation that, given time and encouragement, historical accident would make her policy more favourable to Britain than not. From this point of view, interference with British Guiana had to be set against the warning given to other colonizing Powers that South America was not open. Germany in South America would be more menacing to the British position than the United States in jingo mood. The ambivalence of British policy was due to a conflict of immediate and long-range interests.

This kind of long-range calculation fits well with all we know of Salisbury's character, though evidence for his reasoning as opposed to his policy is slight. The attitude of the country, however, owed little to calculation. It had far more in common with Chamberlain's than with Salisbury's approach.

Public opinion was particularly important in Anglo-American relations at this time, for reasons already indicated, and can be particularly easily studied. Merely because the United States still came into contact with Great Britain — still came into contact with any Great Power — only in the most peripheral way,

---

[1] See 'Lord Salisbury at the Guildhall' in *The Spectator*, LXXVII, 14 November, 1896, p. 664.

both parties to the dispute had, in terms of power politics, a great deal of room for manoeuvre; and where that room was limited it was limited as much by the prejudices of public opinion as by any other factor. The value of the despatches in *The Times* in this context is not that we know them to have been inspired and to have been based on information which Smalley got from Olney and sent home for the information of both Salisbury and the public, though that is of interest. It is that *The Times*, hardly more than its less official but well-informed and thoughtful rivals, expressed admirably the sort of prejudices and considerations on which Salisbury's colleagues if not he himself acted; they reflected as well as informed the opinions of educated England, and, as the publicity of this crisis makes clear, the information they gave was itself shaped in large measure by preconceived ideas. These ideas can most usefully be studied during two comparatively brief periods: the month or so after Cleveland's message broke on the world, when there was a real war scare; and the period of the actual settlement in October 1896. Between these limiting periods the considerable weight of British government activity was directed towards keeping the matter out of the papers and preventing questions from being asked in Parliament.

Parliament was not in session when Cleveland's message was made public; not till March 1896 is there any reference in Hansard to the dispute. By then, of course, the crisis was already fading. Sir E. Ashmead-Bartlett asked mildly whether there was any truth in a report by *The Times* on 12 March that the question had been settled, and was told there was not. On 23 April, the government was tackled more seriously. Henry Labouchere, the noted radical, made a serious attempt to get information about the state of the negotiations, but Curzon, then Parliamentary Under-Secretary of State for Foreign Affairs, declined to make any statement beyond admitting that they were going on, a piece of reticence which drove Harcourt himself to give notice of a question. When it came, however, though it got attention from Arthur Balfour, Harcourt's question fell very flat. He asked 'whether arrangements have been made, or will without delay be concluded, with the government of the United States for the settlement by arbitration of the matters in dispute respecting the boundary of Venezuela'. Harcourt was always treated with more deference than lesser men, but nevertheless Balfour turned his question. 'I am afraid that I cannot give the right hon. Gentleman further information, and the right hon. Gentleman, I am sure, will agree with me that to discuss negotiations that are still being conducted would not be expedient. ["hear, hear!"]'[1]

Five questions asked in June showed the anxiety of the House for arbitration, and that agreement should be reached quickly, but no desire to embarrass the government; except perhaps the last, which asked 'whether the Venezuelan government has repeatedly offered to submit the whole matter in dispute to arbitration; and, if so, why these offers have not been accepted by Her Majesty's government'. The form of the question enabled Curzon to evade it — no recent negotiations with Venezuela had taken place, only with the United States — but all these questions make it clear that such pressure as there was on the government was not because it had given way too readily, but because it had not given way readily enough.[2]

As indicated above, Salisbury was anxious that the matter should not become a party issue, and in fact the Opposition behaved with great discretion; but since he was willing to accept United States intervention, it was agreeable to find Parliament and the country so ready to follow him. This explains his willingness to 'let Parliament have its say first'. Shortly before Parliament adjourned, he took the unusual step of laying papers on an incomplete negotiation, and felt called upon to defend his action.

> We have need [he said], to know what is the trend of public opinion on these matters. We desire, in a question which is certainly not one of Party, that the best intellects that we have on both sides should apply themselves to a matter that affects the welfare of the human race in a singular degree, and especially the good relations of a State with which we so desire to be on good terms as the United States of America.[3]

From the context it appears that Salisbury was speaking of the negotiations for a general arbitration agreement, which were

---

[1] *The Parliamentary Debates* (Fourth Series), 1896, XXXVIII, p. 784, XXXIX, pp. 1527, 1736.
[2] ibid., XLI, pp. 848, 1338, 1432, XLII, p. 265.
[3] ibid., XLIII, p. 6.

being conducted simultaneously with those on Venezuela; but the papers laid were 'Venezuela, No. 3 (1896)' and dealt exclusively with the more specific controversy. The conjunction of the two negotiations made it easier for Salisbury to claim that that on Venezuela was advancing 'with entire friendliness on the part of both Governments'; but he went further when he said that 'the United States has assumed the attitude of the friend of Venezuela, and we have been rather glad to negotiate with the United States rather than with Venezuela', and emphasized his point by adding that 'the United States has shown a disposition to adopt as its own questions affecting many Republics in South America. I do not in the least quarrel with that disposition . . .'.[1] His statement was received with cheers. Finally, in August, Balfour was able to reply to a question from Harcourt, 'The latest proposals of Mr Olney are still under consideration by the government, and are regarded by them as opening the way to an equitable settlement. ["Hear, hear!"] The government have every expectation that the pending negotiations will lead to an early and satisfactory result. [Cheers.]'[2]

If Hansard is only mildly enlightening, the Press is more so. Both Cleveland and Salisbury had supporters and opponents at home, all able to express their opinions with vigour. On the whole, however, British opinion was remarkably uniform. Perhaps its tenor cannot be better expressed than in this private letter from James Bryce to Theodore Roosevelt.

The news of this so-called 'war-scare' met us at Madeira on our way home, and I have not yet had time to read the dispatches nor what passed in Congress nor what the papers have said. But I confess myself astonished at four things.

(1) The apparent existence of ill-will towards Britain in a large part of your population. What in the world is the reason? There is nothing but friendliness on this side.

(2) The notion that we want to interfere with American rights or with the balance of power in the New World. Nothing further [*sic*] from people's minds here. Our hands are more than sufficiently full elsewhere.

(3) The sympathy with a corrupt military tyranny like that of

---

[1] *The Parliamentary Debates*, (Fourth Series), 1896, XLIII, pp. 2, 5.
[2] ibid., XLIV, p. 851.

Venezuela, a government which our Foreign Office has found it not possible to deal with. They are not a civilized government at all.

(4) The total want of all diplomatic courtesy and decorum shown by Cleveland and the State Department — according to what I hear — for I have not read the papers.

All these things amaze me so much that I should be grateful for your remarks on them.

As to the Monroe Doctrine, I have never been able to see how it applies at all to such a case as this: If the U.S. are going to assume a protectorate over all Central and South America, and see that these so-called Republics behave like civilized States, that is another matter. Then other countries will know whom they have to deal with. But the U.S. have not done so — and certainly that is not the Monroe Doctrine — This by the way, however. The subject is too big a one for a letter.

People here seem to have been taken utterly by surprise. Not one man out of ten in the House of Commons even knew there was such a thing as a Venezuelan question pending.[1]

Bryce expressed perfectly the first reaction of the British public, based on general ignorance that there was a Venezuela question — astonishment at the tone and content of Cleveland's message, surprise that there *was* a Venezuelan side to the case, distress that apparently Americans did not feel wholly well disposed towards them, and complete lack of interest in South America.

The pattern of British contrasted sharply with that of American thinking. Olney had his supporters and his critics; Salisbury had his. It might be supposed that an American opponent of Olney would see eye to eye with a British supporter of Salisbury, objecting to gratuitous American intervention in a dispute between two other states; and roughly speaking, this was so. But Olney's supporters did not have anything in common with Salisbury's critics. The arbitration question with which that of the Venezuela boundary became connected confused the issue and affected the terms of the discussion. Salisbury's critics, in general, attacked him for

---

[1] 1 January, 1896. Printed in H. A. L. Fisher, *James Bryce (Viscount Bryce of Dechmont, O.M.)* (New York, 1927), Vol. I, pp. 318–19. Bryce also laid this view before the American public with an article in the *North American Review*, CLXII, January 1896 on 'British Feeling on the Venezuelan Question'.

opposing an unlimited arbitration, both because it would avoid a conflict with the United States, and because they believed in arbitration. Olney's supporters had only the most secondary interest in arbitration — their real interest was in the strong defence of American interests, widely interpreted. From this fact it is clear just how wide apart these two opponents were. What divided them was not the different national interests they supported, but the different stages of imperialism they represented.

Represented is the word, for it would be impossible to describe either Olney or Salisbury as an imperialist without many reservations. Olney trod firmly on any attempts to extend American activity in the Caribbean;[1] he claimed to have narrowed rather than expanded the scope of the Monroe Doctrine;[2] and he later defended his action in Venezuela on grounds which owe nothing to imperialism.[3] Salisbury was all too vulnerable to the charge of lack of interest in British overseas possessions. But both men were supported, when they were supported, by imperialists, and opposed, when they were opposed, by anti-imperialists. The jingoes whom Godkin pictured circling hand in hand round Olney and Cleveland[4] were not doing so because Olney had interpreted the Monroe Doctrine more narrowly than before. They thought he had widened it and approved his act. There is no need to analyse American opinion in detail in order to say that the vast majority of the country supported Olney, viewing war with England not with enthusiasm but as, though regrettable, necessary if there were no other way of establishing the paramount position of the United States in the western hemisphere. Breckenridge for instance, writing to Olney on the attitude of

---

[1] James, *Richard Olney*, pp. 167–70.

[2] 'It is sometimes asserted that this administration by its stand upon the Venezuela boundary question enlarged the Monroe Doctrine. Nothing could be further from the truth. It, in reality, defined it and confined its application within narrower limits than had ever been fixed by previous administrations or public men.' Olney to A. E. Keet (editor of the *Forum*), 15 January, 1897: Olney Papers, Vol. 71.

[3] Olney's explanation, as given to R. H. Dana, is quoted in James, *Richard Olney*, p. 138. See also Olney to Knox, 29 January, 1912: Olney Papers, Vol. 117.

[4] The *Nation*, LXI, 26 December, 1895, p. 456.

D

Russia, reported himself as saying to the Emperor that 'Russia had given us the most conclusive evidence in disposing of Alaska that she would never contest or envy our influence upon our continent, and that it was of course to be regretted that other powers were not as reasonable and generous about our logical and necessary sphere of influence'.[1] Or take Andrew Carnegie, himself a strong arbitration man but one who regarded both America and Britain as given to land-grabbing:

> Great Britain, as far as the other half of her race is concerned, may still acquire any land she can in Europe, Asia and Africa, and Americans will regard the spread of her people with pride and satisfaction, if she will kindly permit them hereafter, to superintend territorial changes upon the American continent, and uphold the doctrine of peaceful arbitration upon it. Nor can she fairly grudge her race here one continent when she has freedom to roam over three.[2]

This last quotation illustrates not only the assertion of the American right to superintend change on her own continent, but some of the ideas which enabled Britain to retreat so rapidly and with so little sense of injury. Essential to all these ideas was the sense of kinship which made the prospect of war so intolerable that almost any solution was preferable. This provided a peculiarly strong motive for finding a solution; but more, it allowed of some arguments which could not have been used had any other country been concerned, and greatly modified others.

A man like Harcourt, for instance, was enabled to insist from the first that the whole demand should be conceded, and that if one were going to arbitrate there was no point in debating details. Harcourt argued that if Britain had a good case there was no reason for not submitting it to an impartial tribunal.[3] This was specious reasoning. It accepted without demur the right of the United States to intervene and implied that the intervention was disinterested. Harcourt was not typical: most agreed that un-

---

[1] 14 January, 1896: Olney Papers, Vol. 43.

[2] Andrew Carnegie, 'The Venezuelan Question' in the *North American Review*, CLXII, February 1896, pp. 141–2.

[3] See his speeches at Bournemouth and London, reported in *The Times*, 12 March, 1896, p. 7c and 6 May, 1896, p. 12b.

limited arbitration was out of the question. Even these, however, readily agreed that to protect the rights of settlers on disputed ground was all that was necessary, and did not closely inspect the final arrangements for that purpose.

Harcourt went further when he urged, 'I have very little doubt that there are plenty of malign influences at work in U.S. to promote war. That is all the more reason why we should not halt or stumble on the road to peace. . . .'[1] With this everyone agreed, though opinion might differ on the best way of reaching the end. It was widely reported that there was a large party in the United States spoiling for a fight.

> In this country [said *The Saturday Review*], the party which desires war with the United States could be put into a first-class carriage, if such a party exists at all; in the United States, on the other hand, there is beyond doubt a very large and powerful party which does deliberately desire war with somebody, and by preference with the United Kingdom. This latter party is happily not by any means identical with the people of the United States; but one thing only is required to make it so: namely a good cause. . . .[2]

From this it followed that great pains should be taken to deny the war party in the States a good cause. The existence of the party was known, but it was not resented or taken as evidence of real hostility. It was treated as an embarrassing circumstance with which Cleveland and Olney had to deal and which would stiffen their policy and that of their successors. By implication the views of the war party were not really those of the American people. Moreover, warmongers and jingoes who desired war 'with somebody' could hardly be regarded as pursuing a policy — they had merely waxed fat and kicked. This minimized the importance of the whole dispute.

Of the possible argument for a joint Anglo-German policy in America, outlined above, no mention was made, or rather it was never carried to its conclusion. It was well recognized in Britain

---

[1] Harcourt to Morley, 26 January, 1896. Quoted in Gardiner, *Life of Harcourt*, II, p. 399.

[2] H. O. Arnold-Forster, 'The Salisbury-Olney Correspondence' in LXXXII, 22 August, 1896, p. 180. See also 'Appearances in America' in *The Spectator*, LXXVI, 4 January, 1896, p. 6; and ibid., 11 January, 1896, p. 38.

that British support of the Monroe Doctrine was a source of irritation in Germany. It was even held that Anglo-German rivalry
was partly due to German knowledge that Britain would support
the United States in any German-American dispute, so shutting
Germany out from the only likely region not pre-empted by
Britain herself.[1] At that point no one suggested a change of
policy. Rather it was argued that British support for the Monroe
Doctrine should be made known. If the American people only
knew what British policy was, their absurd ideas about British
expansion in America would disappear. American sentiment could
only be due to ignorance.

This comfortable hypothesis modified the British attitude to the
Monroe Doctrine itself. On the whole, the American use of that
doctrine was hailed with pleasure, even if it had been wrongly
introduced into a dispute to which it had no relevance. It was
treated, illogically enough, as the American definition of their
sphere of paramount interest. As Carnegie suggested, it limited
the American sphere: the United States would control the Americas, but not stray beyond them. That meant that concessions to
the United States would not be merely the first of ever larger
concessions. There would be a limit. On the other hand, the new
Monroe Doctrine did insist on American hegemony in South
America. This implied, or so British opinion held, some degree of
responsibility for the behaviour of the South American republics,
who had an evil reputation for maltreating foreign nationals and
not paying debts. It was noted that the United States did not
support the extreme Venezuelan claim and that twice in the
course of the negotiations the threat of leaving her to conduct
them alone was used to bring Venezuela to reason.

From this it was a short step to the idea that American super-
vision of South American republics would actually be profitable to
Britain, which had no important interests there beyond the collec-
tion of debts. As Salisbury said, 'we have been rather glad to
negotiate with the United States rather than with Venezuela.'
Yet this conclusion was based on the assumption that American

---

[1] See 'The Meaning of the Venezuelan Settlement' in *The Spectator*,
LXXVII, 14 November, 1896, p. 665; and, for an expansion of the point,
'The Foundations of our Foreign Policy', ibid., LXXXVII, 7 December,
1901, p. 888.

activity would be reasonable and pay due regard to the rules of international law. In the face of American intervention in Venezuela this was a large assumption, and it was not one that Great Britain was prepared to make of other Powers in other parts of the world.

The exception made in favour of the United States, so far as it did not spring merely from emotional sympathy, was perhaps a result of the sense of progress so strong in the minds of the men of the time. The expansion of Britain took on the force of natural law, but if the expansion of Britain was a good thing it was difficult not to admit the same of the expansion of America, regarded as the daughter country, of one blood and bone. The growth of the United States was in some sense fore-ordained, to oppose it wicked as well as stupid; and a retreat in the face of natural law was not really a retreat at all. The real question became that of where the dividing line between the areas of Britain and America should be drawn. Venezuela was obviously in the American area. The same general pattern of British reaction can be traced in the brushes between Britain and America in these years — surprise that any conflict should have arisen, annoyance at the brusquerie of the United States, resolution to defend an old position against unwarranted attack, wry admiration of the vigour and determination of a new country, retreat, a growing conviction that it was to Britain's real interest that the United States should have acted as she did. There is something proprietary about the British attitude towards the first steps of the United States to the status of a Great Power. This picture of Anglo-American relations had only the most limited content of truth, of course, but the readiness with which the British accepted it goes far to explain why the Venezuelan crisis left no bitterness for later years.

Salisbury's announcement that agreement had been reached stirred only the faintest ripples of public comment. The impression made is that Englishmen had long decided that some decision would be reached without war, and had ceased to care deeply what that decision was. Even while recognizing (as they had much earlier) that the Monroe Doctrine had been tacitly accepted by Great Britain, and that an American protectorate over her hemisphere had been 'established as a working clause in inter-

national law',[1] and that this was a triumph for American diplomacy — even while recognizing all this, they did so only to point
out the difficult responsibilities involved for the United States
and the extent to which she might come into conflict with the
European Powers. *The Economist* could bring itself to only modified praise, grumbling, 'We shall probably be held in Europe to
have given up a principle of some value, and in America to have
shrunk from our original contention, which was that we could
not arbitrate about territory clearly our own, out of fear of a
collision with the United States.'[2] But even *The Economist* hailed
the settlement with relief. Perhaps *The Spectator* may have the
last word. It warned that arbitration was still to come and continued, 'Still, a very difficult and complicated affair has so far
been conducted to a reasonable termination without embittering
the relations of the two Anglo-Saxon Powers, and without any
apparent submission of the one to the other, and that is much.'[3]

NOTE
(See note 1 on p. 15)

Apparently Salisbury had originally intended to send the first despatch only, passing over Olney's defective history in silence. In his
letter to Salisbury of 4 November Hicks Beach criticized a draft Salisbury had sent him of his reply to Olney. The draft is not preserved,
nor is Salisbury's reply to the criticism, if any, but all Hicks Beach's
strictures refer to the first of the despatches finally sent (which Salisbury apparently left unaltered) and among them Hicks Beach says,
'. . . whatever our historical view may be, I submit that it should be
stated in reply to Olney's despatch; otherwise it seems to me that there
is great danger that the American people, and even public opinion
elsewhere, will take Olney's history as uncontradicted by us; and will
therefore be disposed to accept the conclusions which he draws from it.'
Salisbury's second despatch of 26 November begins, 'In my preceding
despatch of to-day's date I have replied only to the latter portion of Mr
Olney's despatch of the 20th July last, which treats of the application

---

[1] 'The Meaning of the Venezuelan Settlement' in *The Spectator*,
LXXVII, 14 November, 1896, p. 666.
[2] 'The New Horizon' in *The Economist*, LIV, 14 November, 1896,
p. 1488.
[3] Lord Salisbury at the Guildhall', in *The Spectator*, LXXVII, 14
November, 1896, p. 664.

of the Monroe doctrine to the question of the boundary dispute between Venezuela and the colony of British Guiana. But it seems desirable, in order to remove some evident misapprehension as to the main features of the question, that the statement of it contained in the earlier portion of Mr Olney's despatch should not be left without reply.' It seems reasonable to suppose that this despatch was written under the pressure of Cabinet criticism. Salisbury, in public as in private life, was apt to consider a dignified silence preferable to debate.

CHAPTER THREE

The Hay-Pauncefote Canal Treaty

I N 1898, American opinion held strongly that a transisthmian canal should be built. The conviction had long been growing both because of the commercial advantages of a canal and because it was an obvious way of linking the east and west coasts of the United States. The idea had been opposed by railroad interests which saw their trade threatened by a sea route shorter than that around the Horn. This opposition, the technical difficulties of building a canal, and inertia, had been enough to prevent action; but the growing imperialism of the United States, the influence of the writings of Mahan, and the experience of the Spanish-American War, notably the celebrated voyage of the battleship *Oregon* round the Horn to reach action, combined to make the demand for the building of a canal pressing.

The diplomatic obstacle to its building by the United States (apart from the negotiations with the Central American governments involved) was the existence of the Clayton-Bulwer Treaty of 1850, which laid down not only that any isthmian canal should be built by Great Britain and the United States together, but also a variety of regulations for the operation and control of the canal when built.

This treaty was still in force in 1898. Attempts were made by unscrupulous American politicians to argue that it had lapsed and could be ignored, but this was not the view of the best American opinion. In 1894 Olney, then Attorney-General, had written a memorandum making this clear, of which he sent a copy by request to John Hay, the new Secretary of State, in 1898.[1]

---

[1] Olney to Hay (personal), 15 November, 1898: Library of Congress, Hay Papers, General Correspondence, 1898.

Though there was a great deal of talk about the possibility of the United States abrogating the treaty, some of it supported by arguments whose only basis was that the treaty was an old one, Hay and his colleagues were very anxious to stick to the letter of the law.

They had no reason to suppose that this would be difficult. The President mentioned the canal question in his message to Congress in December 1898, and two days later Hay wrote to Henry White, then chargé d'affaires in London, suggesting that he enquire the views of the British government.[1] White did so, and reported Salisbury as fully alive to the advantages of a canal under the protection of one nation and that one the United States, if it were open equally to the commerce of all.[2] As a result negotiations began in Washington between Hay and Pauncefote.[3]

Salisbury's favourable reaction had been made privately and without consultation. There was, White reported, a strong feeling in Britain that the proposed new treaty would benefit only the United States. It would be, if not actually harmful to Great Britain, a gesture of goodwill for which concessions might reasonably be expected elsewhere. The United States had steadily refused to make any concessions to Canadian interests in the questions under consideration by the Joint High Commission, and Canadians would be angry if a means of applying pressure to the United States were not used. Chamberlain stated the view frankly and added that a general feeling that the United States had of late been getting the better of Great Britain in diplomatic exchanges would make so large a concession politically awkward.[4] Moreover, while the Alaska boundary question remained unsettled, there was always a possibility of trouble flaring into war. It might

---

[1] Hay to White, no. 976, 7 December, 1898: N.A., S.D., to London, Vol. 33.

[2] White to Hay, 23 December, 1898. Quoted by Allan Nevins, *Henry White: Thirty Years of American Diplomacy* (New York, 1930), pp. 144–5.

[3] A. L. P. Dennis, *Adventures in American Diplomacy, 1896–1906* (New York, 1928), p. 158; Nevins, op. cit., p. 145. British policy is examined at length by J. A. S. Grenville, 'Great Britain and the Isthmian Canal, 1898–1901' in the *American Historical Review*, LXI, October 1955.

[4] White, memorandum for Hay, 4 February, 1899. Quoted by Nevins, op. cit., p. 147.

well be asked why Britain should connive at the effective doubling
of the United States fleet by a canal when relations between the
two countries were so strained.[1]

These considerations gave the British government pause, but
by the middle of January 1899 Hay was able to forward to White
a draft treaty substantially agreed upon by Pauncefote and himself. Although Hay had told Senator Morgan confidentially that
he did not expect the negotiations with Great Britain to take long,
and that he saw no reason why study of the Senate Canal Bill
should be checked,[2] he was not so confident as that suggested. In
writing to White about his draft treaty he emphasized that it
should be considered quickly, before the Senate had time to
commit themselves to opposition, and asked whether this could be
urged on the Foreign Office. With the Senate in mind, Hay and
Pauncefote took pains to cast their agreement in such general
terms as to make opposition very difficult.[3]

Hay's hope of reaching agreement with Britain so quickly that
Senate opposition to *any* treaty fettering American action would
not have time to develop was foiled when in February British
agreement on the canal question was definitely tied to arbitration
of the Alaska boundary.[4] Although Salisbury and Chamberlain
later modified this and repeatedly assured White and Choate, the
American Ambassador, that they would consent to abrogation of
the Clayton-Bulwer Treaty even without agreement on Canadian
questions,[5] they showed no eagerness to bring a new treaty before
Parliament, and Hay had to wait for the rest of the year without
making any progress.

In January 1900 Hay broached the matter again, arguing that
now that a *modus vivendi* had been reached with Canada, making
differences less acute, Salisbury might 'see his way clear to con-
senting to the convention agreed upon between Lord Pauncefote

---

[1] White to Hay (tel.), 26 January, 1899 and no. 694, 17 February,
1899. Cited by Dennis, op. cit., p. 158.
[2] Hay to Morgan (confidential), 27 December, 1898: Hay Papers,
Letter Book I, p. 73.
[3] Hay to White, 13 January, 1899: Hay Papers, L.B. I, p. 105.
[4] White to Hay (tel.), 15 February, 1899: N.A., S.D., from London,
Vol. 196.
[5] White to Hay, 29 August, 1899. Cited by Nevins, op. cit., p. 149;
also ibid., pp. 146–7.

and myself'.[1] When Choate spoke to Salisbury, however, he (Salisbury) was firm that Chamberlain must be given a chance to be heard for Canada. The Canadians were angry at the United States attitude on Alaska. When reminded of his assertions that he would not allow Canadian objections to hold up the canal treaty indefinitely, Salisbury replied that the part played by Canada in the Boer War had changed the situation, which must now be considered anew on its merits.[2]

The letter to Choate cited above gives Hay's reason for anxiety. The previous year Congress, failing to agree on a Canal Bill, had set up a Commission to examine the merits of the various possible routes across the isthmus. That had promised a delay of one or even two years; but now Congress was impatient at the result of its own work, and Representative Hepburn had introduced in the House a new bill which the influential Senator Morgan thought he could get through the Senate. This bill ignored the Clayton-Bulwer Treaty and in many respects violated it; for this reason Hay was anxious that it should not pass, and that it should be forestalled by some diplomatic arrangement, so that at least the Administration would be clear of complicity in 'violent and one-sided abrogation' of the Clayton-Bulwer Treaty. It would be un-fortunate, wrote Hay, if England were to veto a work of such importance — 'and the worst of all for international relations is that the veto would not be effective'.[3]

These arguments were urged by Choate in London with good effect, and it seems clear that in spite of regard for Canadian opinion neither Salisbury nor Chamberlain was disposed to stand in the way of the treaty. The Canadian views were received in London on 2 February and at a Cabinet meeting immediately afterwards it was agreed to authorize Pauncefote to sign, which he did on the 5th.[4]

---

[1] Hay to Choate (private and confidential), 15 January, 1900: Hay Papers, L.B. I, p. 361.
[2] Choate to Hay (private and confidential), 27 January, 1900: Hay Papers, Box 19.
[3] Hay to Choate (private and confidential), 15 January, 1900: Hay Papers, L.B. I, p. 361.
[4] Choate to Hay (private and unofficial), 2 February, 1900; same to same (tel.) (private and confidential), 3 February, 1900; same to same (private and unofficial), 7 February, 1900: Hay Papers, 19.

The first Hay-Pauncefote Treaty modified the Clayton-Bulwer Treaty effectively in one respect only — it withdrew the British claim to a share in the building and maintenance of the canal. The Suez Canal had been built and neutralized since the signing of the Clayton-Bulwer Treaty. The neutrality terms of the new treaty therefore followed those governing the Suez Canal, and the other Great Powers were to be invited to adhere to it, making its resemblance to the Suez treaty still closer. The changes in the neutrality terms were verbal rather than real, and the Clayton-Bulwer Treaty remained in force except as it conflicted with the new one.

In spite of the care taken to modify the Clayton-Bulwer Treaty as little as possible, there were valid British objections to the new instrument. This was not by the desire of Hay or the inadvertence of Pauncefote. Hay was most anxious to emphasize that the United States sought no advantage and took none,[1] and Pauncefote, an exceptionally skilful diplomatic draftsman, saw to it that there were no loopholes in the wording. Nevertheless there could be no doubt that the United States would be the chief beneficiary, both commercially and navally. Since the completion of the Suez Canal British interest in the American route to the East, never very great, had declined. She did not greatly care, from a calculation of positive advantage, whether the canal were built or not. It remained only to consider whether there were disadvantages in its building by the United States, and if so whether they made opposition to that country worth while.

The most specific British objection was one which the Spanish-American War had emphasized—the great advantage which would accrue to the United States from being able to concentrate her Atlantic and Pacific squadrons in one ocean at need without having to send them round Cape Horn, an advantage which no other nation would share and one of the chief reasons for American eagerness to build the canal. Without a canal the British Pacific squadron held a temporary advantage over the American, which would be valuable in war and which the construction of a canal would destroy. This would be the effect of a canal whatever the regulations under which it was built, even those of the

---

[1] Hay to White, 13 January, 1899: Hay Papers, L.B. I, p. 105.

Clayton-Bulwer Treaty. The canal could, of course, be blockaded outside the neutral zone, as the Americans were the first to point out. But this itself was an added task for any fleet. Other advantage gained from the canal might make the liability worth while, but Britain gained very little. The British government, in fact, found themselves faced with an invidious choice. They could either hold up the building of a ship canal generally held to be a great work of civilization, by maintaining their strict rights under the Clayton-Bulwer Treaty, or try to argue that the relinquishing of those rights, which Britain did not intend to use, constituted a concession for which something should be given in return.

It was for this reason as much as from any real conviction that the Canadian case on Alaska was a good one that Salisbury and Chamberlain made such effort as they did to tie the two questions together.[1] There was a logical connection between them which the American negotiators would never admit, shrewd tactics since they were negotiating from strength and were able to succeed in gaining the main points of their contention in both negotiations. The British government delayed and made the futile attempt to get concessions in return for the Hay-Pauncefote agreement; it made little effort to criticize the instrument itself. Nor could criticism have been effective. The new treaty admittedly modified the old as little as possible, and gave no advantages to the United States which the Clayton-Bulwer Treaty would have kept from her once the canal was built. Effective criticism would have involved the admission that Britain did not want the canal built — and the canal was universally accepted in that day as a boon to civilization. Hay's anxiety to avoid having his draft amended in London was needless.[2] He and Pauncefote had done good work. All the initiative came from the United States — Hay drew up the treaty, Salisbury accepted it.

The Convention as signed went before the Senate for ratification in the usual manner, and there Hay's hope that it might prove general and inoffensive enough to pass without modification was quickly proved false. It came under heavy criticism both in

---

[1] Salisbury to Pauncefote (tel.), no. 22, 2 February, 1899: P.R.O., FO 5/2393.
[2] Hay to White, 13 January, 1899: Hay Papers, L.B. I, p. 105. Although action on it was delayed for a year the draft was not altered.

the Senate and in the United States generally. Criticism took two main lines. The first attacked the clause of the treaty laying down that the other Powers should be invited to adhere to the treaty when ratified. This invocation of European Powers to the guarantee of a treaty operative exclusively in the western hemisphere seemed to many Senators at variance with the Monroe Doctrine. The more important criticism, however, was that the existence of a neutralized canal would strengthen as against the United States any Power with a navy larger than hers. Under the terms of the Hay-Pauncefote Treaty, it was held, any such Power could effectively blockade the canal against United States warships by waiting for them just outside the neutral limits. The United States, on the other hand, though possessing equal rights, would in fact be unable to prevent larger foreign squadrons from passing through the canal. On this kind of argument, only against a Power like Spain with no squadron large enough to blockade it effectively, would the canal be of value to the United States. No American was willing to spend American money on the building of a canal of such limited value. This sort of opposition to the treaty was brilliantly led by Theodore Roosevelt, then Governor of New York, who explained his position in a letter to Hay:

> My objections are twofold. First, as to naval policy. If the proposed canal had been in existence in '98, the Oregon could have come more quickly through to the Atlantic; but this fact would have been far outweighed by the fact that Cervera's fleet would have had open to it the chance of itself going through the canal, and thence sailing to attack Dewey or to menace our stripped Pacific coast. If that canal is open to the war ships of an enemy it is a menace to us in time of war; it is an added burden, an additional strategic point to be guarded by our fleet. If fortified by us, it becomes one of the most potent sources of our possible sea strength. Unless so fortified it strengthens against us every nation whose fleet is larger than ours. One prime reason for fortifying our great seaports is to unfetter our fleet, to release it for offensive purposes; and the proposed canal would fetter it again, for our fleet would have to watch it, and therefore do the work which a fort should do; and which it could do much better.
>
> Secondly, as to the Monroe Doctrine. If we invite foreign powers to a joint ownership, a joint guarantee, of what so vitally concerns us but a little way from our borders, how can we possibly object to

similar joint action say in Southern Brazil or Argentina, where our interests are so much less evident? If Germany has the same right we have in the canal across Central America, why not in the partition of any part of Southern America? To my mind, we should consistently refuse to all European powers the right to control, in any shape, any territory in the western Hemisphere which they do not already hold.

As for existing treaties — I do not admit the 'dead hand' of the treaty-making power in the past. A treaty can always be honorably abrogated — though it must never be abrogated in dishonest fashion.[1]

This is the classic statement of the views which dominated the Senate opposition to the first Hay-Pauncefote Treaty. Roosevelt expressed those views not only in public and to Hay but repeated them with good effect to influential Englishmen, both through Henry White and in personal correspondence, and British opinion accepted with very little demur many of his questionable assumptions.[2] Though not everyone took this line and Whitelaw Reid in the *Tribune* was notably vigorous in defence of the treaty,[3] opposition was strong enough to induce Hay, never tenacious of office, to resign on 13 March, a resignation refused, as usual, by McKinley.[4] In June the Senate adjourned,[5] without having taken a final vote, and did not meet again till December. During the summer there was more than enough to distract both British and American attention from the subject of the canal. The British were still deeply involved in the Boer War, the Americans in an election campaign; but overshadowing everything else was the Boxer rising, the siege of the legations in Peking and their relief in August, and the involved international negotiations which followed.

---

[1] Roosevelt to Hay (personal), 18 February, 1900: E. E. Morison (ed.), *The Letters of Theodore Roosevelt* (Cambridge, Mass., 1951), Vol. II, no. 1522.

[2] Roosevelt's letter to Hay has been printed before, in H. C. Hill, *Roosevelt and the Caribbean* (Chicago, 1927), pp. 32–3 and Dennis, *Adventures*, pp. 160–1. See also Roosevelt to C. A. Spring Rice (personal), 2 March, 1900, and to A. H. Lee (private), 24 April, 1901: Morison (ed.), *Roosevelt Letters*, II, no. 1539 and III, no. 2028. Roosevelt's public protest was sent to the Press on 12 February, 1900.

[3] Hay to Reid, 7 February, 1900: Hay Papers, L.B. I, p. 386.

[4] Dennis, *Adventures*, p. 161.

[5] Not March, as stated in Nevins, *Henry White*, p. 153.

Nevertheless Hay was not idle during the summer. He consulted Senator Morgan and got from that formidable veteran a draft treaty acceptable to him. He got other drafts from Admiral Walker and Judge Pasco, leading members of the Canal Commission set up by Congress in 1899; and all these drafts were worked up into a final project by Hay and John Bassett Moore, already probably the leading international lawyer in the United States and an unofficial State Department adviser.[1] At this time, of course, the first Hay-Pauncefote Treaty was still under consideration by the Senate; but Hay was convinced that it would be rejected, since what he always feared most had come about — it had become an issue in the election campaign. Bryan, the Democratic candidate, had 'in mere ignorance and malice' attacked it in his letter accepting the nomination, making it a political issue and lining up the Democrats against it.[2]

When the Senate reassembled in December, it ratified the treaty with three amendments, which in their effect followed closely the lines of criticism set out by Roosevelt. The first was of small importance and did no more than to make the abrogation of the Clayton-Bulwer Treaty specific. The second was of the greatest importance. After the five sections of the treaty which laid down the rules for the neutralization of the canal, it inserted a rider negating those rules to the benefit of the United States. 'It is agreed, however,' ran this amendment, 'that none of the immediately foregoing conditions and stipulations in sections numbered 1, 2, 3, 4, and 5 of this Article shall apply to measures which the United States may find it necessary to take for securing by its own forces the defence of the United States and the maintenance of public order.' The third amendment struck out the clause stipulating that the adherence of other Powers should be invited.[3]

Plainly these amendments altered the treaty as sent to the Senate so thoroughly as to constitute a rejection of it. Even

---

[1] Hay to McKinley, 23 September, 1900: Hay Papers, L.B. II, p. 14.
[2] ibid.
[3] The amendments were contained in Hay to Pauncefote, 22 December, 1900, enclosed in Pauncefote to Lansdowne, 24 December, 1900: *Parliamentary Papers*, 1901, XCI, State Papers, United States. No. 1 (1901), (Cd. 438), no. 1.

before any official notification of the Senate resolution reached him Lansdowne wrote to Pauncefote that the so-called 'Davis amendment' (the second) to the treaty must be rejected by Her Majesty's Government, for although its practical effect was not yet clear the moral effect of allowing the Clayton-Bulwer Treaty to be virtually abrogated had to be considered. Pauncefote replied that no one in Washington had any hope that Britain would accept the amended treaty but that it was possible that any further action might be postponed for a year if the President could resist the clamour for abrogation which sprang, Pauncefote thought, from intoxication with prosperity.[1]

The most remarkable thing about the handling of the treaty at this stage is the complete lack of any co-operation between the American Senate and Administration. Hay's immediate reaction to the Senate amendments was to write a long private letter to Choate explaining how they had come about and suggesting the line of argument he should follow with the British government. When the attack on the treaty began, he wrote, the Republican leaders in the Senate began to be fearful of its influence on the Presidential canvass, added the 'Davis amendment' to satisfy the jingoes and then dropped the matter till after the election. When the Senate reassembled, there proved to be enough opposition to defeat the treaty as it stood, opposition which showed itself in a whole crop of new amendments. Of these the Republican leaders selected two, which they thought relatively innocent, to submit to the President,

> ... who asked me to meet a committee, consisting of Lodge, Aldritch and Foraker, at the White House. They told their story — that the treaty would be rejected if these additional amendments were not adopted; that with these amendments, they could not only carry the treaty through, but could prevent any hostile legislation pending further negotiations with England. The President said the treaty was right as originally drawn, that it ought to be ratified without amendment; but as this seemed impossible we were willing to do our best to persuade the British Government to accept the

---

[1] Lansdowne to Pauncefote (tel.), no. 227 (secret), 14 December, 1900: P.R.O., FO 115/1168. Same to same (confidential), 14 December, 1900 and Pauncefote to Lansdowne (private), 21 December, 1900: Foreign Office Library, Lansdowne Papers, Vol. 28 — United States.

E

Davis Amendment; but that he did not think they would accept the other two. Upon which Lodge said 'That puts the onus of rejecting the treaty on England!!' But they all agreed that if the treaty were rejected now, it would be impossible to prevent the violent repudiation of the Clayton-Bulwer Treaty by act of Congress. To this proposition the President made no reply, leaving to the Senate itself the responsibility of its action. . . .

Yesterday the Senate voted. They adopted, as you know, besides the Davis Amendment two others, one inserting the words 'which is hereby superseded' after 'Clayton-Bulwer convention' in the Second Article; and the other striking out Article III.

I deeply regret the adoption of all these amendments. They deform and disfigure the Treaty; they take much from the grace and value of the concession which Great Britain has made us; but beyond the matter of taste and good manners, I consider them of little moment. They give no additional advantage to us; they demand no sacrifice from Great Britain. The Davis Amendment is a mere *brutum fulmen*; it leaves intact the provision against the fortification of the Canal; it reserves to us in vague terms a right which can never be exercised. The omission of the IIId Article hurts nobody but ourselves. It deprives us of the enormous advantage we should have in a universal guarantee of the neutrality of the Canal, and does not in any way injure Great Britain. The amendment in the Second Article 'which is hereby superseded' seems grammatically to refer to the VIIIth Article of the Clayton-Bulwer Convention, and its effect is to substitute the 2nd Article of the present Convention for the 8th of the former one. The most it can be made to mean is that the Clayton-Bulwer Convention, when it conflicts with the present Convention, is superseded to the extent of such conflict.[1]

This letter is special pleading of the most specious kind. In part it is a deliberate misreading of the Senate amendments. The insertion in the Second Article to which Hay refers does not read 'which is hereby superseded' but 'which Convention is hereby superseded', plainly referring to the whole of the Clayton-Bulwer Treaty, and making nonsense of Hay's effort to limit its reference by misquoting it. The most cursory study of the Senate debate on this amendment makes it clear that it was designed to abrogate the Clayton-Bulwer Treaty, and that this was thought important

---

[1] Hay to Choate (private and personal), 21 December, 1900: Hay Papers, L.B. II, p. 67.

just because it might otherwise have been held, as Hay now tried to hold, that any part of the Clayton-Bulwer Treaty not conflict-ing with the new convention remained in force. The position of the Davis amendment certainly gave support to Hay's account of its origin and it undoubtedly did leave intact the provision against fortification; but by doing so it introduced an internal contradiction into the treaty. The new version suggested strongly that there were rival interpretations of a point which was being deliberately left vague, no satisfactory way of drafting the treaty. As for Hay's point about the omission of the Third Article, no-thing could reveal more clearly the enormous divergence between him and the Senate opinion responsible for the omission, opinion shared fully by Roosevelt in the letter quoted above. Hay re-garded, or claimed to regard, the neutrality guarantee as an advantage to the United States. The Senate opponents of the treaty were clear that it was a disadvantage, since the first act of the United States in any war in which she took part must be to close the canal.

Hay and Choate, in short, found themselves in the unfortunate position of trying to persuade the British government that amendments to the treaty which the Senate thought of the first importance were of none at all, were mere matters of wording, due to nothing worse than ignorance and malice in the Senate. This was simply not true, and their efforts placed them in a posi-tion which they occupied with little grace. Lansdowne reported in January the odd behaviour of Choate, who asked for an inter-view on the subject and then admitted to being uninstructed. The reason did not escape Lansdowne. Both Hay and Choate were nervous, he thought, and anxious to be reassuring in private while gaining credit for being aggressive in public.[1]

A large part of Hay's desire to see the amendments accepted in London was due to his conviction that their rejection, even if accompanied by counter-proposals, would induce the Senate to abrogate the Clayton-Bulwer Treaty at once. Urgency was added to his desire by the fact that the amended convention would lapse on 5 March if not ratified by then, so that delay was a form of

---

[1] Lansdowne to Pauncefote, 17 January, 1901: Lansdowne Papers, Vol. 28 — United States.

rejection; and he knew or suspected that some Senators were becoming impatient. He cited in support of his view the activity of a man like Senator Morgan, who had supported the treaty, but who was now led by his zeal for an immediate start on the canal to demand action on the Hepburn bill.[1] To the force of arguments like this Pauncefote was fully alive, and Hay reported him as in favour of 'acceptance of the amendments en bloc as a choice of evils'.[2]

That was putting it too strongly. Pauncefote was aware that it had already been decided that the amendments should be rejected and was less inclined than Hay to tremble at the prospect of Senate action. In the middle of January he was already reporting, in spite of Hay's gloom, that there was no likelihood of any further Senate action that session. He was aware that if the treaty lapsed in March, the Senate adjourned at the same time; and in February, consulted as to the best date for communicating the British rejection of the amendments, he advised doing nothing till after the adjournment, though he admitted that delay might possibly irritate the Senate into action.[3] The American sense of urgency was not shared in London. Choate's letters to Hay in January and February record steady pressure on Lansdowne to answer his note of 4 January in which the amendments had been transmitted — pressure which had no effect. Lansdowne took refuge in evasion. Though the Queen's death disorganized the work of government to some extent, he was in fact considering his reply with great care. He sent parts of it to Pauncefote for approval, and it was closely discussed at two Cabinet meetings on 22 and 26 February.[4] Pauncefote's judgment was vindicated by the event. The Senate adjourned 'without committing any further enormity'.[5]

Lansdowne finally set out the grounds of his rejection of the

---

[1] Hay to Choate (personal), 11 January, 1901: Hay Papers, L.B. II, p. 81.

[2] ibid.

[3] Pauncefote to Lansdowne (private), 18 January and 8 February, 1901: Lansdowne Papers, Vol. 28 — United States.

[4] Choate to Hay, various private letters, January and February 1901: Hay Papers, 19. Lansdowne to Pauncefote (secret), 19 February, 1901: Lansdowne Papers, Vol. 28 — United States.

[5] Pauncefote to Lansdowne (private and confidential), 1 March, 1901: ibid.

Senate amendments in a long formal despatch dated 22 February, 1901, but not handed to Hay till 12 March.[1] This reviewed the history of the negotiation, pointed out that the first Hay-Pauncefote Treaty was the work of the State Department, accepted without conditions by the British government, and went on to consider the effect of the new amendments. With regard to the first amendment, specifically abrogating the Clayton-Bulwer Convention, Lansdowne pointed out that in its absence those parts of that convention not superseded by clauses of the new agreement would remain in force. The most important of these was Article I.

> Under Article I of the Clayton-Bulwer Treaty [wrote Lansdowne], the two Powers agreed that neither would occupy, or fortify, or colonize, or assume or exercise any dominion over any part of Central America, nor attain any of the foregoing objects by protection afforded to, or alliance with, any State or people of Central America. There is no similar agreement in the Convention. If, therefore, the Treaty were wholly abrogated, both Powers would, except in the vicinity of the canal, recover entire freedom of action in Central America. The change would certainly be of advantage to the United States, and might be of substantial importance.

This was fair comment on the effect of the abrogation of the Clayton-Bulwer Treaty, and was amplified by Pauncefote:

> I have impressed as well as I could on Mr Hay and others that the framers of the Clayton-Bulwer Treaty foresaw that whichever of the two High Contracting Parties annexed the Isthmus would have absolute control of the Isthmian Canal and for that reason they composed Art. I with the greatest elaboration. It is the foundation stone of the edifice which the U.S. Senate have naturally been anxious to dislodge by their first amendment.[2]

The noteworthy thing about these opinions is their assumption that the United States could only gain from freedom of action in Central America. Freedom of action to Great Britain meant

---

[1] Hay to Choate, 13 March, 1901: Hay Papers, L.B. II, p. 118. Lansdowne's dispatch is printed in *Parliamentary Papers*, loc. cit., no. 2. It was slightly modified for publication to avoid a possible inference from Lansdowne's draft that Hay and Choate had not been supporting the amendments vigorously in London. (See the exchanges in the Lansdowne Papers, Vol. 28 — United States.)

[2] Pauncefote to Lansdowne (private and confidential), 1 March, 1901: Lansdowne Papers, Vol. 28 — United States.

nothing, a mere theoretical freedom which circumstances would prevent her from exercising. The Caribbean was not an area in which Britain intended to take an interest. On the United States, on the other hand, the Clayton-Bulwer Treaty placed a real, not merely formal, restriction and it was not unnatural that the relaxing of it should be regarded in Great Britain as a major concession. The divergence of views on this clause of the Clayton-Bulwer Treaty represented the shift of power which had taken place in the Caribbean since 1850.

The first of the Senate amendments was not, however, the most important, nor the one to which most attention was directed. Lansdowne next turned to the Davis amendment. This had been defended on the ground that similar rights of defence had been reserved to the Sultan and the Khedive in the Suez Canal Convention. Lansdowne pointed out forcibly and at length the difference between the two cases and claimed:

> Were this amendment added to the Convention the United States would, it is presumed, be within their rights, if at any moment when it seemed to them that their safety required it, in view of warlike preparations not yet commenced, but contemplated or supposed to be contemplated by another Power, they resorted to warlike acts in or near the Canal — acts clearly inconsistent with the neutral character which it has always been sought to give it, and which would deny the free use of it to the commerce and navies of the world.

And again:

> The situation which would be created by the addition of the new clause is deserving of serious attention. If it were to be added, the obligation to respect the neutrality of the Canal in all circumstances would, so far as Great Britain is concerned, remain in force; the obligation of the United States, on the other hand, would be essentially modified. The result would be a one-sided arrangement under which Great Britain would be debarred from any warlike action in or around the Canal, while the United States would be able to resort to such action to whatever extent they might deem necessary to secure their safety.

It may be contended that if the new clause were adopted, section 7 of Article II, which prohibits the erection of fortifications, would sufficiently insure the free use of the Canal. This contention is, however, one which His Majesty's Government are quite unable to admit . . . it would be impossible to determine what might be the effect if one clause permitting defensive measures, and another forbidding fortifications, were allowed to stand side by side in the Convention. . . . Such an enactment would strike at the very root of that 'general principle' of neutralization upon which the Clayton-Bulwer Treaty was based, and which was reaffirmed in the Convention as drafted.[1]

Last, Lansdowne pointed out that the effect of this amendment was strengthened by the third. This not only deprived Great Britain of the support of other Powers in upholding the neutrality of the canal, but turned the Convention into a self-denying ordinance for Great Britain, for it submitted her to an undertaking not to interfere with the canal, an undertaking from which the United States would be exempt by treaty and which the other Powers, non-signatory, would be entitled to disregard.[2]

These were all valid objections to the Senate amendments and disposed finally of Hay's feeble efforts to pretend that they were of no importance. They demonstrate conclusively that while Hay had already got more than many observers thought possible — the modification of the Clayton-Bulwer Treaty — he was far behind the new demands of the United States. What Americans had accepted in 1850 they would not accept now. Lansdowne's despatch, firm though its tone is, shows clearly that the only British reply was to cite the restrictions which the Clayton-Bulwer Treaty had placed on both countries, in the hope of retaining them to restrict the activity of the United States. Its vigour is a negative vigour. The treaty as amended would have made Great Britain in the first instance and the other Powers only less so entirely dependent on the good will of the United States in the Caribbean. For that very adequate reason the amended convention was rejected. As Lansdowne significantly said, 'So far as Her Majesty's Government were concerned there was no desire to procure a modification of that Convention [the Clayton-Bulwer Treaty].'[3]

---

[1] Lansdowne to Pauncefote, 22 February, 1901: *Parliamentary Papers*, loc. cit., pp. 6, 7.
[2] ibid., p. 7.
[3] ibid., pp. 3–4.

Lansdowne's despatch was admitted in the United States to be 'an able and very temperately written document'.[1] The difficulty was to see how it could lead to further negotiations, but Hay was able to avoid dealing with it in detail since the convention had now lapsed. Choate reported from London that opinion in Britain was firm against the amendments; and their rejection was taken surprisingly well in the United States. A new treaty was drawn up by the State Department on the basis of all the various drafts available and this was worked over in extended conversations with both Pauncefote and leading Senators. This was sent to Choate on 27 April; but by then Pauncefote had already sent some comments on it to London, and asked permission to come home for consultation. The final work on the new agreement was done in London by Lansdowne, Pauncefote, Choate and Henry White.[2]

Hay wrote to White that if agreement were not reached by December, the Clayton-Bulwer Treaty would certainly be abrogated — his old cry. White took the letter to Salisbury at Hatfield, and protested so vigorously when Salisbury suggested compensation in Alaska that Salisbury — according to White — was convinced.[3] It is, however, very doubtful whether Salisbury or anyone else was seriously considering compensation in Alaska at this stage. It is true that just at this time Hay produced a new Alaskan scheme, and that this was given by Lansdowne as a reason for meeting Hay half way.[4] It is true, too, that the possibility of getting more favourable terms if the two questions could be connected was used as an argument in urging Canada to settle the

---

[1] White to Hay, 9 March, 1901: Henry White Papers.

[2] Pauncefote to Lansdowne (private), 25 and 26 April, 1901; same to same (tel.), 28 April, 1901; Lansdowne to Pauncefote, 7 May, 1901: Lansdowne Papers, Vol. 28 — United States. The dates on Lord Pauncefote's letters and telegram cannot all be accurate. Choate's letters to Hay during the summer of 1901 are in the Hay Papers, 19. See the memorandum by Lansdowne, 3 August, 1901, in *Parliamentary Papers*, 1902, CXXX, State Papers, United States. No. 1 (1902), (Cd. 905), no. 2.

[3] Hay to White, 18 June, 1901; White to Hay, 24 July, 1901. Cited by Nevins, *Henry White*, p. 158.

[4] Pauncefote to Lansdowne (private), 10 May, 1901: Lansdowne Papers, Vol. 28 — United States. Memorandum by Lansdowne, 6 July, 1901: ibid. (Printed as appendix to this chapter.)

Alaskan question later in the year.[1] That argument was probably disingenuous. The first Hay-Pauncefote Treaty had already been negotiated without reference to Canada, after some delay due to regard for Canadian wishes. Canada had conceded the issue then — to her credit, as Choate admitted — and it was not likely that it would be reopened.[2] Moreover, there is no evidence in the British documents to suggest that any serious attempt was made to connect the two questions. Hay's draft was considered on its merits, modifications were suggested, these were modified in turn, and so on. The discussion was purely technical, and friendly. No great difficulty was found in reaching a form of words acceptable to both sides. The impression left is that Lansdowne had decided to meet Hay's wishes before the negotiations began. Nor does the threat of Senate action appear to have been particularly effective. Hay cried 'wolf' a little too often. In the negotiations there was no haste, but no unnecessary delay.

Hay's own view of his new draft were given in the letter he sent with it to Choate, indicating the line of argument he thought Choate might use:

> I have drawn this up with very great care, after serious and extended conversations with Lord Pauncefote and with leading members of the Senate. You will see by a careful perusal of it and comparison with the extinct treaty, that it contains substantially all that was asked for in the amended treaty, but in a form which, I hope, will not be objectionable to the British Government. The provision superseding the Clayton-Bulwer treaty is, as you see, contained in a special article, instead of being introduced in a parenthesis. In Article III, you will notice that the United States 'adopts' the rules of neutralization, instead of making it a joint guarantee in company with England. The seventh section of Article III is left out entirely, and the provision for the military police of the canal is transferred to Section 2. The question of fortification is thus passed sub silentio. I hope it will not be considered important enough for the British Government to take exception to this omission. The fact is that no Government, not absolutely imbecile, would ever think of fortifying the canal, and yet there are several members of the Senate so

---

[1] Below, ch. iv, p. 105.
[2] Choate to Hay (private and unofficial), 2 and 7 February, 1900: Hay Papers, 19.

morbidly sensitive on the subject that it might seriously injure the passage of the treaty through the Senate if this provision were retained after the omission of the Davis amendment. In this new redaction, the Davis amendment disappears, as you see, entirely. By eliminating the words 'in peace as well as in war' in the first section of Article III, and by the omission of the seventh section, it has been thought by many senators that the necessity for the Davis amendment has disappeared. The third section, omitted by the Senate, is also omitted in this new draft. If we release Great Britain from the obligation of the joint guarantee, there is no reason why the rest of the world should not be released in like manner, and the United States assume alone the duty of guaranteeing the neutrality of the canal. Nobody loses by it except ourselves.[1]

This can usefully be compared with a long memorandum which Lansdowne prepared for the Cabinet, in which he urged strongly the acceptance of the new proposals with only minor modifications. (This is too long to reproduce here and has been reserved for an appendix.) In the new draft, the Clayton-Bulwer Treaty was specifically abrogated, not in a parenthesis, but in Article I. Lansdowne now argued in his memorandum that this was unobjectionable, because his objection to abrogation by Senate amendment had been one of form rather than of substance. It is true that his protest had been based on the validity of the Clayton-Bulwer Treaty as an international contract, so that the Senate action was a breach of international usage; nevertheless he had gone on to draw attention to a point of 'substantial importance', the clause limiting the freedom of action of both parties in Central America.[2] That was not replaced. Even Pauncefote's insertion in the treaty, temporarily called Article III A, which extended the rules laid down to cover 'all inter-oceanic communications' across the isthmus did nothing to replace it; and this itself was later weakened to meet American objections.[3] Lansdowne was

---

[1] Hay to Choate (private and personal), 27 April, 1901: Hay Papers, L.B. II, p. 142. Hay's draft treaty, the draft as modified by British amendments, and the treaty as finally signed and ratified are all printed in *Parliamentary Papers*, loc. cit.

[2] Lansdowne to Pauncefote, 22 February, 1901: *Parliamentary Papers*, 1901, XCI, loc. cit., p. 5.

[3] *Parliamentary Papers*, 1902, CXXX, loc. cit.

now concerned to minimize for the benefit of the Cabinet a concession to which he had objected in February.

That was not, however, the most important modification. To continue in the order in which Hay took his points, the United States now 'adopted' the rules of neutralization, releasing Great Britain from her share in their guarantee. At the same time, the old Article III (deleted by the Senate), which had invited the adherence of the other Powers to the treaty, was not restored. Taken together these modifications represented an attempt to meet both the wishes of the Senate and the British objections to them. As his letter quoted shows, Hay regarded his new version as placing Britain and all other countries in the same position. Lansdowne and Pauncefote did not agree. They pointed out that though Britain now had no responsibility for maintaining the neutrality of the canal, she was committed to observing it; and that other Powers were not. Pauncefote proposed to solve the problem by guaranteeing free and equal use of the canal only to those Powers 'which shall agree to observe these rules'. This was further amended by Choate to 'observing these rules'.[1]

The difference between these versions was not merely verbal. Pauncefote's was open to the same objection as the first Hay-Pauncefote Treaty — it invited the adherence of other nations to the treaty. True, they were not now to join Britain in a guarantee of the canal's neutrality, but they would be invited to pass on the position of the United States as guarantor — exactly what the Senate wished to avoid. Choate's form left the United States alone to decide what observation of the rules involved and when they had been broken. Only Britain was directly affected by the treaty. Yet Lansdowne not only accepted Choate's amendment, but apparently had no anxiety over doing so. It was not treaty rights against the United States that he was concerned to maintain, but Britain's equality with other Powers. He was quite prepared to rely on the United States for control of the canal, and the readiness with which Choate's form was accepted makes it clear that the implication to which Choate took exception in the earlier draft had been no part of Pauncefote's intention. Provided the

---

[1] ibid.; Choate to Hay (private and confidential), 16 and 20 August, 1901: Hay Papers, 19.

right of other Powers to use the canal was made contingent on their submission to the same restrictions as Britain, those restrictions could be administered and enforced by the United States. On the other hand, it was not the intention of Roosevelt and the Senate to place Britain under peculiar disadvantages. There was, therefore, no difficulty in reaching agreement.

The magnitude of the difference between American and British thinking is revealed by Choate's comment on Pauncefote's amendment. He took the view that the neutrality rules restricted not Britain but the United States; that Britain alone had some claim to impose conditions in return for the abrogation of the Clayton-Bulwer Treaty; and that if the conditions she imposed were neutrality for all nations instead of concessions for herself, she could not argue that she was placed at a disadvantage thereby.[1] He regarded his insertion of 'observing these rules' as an unimportant sop to British sentiment which was, if anything, a further advantage to the United States. The change from the first Hay-Pauncefote Treaty was enormous.

The new treaty, then, was in one way even more effective than the Senate version had been, for it made explicit that the rights of other Powers in the canal were limited equally with those of Britain; but it did meet the British objection to the work of the Senate, as stated by Lansdowne in February. Britain's disadvantage, real or supposed, relative to other Powers *had* been his main complaint. His advocacy of the new treaty as it affected the fortification of the canal is less satisfactory. The Davis amendment had waived the neutrality clauses in favour of the United States; but the clause forbidding fortification had been retained, and followed the Davis clause. This introduced, as Lansdowne said, an internal inconsistency into the treaty. Now the Davis amendment was removed, but so was the clause forbidding fortification; and, most important, the words 'in time of war as in time of peace' disappeared from Clause 1 of Article III which declared that the canal 'shall be free and open'.

The significance of the new wording is set out in a letter to Hay from Choate, who was anxious to know if he had correctly

---

[1] Choate to Hay (private and confidential), 16 August, 1901: Hay Papers, 19.

interpreted Hay's intentions. The new treaty was not intended to
apply to a state of war between Britain and the United States.
Such a war would, as usual, suspend the operation of the treaty
and the canal would not be neutral ground between the combatants.

> Suppose the two hostile fleets to rendezvous in the neighbourhood
> of the canal, as upon the outbreak of war they would be likely to do,
> each would certainly do its best to destroy the other wherever it
> could be found whether within or without the three mile limit, and
> I understand your purpose to be that this Treaty shall not in that
> case stand in the way, that in case of war, notwithstanding the elision
> of the Davis Amendment each of the contracting parties is left free
> to defend itself whenever and wherever, as best it can [*sic*] — or as
> Lord Lansdowne put it in a desultory talk we had, 'In case we get in-
> to a war with you we both fall back on our reserved rights.' . . . In
> this view or construction the word 'belligerent' wherever used in
> Article III would not include the United States and Great Britain
> when engaged in war with each other. Nor would the first clause of
> section 2 of that article, that 'the canal shall never be blockaded, nor
> shall any right of war be exercised nor any act of hostility be com-
> mitted within it' or (sect. 5) in 'waters adjacent to the canal within
> three marine miles of either end' apply to either of the combatants
> in such a war.

To this general view the sixth section of Article III, protecting the
plant and works of the canal from injury even in time of war
would be an exception. Hay confirmed that Choate had understood him correctly.[1]

In the same letter (24 July), Choate emphasized that he realized
that no treaty under which a British warship could pass the canal
in time of war with the United States, would get through the
Senate; in other words the right to fortify the canal, though
'passed sub silentio' was reserved to the United States. Lansdowne
admitted this (see sub-head B of his memorandum), and was
reduced to arguing that it was of no importance. Hay for his own
reasons naturally took the same line. They may both have been
right, and certainly the interpretation of the treaty given by

---

[1] Choate to Hay (private and confidential), 24 July, 1901 and 16
August, 1901 (referring to Hay to Choate, 5 August, 1901): Hay
Papers, 19.

Choate (and accepted by Lansdowne at the end of his memorandum) made the mere question of fortification of secondary importance. A small amount of work would make the canal too dangerous for hostile shipping, and in time of war the United States, in the absence of the former specific injunction to the contrary, would immediately be set free to take any steps thought necessary. On the other hand, the offensive power of Britain against the canal would be greatly lessened by the treaty obligation, which was retained, not to damage the plant or works.

Whether Hay and Lansdowne were correct or not in thinking the right to fortify of small importance, there was a large body of opinion in the United States which held otherwise. Nor does Lansdowne's argument altogether convince. He claimed that the control of the canal in war-time would not depend 'upon the presence or absence of such works'. It is true that fortification of the canal would not give control of the passage in the face of a strong blockading force; but it had never been contended that it would. The purpose of fortifying the canal was the negative one put by Roosevelt — if the canal were not fortified 'our fleet would have to watch it, and therefore do the work which a fort should do; and which it could do much better'.[1] Nothing in the extended quotation from a technical paper given by Lansdowne contradicts Roosevelt's argument. Furthermore, Lansdowne's appeal to the opinion of his own technical experts misses the point. Their opinion was that no belligerent would attempt to pass the canal 'unless he could be sure that the passage could be made with safety. The latter condition is never likely to be present while the United States hold the banks'.[2] The question was not one of the extent of fortification which would make it unsafe to try to pass the canal, but of the presence or absence of a contractual obligation to keep the canal neutral even in time of war between the two signatories. That question was never adequately discussed — it was no answer to say that a sufficient naval force could also close the canal. In the first Hay-Pauncefote Treaty the neutrality of the canal in time of war was guaranteed. In the second it was not.

The work done on the treaty throughout the summer of 1901 was chiefly concerned with minor matters on which the drafts-

---

[1] Above, p. 54.   [2] See Appendix.

men exercised their ingenuity at some length, but on which agreement was never in real doubt, since they were not points of present difference, but those on which the treaty might later be open to misinterpretation.[1] At one stage Choate recorded his impression that Lansdowne and Pauncefote had been 'preparing a wholly new draft, which will have to be submitted directly to you'[2] but, as comparison of Hay's draft with the final treaty shows, this fear proved illusory. By the middle of September Hay was becoming anxious, and Choate promised to press his views as hard as possible in the hope of reaching a decision.[3] This did not, however, indicate any serious divergence of views, but merely that the British government were in no hurry, and that Pauncefote was tightening up the language of the treaty. At the end of September, for instance, it occurred to him that the route now chosen for the canal might be by Panama rather than Nicaragua, and the treaty had to be amended for that reason. Hay, of course, had no objection to making the treaty applicable to any canal that might be built.[4] When in September McKinley died and Roosevelt succeeded, he approved Hay's draft and the later correspondence — there could be no better indication that the United States was getting all anyone could ask.[5]

As a result of all this work the treaty was sufficiently advanced to enable Choate to go on leave in October. He sent home on the 2nd the final version of the amendments, which Lansdowne was to submit to the Cabinet without delay. The last sentences of his telegram read, 'Hope for the approval of the Premier and the Lord Chancellor which would I think be conclusive, though no Cabinet meeting till November. Have gone through whole matter

---

[1] In spite of all the technical skill employed, the drafting of the treaty was loose enough to cause controversy later, as in the 1912 dispute over toll charges. See L. Oppenheim, *The Panama Canal Conflict between Great Britain and the United States of America* (Cambridge, 1913).

[2] Choate to Hay (private and confidential), 3 August, 1901: Hay Papers, 19.

[3] Same to same (private and confidential), 13 September, 1901: Hay Papers, 19.

[4] Same to same (tel.), (confidential), 27 September, 1901: N.A., S.D., from London, Vol. 203; same to same (private and confidential), same date: Hay Papers, 19.

[5] Hay to Choate (tel.), 21 September, 1901: N.A., S.D., to London, Vol. 34.

with Senator Lodge, who approves absolutely and thinks it will pass Senate.' And on the 5th he had more good news: 'Yesterday . . . I learned that we are not to expect any opposition from the Lord Chancellor who was the one member of the Cabinet from whom I thought opposition was most likely.'[1] The treaty was signed on 18 November.

The important result of the modifications was that every point contended for by the Senate was conceded in the second Hay-Pauncefote Treaty, and conceded without a struggle. It appears as if Pauncefote, Lansdowne and the Cabinet felt that a war with the United States was a contingency so remote that it need not be closely considered, and so disastrous that if it came, concessions on the canal would prove of no importance. Except in the single event of war between Britain and the United States, the stronger the grip of the United States on the canal the better for Britain. Lansdowne withdrew completely from the position taken in his despatch of February.

There are indications that even at that time his real reasons for rejecting the Senate amendments were not quite those laid down in his despatch. A private letter to Pauncefote suggests that *amour-propre* rather than any more important consideration lay behind the rejection.

> Many thanks for your interesting letter of the 8th.
>
> I send you herewith a copy of the draft despatch — not yet finally approved by the Cabinet — of which the last words were telegraphed to you. They go, I think, as far as we could be expected to go without loss of self respect.
>
> Remember that from the U.S. Govt. we have had no hint of a desire to negotiate, no official intimation that the Senate amendments were offered, as Mr Choate told me privately, for our consideration. They have been thrown down upon the floor with an intimation that we are expected to pick them up and swallow them.
>
> The attitude of the public here would I think have been different, if the U.S. Govt. had approached us differently, had endeavoured, e.g., to shew us that the Davis amendment was not intended to

---

[1] Choate to Hay (tel.), (confidential), 2 October, 1901; same to same (private and confidential), 5 October, 1901: N.A., S.D., from London, Vol. 203.

interfere with the neutrality of the Canal and that they were ready
to reconsider its language, and, if necessary, to add safeguards such
as those to be found in the Suez Canal Convention.

Again, if the Clayton Bulwer Treaty stinks in American nostrils,
and it would strengthen Mr Hay's position to be able to announce
that he had succeeded in getting rid of it altogether, an attempt
might have been made to preserve in the new convention everything which was worth preserving in the older contract, which
might have been abrogated by mutual consent.

But none of these things have been done.

I am, as you know, sincerely anxious that we should remain on good
terms with the U.S. I do not attach too much importance to the
extravagances of individual Senators — above all I should be sincerely grieved if Mr Hay's resignation were to be the result of what
has taken place. But we can scarcely be expected to accept without
a murmur proposals which we believe to be inconsistent with the
'general principle applicable to all trans-Isthmian canals' to which
you refer, and we have surely a right to ask that our temperate
criticisms shall be examined and discussed with equal temperance,
before a 'Hepburn Bill' is passed, or the Clayton Bulwer Treaty torn
up by a precipitate resolution of the Senate.

I think the Cabinet will accept the despatch as now drafted, but I
am for the moment holding my hand in the hope of hearing again
from you after you have had time to consider the effect which would
be produced by the intimation with which the draft concludes.

.   .   .   .

P.S. You can, if you think well, speak to Mr Hay in the sense of what
I have written above. But as Mr Choate has not allowed me to treat
his explanations as those of his Government, so you must be careful
not to allow anything which you may say to be regarded as an
overture from us.[1]

Lansdowne's readiness to accept the modifications of the Hay-
Pauncefote Treaty demanded by the Senate was shared by British
public opinion. Few Foreign Secretaries have needed large public
successes more than Lansdowne. His appointment came as a surprise, for Balfour had usually deputized for Salisbury, and Lansdowne had not even been particularly active in the shaping of

---

[1] Lansdowne to Pauncefote (secret), 19 February, 1901: Lansdowne
Papers, Vol. 28 — United States.

foreign policy. The appointment was more surprising because the failure of the British army in the Boer War was largely laid to the charge of Lansdowne's administrative incompetence as War Minister. It was held to imply that Salisbury intended to keep control, and wanted a competent subordinate to take the burden of routine rather than a man of independent mind. That judgment was severe, and Lansdowne proved more independent, and more successful, than many had thought. Yet he necessarily took office with a sensitive regard for his own position and so for that of Great Britain. The large concessions he made to the United States over the isthmian canal aroused no criticism at all. Hardly a dissentient voice was raised.

This general approval was not due to weakness, or to any feeling that Britain must make concessions somewhere, to someone, and could most economically make them to the United States. The Boer War had been a triumph for isolation. British policy was widely unpopular in Europe; British defeats in the early stages of the war had stimulated sympathy for the Boers; yet the European Powers had early realized that they could do nothing. The Royal Navy prevented them from getting any men to the support of the Boers, but more important none of them had any interests in South Africa vital enough to induce her to make the European concessions that were the price of joint action. France would do nothing unless Germany agreed. Germany demanded a Russian guarantee of Alsace and Lorraine before moving, and had no real desire to alienate Britain finally merely for the sake of the Boers. Russia felt isolated action to be risky — and ineffectual — and could not pay the German price without losing the French *entente*. If, towards the end of the Boer War, the British were worried, it was about the poor performance of their army in South Africa, not about their world position. They were in no mood to feel that concessions to the United States were necessary.

The canal negotiations got little attention in Parliament. One question was asked in 1899, and one when the first Hay-Pauncefote Treaty was signed, enabling St John Brodrick, Curzon's successor as Under-Secretary at the Foreign Office, to explain that there had been 'no question of compensation, the advantages in the former Convention relative to the neutrality of the canal,

and the protection of commerce under conditions of entire
equality, being fully maintained'.[1] The Senate amendments produced one serious question in December 1900, when Mr Norman,
Liberal, asked

> whether Her Majesty's Government has any reason to believe that
> other European Governments would agree to regard as neutral a
> ship canal in Central America occupied and fortified by the United
> States Government; whether Her Majesty's Government has reason
> to believe that the Republic of Nicaragua accepts the view ex-
> pressed by the United States Senate Committee on Foreign Rela-
> tions, that the relationship between the United States and Nicaragua
> is analogous to that between Turkey and Egypt at the time of the
> construction of the Suez Canal, namely, the relationship between
> suzerain and vassal; and whether Her Majesty's Government
> understands that the United States Government associates itself
> with the protocol signed by all the Great Powers of Europe at the
> London Conference on 13th March, 1871, to the effect that it is an
> essential part of the law of nations that no Power can liberate itself
> from the engagements of a Treaty except with the consent of the
> contracting parties, by means of an amicable arrangement.

Beyond saying that the government had not consulted any European Power, Lord Cranborne, the government spokesman, declined to answer, and the matter was dropped; but by comparison
with the complete lack of interest taken in the negotiations at
any other time, the question is some indication of the feeling
roused by the Senate action.[2] The three questions asked in 1901
were purely formal; one of them was arranged to enable Cranborne to give the news of the rejection of the Senate amendments
the day after Hay had been informed.[3]

When the King's speech of 1902 announced the signing of the
second Hay-Pauncefote Treaty, acceptance was hardly less general.
The Earl of Lytton said:

> . . . I feel sure that your Lordships will rejoice to think that no legal
> or diplomatic technicality has been allowed any longer to stand in
> the way of an undertaking which will benefit the commerce of the
> whole world. According to the terms of the new treaty the United

---

[1] *The Parliamentary Debates* (Fourth Series), 1900, LXXVIII, p. 922.
[2] ibid., LXXXVIII, p. 841.   [3] ibid., 1901, XC, p. 1338.

States have undertaken the construction of the canal and the entire responsibility for the maintenance of its neutrality, and when the canal is completed it will be thrown open, on terms of absolute equality, to the ships of commerce and of war of all nations observing the rules which have been laid down. There are no people for whom we in this country have greater respect, and with whom we are more desirous of maintaining the most intimate and cordial relations, than the great enlightened population of America, and we cannot but hope, therefore, that all future discussions on points of difference between the two countries may be discussed in the same friendly spirit, and may be crowned with an equally satisfactory result.[1]

In general the line taken was that the Clayton-Bulwer Treaty could not meet the changed circumstances of the day, that Britain got all the advantages she required in connection with a canal which was of admitted benefit to commerce, and that friendly relations with the United States had been reaffirmed. Approval of the new treaty was entirely uncritical, no attempt was made to compare it either with its predecessor or with the Clayton-Bulwer Treaty, and none to find out whether Britain really obtained, as Earl Spencer said, 'all the advantages we require.'[2] The assumption that only 'legal or diplomatic technicalities' could have held up the treaty went unchallenged.

Enough evidence has been adduced of American determination to build the canal. As Hay said, a veto would not be effective. A serious consideration in Britain of the likelihood of conflict with the United States and of the advantages and disadvantages of modifying the Clayton-Bulwer Treaty might well have produced the conclusion that it would be better to give way. Britain's resources were not inexhaustible. A diplomatic defeat of this kind would, however, have strained Anglo-American relations far enough to bring the new factor in the international equation to British attention. The final result of the negotiations was the complete concession to the United States of everything asked, without compensation, but obvious though this was it was not treated by the country as being dangerous. No warnings of the menace of America were heard. No suggestions that Britain should prepare to defend her rights were made. The

---

[1] ibid., 1902, CI, pp. 9–10.   [2] ibid., p. 20.

action of the United States was not regarded as threatening.

Even more than those of the government, the protests of the leading journals at the action of the Senate were on points of form rather than of content. Their tone was unruffled, even friendly. They took it upon themselves to remind the United States and its Senate that the path of real wisdom lay in keeping international compacts.[1] They explained to their readers that the agitation of the Senate was not fundamentally anti-British, but sprang from such diverse motives as a desire to emphasize the constitutional power of the Senate, desire (among some Senators) to block the building of any canal at all, a strong sense of America's expanding destiny without any clear idea of its implications, a determination to uphold the Monroe Doctrine without any very good idea of what it was, a desire to accuse the Republicans of being too pro-British (largely with the German-American and Irish-American vote in mind) or a desire to refute that Democratic charge. All these explanations of the Senate amendments are to be found adequately, and accurately, set out in the serious periodicals of the day. The intelligent, politically conscious British public got full, adequate, friendly and unusually well informed comment on the state of American opinion.[2] Further, they were constantly reminded that the Senate, though for certain kinds of activity it functioned together with the Executive, was only part of one branch of the American government, and that though President McKinley had displayed neither tact nor strength in dealing with it, the behaviour of the President and the Secretary of State themselves had been notably friendly and correct.[3] The Press, in short, took care to play down the differences between Great Britain and the United States, and on occasion felt that both the public and government of Britain deserved credit for this restraint.

The flame which blazed up so briskly on the other side of the Atlantic was not fanned on this side, and in the absence of this

---

[1] See 'The Nicaragua Canal' in *The Economist*, LVIII, 22 December, 1900, p. 1810; *The Spectator*, LXXXV, 22 December, 1900, p. 917.

[2] See, for instance, 'America and England' in *The Spectator*, LXXXIV, 14 April, 1900, p. 511.

[3] 'The Nicaragua Canal' in *The Economist*, LVIII, 22 December, 1900, p. 1810.

artificial encouragement it rapidly died down [*The Economist* con-
gratulated itself]. . . . our language towards the United States has
been measured and kindly, and as a consequence of this we have
happily escaped any appreciable disturbance of the mutual goodwill which ordinarily exists between the two countries. That this is
a fortunate result will not be denied by anyone who sets a proper
value upon the maintenance of peace.[1]

Playing down differences is perhaps a poor expression of what
was going on in Britain. The quotation just given suggests the
general opinion that there was something artificial about those
differences, and that rivalry was manufactured in the United
States for internal political ends. The inference drawn was that it
need not be taken too seriously. This inference, justifiable though
it was, reveals a good deal about British thought. It marks the
effect of the repeated protestations of Hay and other influential
men that they would like to follow a friendly policy if only the
Senate and public opinion would allow it. At this time, by way
of contrast, reputable newspaper men in Germany, notably Chirol
of *The Times*, were making themselves unpopular by their persistent, and accurate, reports that, however friendly the attitude of the German government, German public opinion was
hostile to Britain. The analogy between the two cases must not be
pressed too far, but the difference in approach to these similar
phenomena is too great to be overlooked, at a time when the
growth of the new German navy had not yet affected British
opinion. American friendship during the Boer War had made a
good impression, but the attitude of the German government had
been only less correct, and both countries were known to be trying
to keep free of commitments.

The difference in reaction was not a rational one. In part it
came from the idea that while German hostility had its origin in a
real jealousy of Britain's position and a real determination to gain
at Britain's expense, American hostility came from such less
important sources as Irish rancour and the mere brashness of a
'young' country. United States foreign policy, in short, was held
to be still dominated by domestic considerations, German domestic

---

[1] 'The United States *v.* England' in LIX, 23 November, 1901, p. 1726.
That mutual goodwill had only been maintained by British concessions
was overlooked.

politics recognized to be increasingly controlled by the demands of imperialism. The distinction had some validity, but those who drew it never questioned the assumption behind it — that Great Britain and the United States could have no real and important differences, if only Britain would ignore the irrelevant irritations. The irritations were irrelevant because not based on real differences of interest. Therefore the United States could expand without any differences arising. Evidence of congruity of interest was not produced — that congruity was assumed.

These emotions shaped British reaction to the canal negotiations. The motives which were implicit in Lansdowne's handling of them, if not in Salisbury's, became explicit in the Press.

> We want nothing that belongs to America, nor do we claim to interfere with what she considers within her special 'sphere of influence'. Our virtual acceptance of the Monroe doctrine when we agreed to the Venezuelan arbitration has removed the risk of serious quarrel in the future. Indeed, this acceptance has done more than take away the only dangerous source of enmity. It, and the acquisition by America of a Far Eastern and Asian Empire in the Philippines, have brought us together, and shown us that we have a community of interests as well as of blood. The tie of blood is far the stronger, the essential tie, but the other exists. But we need not labour the point. It will, we think, be admitted by all who take the trouble to look into the matter that the British Empire will benefit greatly by the making of the canal, and that being so, the sooner we come to a frank and generous and sensible understanding with America the better.[1]

It is apparent that, so far as the reference to interests is concerned, the argument was a circular one. Britain had no interests conflicting with those of America because she chose to have none. The British and American community of interests in the Far East was largely illusory, and good-feeling was based on British withdrawal from the western hemisphere. The tie of blood, stronger in the imagination of Britons than in reality, was, as *The Spectator* admitted, of far greater importance — 'the essential tie'. It prevented Britain from viewing Anglo-American relations with the eye she turned on her other affairs.

---

[1] 'The Clayton-Bulwer Treaty' in *The Spectator*, LXXXIV, 27 January, 1900, pp. 129–30.

Towards the first Hay-Pauncefote Treaty no one felt anything but approval. Just before it was announced an article appeared in *The Spectator* advocating it. That article was written as if the author had no knowledge of the negotiations then proceeding, but it is incredible that John Strachey, the editor, an influential Unionist and a friend of Theodore Roosevelt, should not have known what was going on, and the article so accurately forecast the content of the treaty that it was probably inspired. It argued that Britain could only gain from the building of a new water-way, that the conditions ensuring neutrality were adequate and that the United States was the obvious country not only to build but also to control the canal. Strachey even dealt with the idea that concessions for Canada in Alaska should have been obtained. As between Canada and the United States, he said, the interests of Canada, a member of the Empire, must have first consideration. But the Hay-Pauncefote Treaty was not a concession to the United States. It was to the larger interests of the Empire to have the canal built, and to those interests the local interests of Canada must give way. This, he felt sure, the Canadians themselves would realize.[1]

The more extreme periodicals were already suggesting that it would be to Britain's advantage to have the canal fortified by the United States, and — absurdly — that if a clause forbidding that had been inserted it was at American request and from American anxiety not to offend the Continental Powers.[2] Nothing of course was further from American thoughts. But it followed from this argument that the insertion or non-insertion of a fortification clause was one for American decision. If the Senate decided to put it in Britain would gain. This attitude greatly strengthened the government's hand when the question actually arose.

The first Hay-Pauncefote Treaty, then, was accepted without

---

[1] 'The Clayton-Bulwer Treaty' in *The Spectator*, LXXXIV, 27 January, 1900, p. 129. See also 'The Nicaraguan Canal' in *The Economist*, LVIII, 10 February, 1900, p. 190; and 'Great Britain and the Nicaragua Canal' in *The Spectator*, LXXXIV, 24 February, 1900, p. 267.

[2] *The Spectator*, LXXXIV, 10 February, 1900, p. 193; also 'Great Britain and the Nicaragua Canal', ibid., 24 February, 1900, p. 267. Nor was *The Economist* in December concerned to oppose the fortification of the canal. See 'The Nicaragua Canal' in LVIII, 22 December, 1900, p. 1810.

demur and without insisting on any British right to concessions
in return; and if the first Hay-Pauncefote Treaty was regarded as
a benefit to the British Empire that attitude sprang from two
related ideas: that Britain had no interests of her own in Central
America, and that the prospects of any conflict with the United
States were so remote as to be negligible. These were assumptions, not conclusions. They were not debated at all.

The action of the Senate in amending the treaty in December
1900, did very little to alter the British attitude, for reasons
already foreshadowed. It was supposed that the only likely even-
tuality would be war between the United States and some third
Power. In that event the more power the United States had to
guarantee the neutrality of the canal in time of war the better.
It would be merely foolish to make the United States the guardian
of the canal and then tie the hands of the guardian.[1] That this
view went together, somewhat illogically, with the comforting
reflection that naval power would still enable Britain to close the
canal at will — a point also made by Theodore Roosevelt in his
desire to emphasize that Senate activity was not aimed at Britain
— did nothing to weaken the force of either.[2] This last argument
either was a muddled one or concealed an assumption never made
specific. No competent American critic ever maintained that
fortification would enable the United States to keep the canal
open against blockade by a stronger naval force. They did maintain that it would enable the United States to keep the canal
closed against a stronger naval force, work for which the American navy would prove inadequate. The American contention that
Britain was the one nation which had nothing to fear from a
fortified canal, since her naval strength was overwhelming and
would not be challenged by America, was disingenuous. Against
any lesser naval Power, the proper defence was a bigger navy,
which the United States would be committed to building anyway.
The fortification of the canal could only be directed against a navy
larger than that of the United States; it was designed to make
other naval Powers blockade the canal, if they thought it necessary,

---

[1] 'The Nicaragua Canal Treaty and the Monroe Doctrine' in *The
Spectator*, LXXXVII, 23 November, 1901, p. 788.
[2] See 'The United States *v.* England' in *The Economist*, LIX, 23
November, 1901, p. 1726.

while the United States was relieved of that necessity. If this new state of affairs was not disadvantageous to Britain it could only be because of the complete abdication of Great Britain in the western hemisphere and the determination not to challenge the United States in the Caribbean.

Precisely this determination, this insistence that accretion of strength to the United States could only benefit Britain, marked all comment on the subject. '. . . the Foreign Office has done in November what it might just as well have done in March,' wrote *The Spectator*, chiding the Foreign Office for its unwillingness to give anything away 'even though we do not want it ourselves, without obtaining an equivalent.'[1] 'If the Senate had simply stated its grounds of objection to the treaty as it was first framed, the English Government would have been quite ready to modify it.'[2] If this was not quite literally true, it was true in spirit, as the signing of the second Hay-Pauncefote Treaty made clear.

The magnitude of the change, then, cannot be measured by the readiness with which it was made, but its acceptance was not due to a sense of weakness. There was a strong body of American opinion which thought that the Senate could do what it liked, since Britain was in no position to oppose anything it might do. This was not the best opinion but it was influential in the Senate.[3] McKinley and Hay, however, had little doubt that the amendments would be rejected from the time when they came under discussion, and the rejection came as no surprise to them even if it surprised the Senate.[4] Certainly no one reading the British Press could be misled into supposing that the amendments would be accepted. But a reading of that Press strengthens the conclusion that it was prestige diplomacy rather than any calculation of interest which dictated their rejection.

The action of the Senate was fully recognized to change the whole content of the treaty. It was pointed out that in the first Hay-Pauncefote Treaty all the advantages of the Clayton-Bulwer Treaty had been retained, that Britain had merely relinquished

---

[1] 'The Nicaragua Canal Treaty and the Monroe Doctrine' in *The Spectator*, loc. cit.
[2] 'The United States *v.* England' in *The Economist*, loc. cit.
[3] *The Times*, 12 December, 1900, p. 5e.
[4] ibid., 8 December, 1900, p. 7e.

a right which she no longer had any wish to exercise, and that this was the real reason for not insisting on any compensation. If this was not quite true, it could pass without much objection. As *The Times* firmly remarked, 'If the concessions to which we have consented are refused, we can only express our regret. Our existing treaty rights remain untouched. . . .'[1] And again, 'It is not the custom of this country to conclude treaties of surrender . . . and that is a custom from which we have no mind to depart.'[2]

If, after that, the second Hay-Pauncefote Treaty was accepted, it was because the calculation of British interest showed it profitable. The calculation was genuine, but its results were determined in advance and by sentiment. Perhaps *The Times* may be quoted as summing up the official and almost universal view:

> So far as Great Britain is concerned, the arrangements which Lord Pauncefote has accepted as satisfactory are not likely to be objected to. . . . This country could not undertake the serious responsibility of maintaining the freedom of the Canal for neutral commerce in time of war, though, while we hold the open seas, we should be able to look after our own interests.[3]

> England undoubtedly waives certain objections she has heretofore pressed, but this waiver is the result, not of dictation, but of negotiations ending in the final and complete agreement of the two Governments on all points.[4]

> In Washington everybody considers the action of the Senate on the Canal Treaty as a new pledge of amity with England. The enemies of the Treaty opposed ratification on that ground . . . . it is regarded as the close of a long period of controversy; it is regarded also as the opening of a new period of better feeling and better understanding between the two countries. Unless this better feeling had already existed no such majority as was obtained would now have been obtainable. . . .[5]

This last quotation, from a highly pro-British American correspondent must be accepted with some reserve. Whether true of

---

[1] ibid., leading article, 15 December, 1900, p. 11c.
[2] ibid., leading article, 19 December, 1900, p. 9e.
[3] ibid., leading article, 19 November, 1901, p. 9b, c.
[4] ibid., p. 5a.
[5] ibid., 18 December, 1901, p. 5b.

American opinion or not, however, the statement was certainly true in reverse. British goodwill towards the United States did more than anything to remove those causes of dispute whose removal gave reality to the sentiment. Of this general process in Anglo-American relations, the canal negotiations provide perhaps the clearest example.

APPENDIX

Memorandum by Lansdowne, 6 July, 1901

Confidential — printed for the Cabinet, 8 July, 1901

Our refusal to accept the amendments inserted by the Senate in the Hay-Pauncefote Convention has led, as we anticipated, to a further proposal on the part of the United States' Government. I circulate, with an explanatory Memorandum by Mr Villiers, a new draft Convention which Mr Hay has prepared in consultation with a number of prominent Senators, and which Lord Pauncefote has been asked to submit to us privately in the first instance.

Lord Pauncefote's opinion may, I think, be summarized as follows:

He thinks the Senate would probably accept the new draft as it stands. He believes that an attempt to recast it would probably be fatal to its chance, and he inclines to the view that with one or two amendments which he suggests, the new addition might be accepted by His Majesty's Government.

We should, I believe, all of us be glad to find an amicable solution of this troublesome question. The conditions are, moreover, more favourable than they were, for whereas the inconsiderate action of the Senate last year justified us then in insisting on our strict rights and in pressing our objections to the utmost, it is open to us, now that we are approached in a very different spirit by Mr Hay, to deal somewhat less strictly with him so far as matters of form are concerned. We ought also to take into account the fact that Mr Hay has laid before us not only this draft of a Convention relative to the construction of the Interoceanic Canal, but also a scheme for determining the Alaska boundary by arbitration, and a draft Treaty dealing with a number of the outstanding Canadian questions which we had hoped to settle in 1899, but which were left open by the Joint High Commission appointed in that year.

On the other hand, however much we may desire an amicable

settlement, it will be impossible for us to abandon abruptly the strong position which we took up in our despatch of the 22nd February, a despatch which was regarded with approval here, and was admitted in the United States to be a moderate and reasonable statement of the British Case.

In form the new draft differs from the old Convention, under which the High Contracting Parties, after agreeing that the Canal might be constructed by the United States, agreed to adopt certain rules as the basis upon which the canal was to be neutralized. In the draft now before us the United States intimate to us *their* readiness to adopt somewhat similar rules as the basis of the neutralization of the canal. I do not know, however, that this change of form is one to which we need seriously object.

The three amendments inserted by the Senate, and objected to by us in our despatch of the 22nd February, 1901, are dealt with as follows:

(A.) *Supersession of the Clayton-Bulwer Treaty.*

As to this amendment we stand where we did, for the Treaty is superseded in the first Article of the new draft.

I pointed out, however, in a Memorandum circulated to the Cabinet on the 15th January, 1901, that the Hay-Pauncefote Convention in its original form contained provisions which did in effect almost entirely supersede those of the Treaty. I showed that there were only two provisions of the Treaty which were not covered by the Convention, and that neither of them were of great importance to us, and I said that if this amendment had stood alone I should have been in favour of coming to terms with regard to it. In our despatch we objected to the amendment, not so much upon the ground that it would be materially injurious to us, as upon the ground that the Treaty was an international contract of unquestionable validity, and that, according to well-established national usage [*sic*], it ought not to be abrogated or modified, save with the consent of both the parties to the contract. So far as this amendment was concerned, our complaint had reference rather to form than to substance.

Lord Pauncefote's new Article III provides for the case in which the sovereignty of the territory through which the canal is intended to pass might fall into the hands of the United States, or of any other foreign Power. I do not see how the United States could object to this stipulation. They could scarcely contend that a change in the ownership of the territories adjoining the canal would relieve them of their obligation to maintain its neutrality.

(B.) *Reservation by the United States of the Right to Defend the Canal.*

To this amendment we objected very decidedly (see despatch, p. 3). The objectionable provision does not appear in the present draft, from which, however, is also omitted Rule 7 of Article II of the original Convention, under which the Contracting Parties were forbidden to fortify the canal. The two Rules were, as I pointed out at the time, antagonistic. I think we may be content to have them both omitted; but attention will, no doubt, be called to the omission of Rule 7, as suggesting that the right to fortify is not renounced.

The Rule against fortification was, I believe, of no practical value to us: the United States would not be likely to spend money on expensive works at the mouth of the canal or throughout its course, nor, if they did, would the control of the canal in time of war depend upon the presence or absence of such works.

(C.) *The High Contracting Parties not to be obliged to bring the Convention to the notice of other Powers and to invite them to adhere to it.*

The Article excised by this amendment has not been restored, and as to it we stand where we did in the spring. It will, I think, be impossible for us to agree to give way altogether upon this point, but Lord Pauncefote's proposal for dealing with the matter seems to me sufficiently to meet the requirements of the case. If his words are added to Article III, Rule 2, it will no longer be possible for us to contend, as we contended in our despatch, that we should be placed in a position of marked disadvantage compared with other Powers.

Any Power which gives its adherence will incur the obligation to observe the Rules described in Article III, and no non-adhering Power will be able to claim a right to use the canal.

The omission of the words 'in time of war as in time of peace', from Article III, Rule I, is the alteration which we shall find most difficult [*sic*] in justifying. The fact that the words occur in the original text renders their disappearance significant. Were it not for this, we might rely upon the fact that there are no limiting words in Article I, which, therefore, might be presumed to apply in time of war as well as in time of peace, that in Article II it is said that the canal shall '*never* be blockaded, etc.', and that in Article VI it is stipulated that the plant, establishment, buildings, etc., of the canal shall 'in time of war as in time of peace' enjoy complete immunity from attacks or injury by belligerents, and from acts calculated to impair their usefulness as part of the canal. But it will not be forgotten that throughout the discussions which have taken place in the United States, prominent politicians have constantly insisted that under no circumstances could the United States preclude themselves from the right of adopting, when their country was at war, whatever measures were best calculated to secure its safety, even if such measures involved temporary deneutralization of the canal. The United States could not, it was said, refuse to take such measures, when the time came, without dereliction of duty, and they would be dishonest if they promised not to take them without the intention of keeping their word.

As a matter of practical politics I do not think we need object. Assuming the United States and Great Britain to be at war and assuming a British ship of war to have forced its way through the squadron which might be watching one end of the canal, could we expect the United States to give that ship facilities for passing through the canal from end to end in order that she might, as soon as she re-entered extra-territorial waters, renew her attack upon American shipping? Or, again, should we, if we were at war with the United States, be in the least likely to risk the safety of our ships by endeavouring, even if the canal were ostensibly open, to pass them through it? The Admiralty, in a paper which was circulated to the Cabinet, have advised us that the real control of the canal will probably remain with that Power which is able to place a superior naval force in a position to command the approaches to its entrances, and that no belligerent, even in superior naval force, would attempt to pass his ships through the canal unless he could be sure that the passage could be made with safety. The latter condition is never likely to be present while the United States hold the banks. It seems to me, therefore, that for all practical purposes, we should in substance gain nothing, even if we were to secure on paper the right of passing our ships through the canal in time of war as well as in time of peace.

I quote in support of this view the following passage from a paper entitled 'An Isthmian Canal from a Military Point of View', read before the American Academy of Political and Social Science:

'An isthmian canal, to be of service to the United States, presupposes that passage to it, through it, and from it is assured. But passage to or from it in case of war with a strong naval Power could only be maintained by a strong naval force. If the canal bristled with guns from one end to the other, it would be of no use to the United States while a powerful hostile fleet dominated the Caribbean Sea. The nation that controls the adjoining seas will in time of war control passage through the canal, no matter which one has possession.'

The despatch of the 22nd February does not seem to me to tie our hands, should we desire to concede this point now. In that despatch, we showed reasons against a unilateral arrangement, under which the United States would enjoy the right, not enjoyed by the other Contracting Party, of taking, even in time of peace, whatever steps they thought necessary for the purpose of defending the canal. Under the present proposal no such right is sought by the United States, although the draft is so worded as to render it possible for them to contend, when war has actually broken out, that they are no longer bound by any of the Rules which govern its neutralization. In such a case, however, we should be entirely emancipated from the restrictions now imposed upon us by the Clayton-Bulwer Treaty, and should find ourselves equally free with the United States to act in whatever way we thought best for our own interest.

L.

Foreign Office, July 6, 1901.

(Foreign Office Library, Lansdowne Papers, Vol. 28—United States).

CHAPTER FOUR

The Alaskan Boundary Dispute

THE boundary between Venezuela and British Guiana had been in dispute for many years before the United States took a hand. It was, on the contrary, an essential part of the American case in the Alaskan dispute that their boundary had been unchallenged till the discovery of gold in the Yukon made it profitable for the Canadians to invent a claim to part of United States territory.

This attitude was tenable because no one had had much interest in the details of the boundary line till gold was discovered in 1897, and the line had never in fact been adequately surveyed. From that time constant complaints by United States officials of Canadian encroachments on their land made a settlement of the boundary, at least a temporary one, important. Had the question been merely one of surveying the boundary and fixing marks under known regulations, it would have been easily settled, but as the very suggestion that a temporary boundary might be valuable shows, this was not so. The circumstances which made a temporary boundary desirable made it almost as difficult to run as a permanent line. If nothing more had been involved in reaching a *modus vivendi* than to avoid conflicts of jurisdiction and to let miners on the ground know their standing, that too could readily have been achieved. No doubt points of detail would have been keenly fought. As it was, both sides were alert to see that likely gold-bearing areas did not pass from their hands by inadvertence; and much debate was held on such questions as whether it was more just and less troublesome for Canada to relinquish temporarily control of some land to which she might later have a claim, or for the United States to give up jurisdiction over American miners settled on that land.[1] Still, the general principles of such agreements were well known: the line should as far as possible get Canadians on one side of it and Americans on the other, and it should not prejudice the later claims of either country. It was plainly to the advantage of everyone to get a line of some kind drawn, and generally speaking the Americans were ready to accept the *status quo* and make it formal. Not so the Canadians. Their reasons bring us to the heart of the controversy.

The discovery of gold, which brought miners and disorder to the region and caused the American initiative, made Canadians aware of the advantages of having a port on the coast readily accessible from the interior by one of the few possible routes. Such a port they could only get by establishing their permanent title to part of the coast. No *modus vivendi* could give it to them, since they were obviously not in possession. Their interest was in the permanent boundary and, as will appear, they regarded American desire for a temporary line as a bargaining counter.

The Canadian claim to a port was a political claim, not something that could be settled by surveyors, and some topographical details must be given to show its basis. From the south-eastern corner of the main bulk of Alaska, where the angle of the Yukon approached most closely to the sea, a panhandle ran down the coast for a distance of some five hundred miles. Alaska had been acknowledged as Russian territory by a Russo-British treaty of 1825; and by the Russians sold to the United States in 1867. By this sale the United States might be presumed to hold under exactly the same terms as Russia, and this contention was never challenged. The question at issue was the proper interpretation of the language of the treaty. This provided that 'the line of demarcation shall follow the summit of the mountains situated parallel to the Coast' over most of the territory in dispute, and the text continued:

That wherever the summit of the mountains which extend in a direction parallel to the Coast, from the 56th degree of north Lati-

---

[1] Hay to Choate, 26 June, 1899; Hay to Reginald Tower [chargé d'affaires in Washington] (private and personal), 3 August, 1899: Library of Congress, Hay Papers, L.B. I, pp. 205, 253; Hay to Choate, 24 July, 1899: N.A., S.D., to London, Vol. 33, p. 227; Choate to Hay (private), 4 August, 1899: Hay Papers, 19; and much correspondence in the P.R.O., FO 5/2415 and 5/2416, *passim*.

tude to the point of intersection of the 141st degree of West Longitude, shall prove to be at the distance of more than ten marine leagues from the Ocean, the limit between the British Possessions and the line of Coast which is to belong to Russia, as above-mentioned, shall be formed by a line parallel to the windings of the Coast, and which shall never exceed the distance of ten marine leagues therefrom.[1]

The coastline was heavily indented with long inlets running as much as two hundred miles inland, the most important of which was the Lynn Canal, and an ambiguity in the wording of the treaty became of great importance. Should the coastline from which the width of the *lisière* was to be measured be regarded as running round the heads of inlets or across their mouths? Or perhaps some compromise between the two? In a coast so deeply indented the second interpretation would give Canada access to the sea at the head of several inlets and break American territory into a series of promontories, while the other would deny the Canadians a useful sea exit from the Yukon and give the United States an unbroken coastline. The machinery for a discussion of the boundary dispute was available. An American-Canadian Joint High Commission was already meeting in Washington to discuss all the questions at issue between the two countries, and to this body the temporary settlement of the boundary was referred.

The Joint High Commission made no progress with the problem. The boundary dispute was one on which the American Commissioners were least inclined to make concessions, feeling that their case was so strong that it was not a proper matter for bargaining.[2] They felt that the Canadians must have some

---

[1] Que partout où la crête des montagnes qui s'étendent dans une direction parallèle à la Côte depuis le 56me degré de latitude Nord au point d'intersection du 141me degré de longitude Ouest, se trouveroit à la distance de plus de dix lieues marines de l'Océan, la limite entre les Possessions Britanniques et la lisière de Côte mentionée ci-dessus comme devant appartenir à La Russie, sera formé par une ligne parallèle aux sinuosités de la Côte, et qui ne pourra jamais en être éloignée que de dix lieues marines.' *British and Foreign State Papers*, 1824–5 (London, 1826), pp. 40–1.
[2] See Hay to Henry White, 3 January, 1899. Quoted in W. R. Thayer, *The Life and Letters of John Hay* (London, 1915), Vol. II, pp. 204–5.

ulterior motive for arguing about it; and in this they were right
to the extent that the Canadians, conscious as they were of their
inferiority in size and power, were trying as a matter of policy to
combine a variety of unrelated issues into a general settlement.[1]
The work of the Commission was further handicapped by Lord
Herschell, the only British member of the Commission, who was
thought by his American colleagues to be needlessly stiff and
aggressive in defence of the Canadian case.[2] Herschell's sudden
death in 1899 might have opened the way to agreement, but it
also caused the abandonment of the High Commission, which was
not called again. Thereafter negotiations were conducted through
ordinary diplomatic channels. Since the decision of the permanent
boundary would inevitably be a lengthy business, negotiations
for a *modus vivendi* were put in hand.

The matter was opened by Hay in March 1899 on the ground
that the Governor of Alaska was reporting a likelihood of
dangerous conflict between Canadians and Americans in the
disputed region. It was Hay's claim that the trouble arose from
expanding Canadian jurisdiction over country in which American
miners were operating, country which they regarded as American
because it lay within the line claimed by the United States and
shown on American maps. The Canadian reply to this charge was
that their posts had not been advanced, and indeed were well
behind the American line, but that the district in dispute was
filling up with Canadians.[3] Apparently the country was rough
and under the control of police patrols. The very different
Canadian and American stories of what was actually happening
and whose citizens were on the ground strongly suggest biased
evidence; but one thing is clear. Since American miners besieged
the State Department with complaints of onerous regulations

---

[1] Pauncefote warned from the beginning that this policy would not
be successful. Pauncefote to Salisbury (tel.) no. 11, 9 February, 1899:
P.R.O., FO 5/2415.
[2] Hay to Henry White (confidential), 3 December, 1898; H. C.
Lodge to White (private), same date: Henry White Papers.
[3] Hay to Pauncefote, no. 1381, 20 March, 1899, enclosed in Pauncefote to Salisbury, no. 99, 21 March, 1899; Pauncefote to Salisbury (tel.)
no. 43, 23 April, 1899; Lord Minto, Governor-General of Canada, to
Pauncefote (private), 25 April, 1899, copy enclosed in Tower to Salisbury,
no. 124 (confidential), 28 April, 1899: P.R.O., FO 5/2415.

against aliens, the Canadians were in fact administering a part of the area on the American side of the American line.

The Canadians were aware of the value to them of American miners' complaints, and were reluctant to give up this advantage, the more so since there seemed no hope of getting the United States to agree on a permanent boundary. In this the Colonial Office supported Canada. The local regulations were certainly severe on alien miners. Chamberlain felt that they might cause hardship; and Laurier, Prime Minister of Canada, was on record as disapproving of them. They were, however, the provincial regulations of British Columbia, not those of the Dominion government, and both Chamberlain and Laurier agreed in refusing to disallow the legislation before arbitration of the boundary was agreed.[1]

By these means they were hoping to bring pressure to bear on the United States government to modify their boundary claim.[2] They felt too — a view shared by the Foreign Office — that Hay's first offer of a *modus vivendi* was much too favourable to the United States. A minute written for the Foreign Office by Cartwright of the American Department put the case strongly. Hay's *modus* gave the United States the utmost they would get as a permanent boundary if their own interpretation of the boundary were accepted. If a formal consent to the *modus* were given, they would be satisfied and avoid arbitration or any definite settlement. The only object of the proposal was to get from the British government a distinct recognition of the situation as it existed.[3] The plain implication was that such a recognition would weaken the Canadian case in an arbitration, if indeed it did not prevent

---

[1] ibid.; also Chamberlain to Minto (tel.), 27 April, 1899; and Colonial Office to Foreign Office (pressing and secret), 28 April, 1899: P.R.O., FO 5/2415.

[2] Laurier also refused to reconvene the Joint High Commission to consider other disputed subjects before arbitration of the boundary was conceded. According to Hay, most of the United States Commissioners agreed that it would do no good to meet again before the governments had come to some arrangement on Alaska. Minto to Chamberlain (secret), 5 May, 1899; Tower to Salisbury, no. 141, 12 May, 1899: P.R.O., FO 5/2415.

[3] Minute by W. C. Cartwright, 23 March, 1899 on Hay's proposals, forwarded in Pauncefote to Salisbury (tel.) no. 27, 22 March, 1899: P.R.O., FO 5/2415.

arbitration altogether. A little later Hay modified his offer, suggesting that if the British Columbia authorities would waive their regulations against alien miners pending settlement, this would facilitate a *modus vivendi* on a line more favourable to Canada.[1]

This suggestion Laurier and the Colonial Office agreed in turning down. They regarded a slightly more favourable *modus vivendi*, which would in any case certainly not give Canada the main points for which she was contending, as of small importance against the pressure which the discontent of American miners could bring on the State Department. The concession would make ultimate settlement of the question less likely.[2] On 4 May Hay again raised the matter, suggesting a new line; and the following day he told Tower, the British chargé d'affaires in Washington, that the United States had decided to send a company of troops to the region. Although on protest by Tower these troops were not sent, this reminder that the United States was in a strong position to enforce its claims should need arise had its effect.[3]

During most of May 1899 discussion of the *modus vivendi* lapsed, though Americans and Canadians were still presumably feuding in the Klondike, because the Canadian determination to concede nothing till the principle of the arbitration of the boundary had been accepted, together with a visit by Pauncefote to London, provided a motive and an opportunity for concentrating on a permanent settlement. 'The Dominion Government,' said the Colonial Office, 'is not prepared to accept any provisional boundary on the Chilkat Pass except as part of an agreement for the reference of the whole question to arbitration.'[4] Not till the Canadians abandoned this position, and they were slow to see that it was hopeless, could there be any more talk of a *modus*. Choate urged it again on 2 June, the more because he was not hopeful

---

[1] Pauncefote to Salisbury (tel.), no. 43, 23 April, 1899: P.R.O., FO 5/2415.

[2] Colonial Office to Foreign Office (pressing and secret), 28 April, 1899: P.R.O., FO 5/2415.

[3] Tower to Salisbury, no. 135 (secret), 4 May, 1899; same to same (tel.), no. 46, 5 May, 1899; Salisbury to Tower (tel.), no. 70, 11 May, 1899; Tower to Hay, 12 May, 1899, copy enclosed in Tower to Salisbury, no. 142, 12 May, 1899; Tower to Salisbury (tel.), no. 47, 17 May, 1899: P.R.O., FO 5/2415.

[4] Colonial Office to Foreign Office (confidential), 22 May, 1899: P.R.O., FO 5/2415.

of any permanent settlement being quickly reached, and this time the Canadian government accepted his proposal, after some discussion but without reference to a general arbitration. What caused this change of attitude one cannot say: probably the realization that they would gain nothing by holding out longer.[1]

Although debate on details dragged on through the summer, from this time the reaching of a *modus vivendi* was only a matter of time. In that debate the Foreign and Colonial Offices played an equivocal role, urging the Canadian case in Washington, but privately arguing strongly that the Canadian government could only lose by delay, because such temporary arrangements are always essentially a recognition of the *status quo*, and the thrusting energy of American miners was daily altering the lines of occupation to Canada's disadvantage.[2] The one possibility of gaining anything by insistence vanished when Senator Fairbanks returned from a visit to Alaska at the end of July and reported that there was less danger of immediate conflict than the United States government had been led to suppose. This greatly strengthened Hay's hand, particularly as winter was approaching to limit activity of any kind. He reprimanded the Governor of Alaska for his alarmist reports, and settled down to wait, confident that time was on his side.[3] The *modus* agreement was finally signed on 20 October.

The settlement of a temporary line left the way clear for the more important debate on the permanent boundary. The weakest part of the Canadian case was that while the coast was of no interest to them they had failed to protest against American actions based on American assumptions.[4] From a study of the treaty itself the Canadian interpretation was at least a possible one. As a matter of equity, based on a presumed natural right of

---

[1] Minto to Chamberlain (tel.), 4 June, 1899, copy enclosed in Salisbury to Choate, 6 June, 1899: P.R.O., FO 5/2415.

[2] Chamberlain to Minto (tel.) (secret), 1 June, 1899: P.R.O., FO 5/2415. This telegram was approved by the Foreign Office before being sent.

[3] Tower to Salisbury (tel.), no. 60, 20 July, 1899: P.R.O., FO 5/2416.

[4] The Canadians, however, maintained that an attempted protest in 1889 had been mishandled by Salisbury and Sir Lionel Sackville-West (then Minister in Washington). O. D. Skelton, *Life and Letters of Sir Wilfrid Laurier* (London, 1922), Vol. II, p. 135, note 1.

egress to the sea, it was stronger still. (The value of that last argument in international law is very doubtful; but the United States took some trouble to ensure that any arbitrators — when arbitration was still in question — should not take it into account.) But when the Canadians were asked to show that they had claimed their boundary since before the 1890s they could not do so. Again and again Choate, skilfully handling the American case, came back to this point, and the Foreign Office had to concede its justice. On 1 August, for instance, in a long conversation with Villiers of the Foreign Office, he reported Hay's rejection of the British proposal that the terms of the Venezuela arbitration should be followed, because the cases were not similar: the Venezuelan boundary had always been disputed, the Alaskan boundary not till 1898 or so. 'To this line of argument we have really no answer', noted Villiers.[1]

The efforts of the Joint High Commission to settle the boundary dispute failed principally because the United States Commissioners regarded the question as a separate one to be decided on its merits, while the Canadians were anxious to combine it with others, especially the modification of the Clayton-Bulwer Treaty. Salisbury and Chamberlain shared this desire, though primarily because they regarded the modification of the Clayton-Bulwer Treaty as a concession, unwelcome to British opinion unless accompanied by a reciprocal concession elsewhere.[2] This anxiety suggests that the Canadians were unsure of their case, but there is no evidence to suggest that the United States at that time regarded it as entirely invented. The lengthy private exchanges between Herschell and Senator Fairbanks at the time of the High Commission show Herschell fully holding his own in the argument. Herschell himself claimed that when he came to study the Canadian case, which had never been systematically done, he found it stronger than he had supposed; and reported that United States reluctance to go to arbitration increased very obviously after Herschell had put that case.[3] The United States Commissioners were very anxious to avoid having a foreign um-

---

[1] Memorandum, 1 August, 1899: P.R.O., FO 5/2416.
[2] See above, ch. iii.
[3] Herschell to Salisbury, no. 9 (confidential), 11 October, 1898. This and much other interesting correspondence of the High Commission,

pire in the event of arbitration, claiming that all umpires had a
tendency to compromise, out of place in a judicial question to be
settled judicially. This was just the argument put forward by
Great Britain in the Venezuela case, when Olney had contended
that an umpire could always be suitably instructed to prevent
compromise. The insistence on a legalistic approach may be held
to indicate great confidence in the strength of their case, but it
marked a change from the line taken by Olney over Venezuela
that if the British case were as strong as claimed they had nothing
to fear from an umpire.

In February, the American documents record a British attempt
to connect arbitration of the boundary with a new canal treaty,
although as early as the 9th Pauncefote was quite clear that the
United States would not agree to this.[1] Shortly afterwards, however, Hay, for the United States Commissioners,[2] made for the
first time the American offer finally accepted, that of arbitration
by six jurists, three appointed by each side, the majority to decide.
In transmitting this offer, Henry White said that the United
States hoped to avoid a foreign umpire, though the possibility of
one might be considered to prevent a deadlock.[3]

There is no evidence of any reply by Salisbury to this proposal
made at a time when the organization of a *modus vivendi* was still
the chief concern. In May Pauncefote went home and in consultation with Choate drew up a plan of arbitration. The towns of
Dyea and Skagway on the Lynn Canal were to be reserved to the
United States and the boundary would then be settled by a
tribunal of seven, the seventh to be chosen by the other six,
appointed by the two governments. Pauncefote's attempt to get
compensation if Dyea and Skagway should prove to be on land
which would have fallen to Canada without a reservation to the

especially Herschell to Senator Fairbanks (confidential), 21 December,
1898 and Herschell to Salisbury, no. 15, 22 December, 1898 are in
P.R.O., FO 5/2421. See also the letters and memoranda of W. C. Cartwright (of the Foreign Office, attached to the Commission) to the
Foreign Office, in P.R.O., FO 5/2422.

[1] Henry White to Hay (tel.), 15 February, 1899: N.A., S.D., from
London, Vol. 196; Pauncefote to Salisbury (tel.), no. 11, 9 February,
1899: P.R.O., FO 5/2415.

[2] The Commission was not at this time in session.

[3] Henry White to Salisbury, 18 February, 1899: N.A., S.D., C8.5/50.

contrary was rejected by Choate. To this plan the Canadians replied with another, that the arbitration should be on the lines of the Venezuelan arbitration, and that if Dyea and Skagway were reserved to the United States, Pyramid Harbour should be similarly reserved to Canada. 'Premier insists on the necessity of retaining for Canada some harbour on the Lynn Inlet', cabled Lord Minto, the Governor-General.[1]

This attitude gave the Canadian game away. It was one thing to attempt to bargain for a harbour on the Lynn Canal in return for concessions elsewhere or to arbitrate in the hope of getting the harbour; it was quite another to insist on arbitration in which the harbour should be reserved. It was becoming increasingly clear that the Canadian government was interested only in a harbour on the coast. Its continued talk of legal rights began to ring hollow. The British departments began to suspect that the Canadian offer to arbitrate the whole coast without reservations, to which they referred when it was pointed out that there was no similarity between Skagway and Pyramid Harbour, was based on the hope of getting a harbour from the foreign umpire in mere equity. 'The Canadian attitude is impracticable', noted Wingfield of the Colonial Office, forwarding their terms to Villiers,[2] and Choate and Hay rejected them at once, refusing to see any reciprocity between Pyramid Harbour and the American towns. Nor was there any. The American claim to Dyea and Skagway was based on the existence there of American settlements. There was no Canadian settlement at Pyramid Harbour. Hay's reply indicated that the earlier proposal agreed between Choate and Pauncefote and sent home by Choate had been accepted by Hay after consultation with the American members of the Joint High Commission, though they felt it involved considerable American concessions. The new proposal, said Hay, meant that if the decision went against Canada she would get a port on the United States coast; if it were in her favour she would get the coast itself. Had the United States been willing to consider such an arrangement, no arbitration would have been necessary.[3]

---

[1] Minto to Chamberlain (tel.), 14 May, 1899: P.R.O., FO 5/2415.
[2] Wingfield to Villiers, 15 May, 1899: P.R.O., FO 5/2415.
[3] Hay to Tower, no. 1454, 19 May, 1899, copy enclosed in Tower to Salisbury, no. 151, 20 May, 1899; Choate to Salisbury, 19 May, 1899;

Although, as their internal correspondence shows, the Foreign Office and the Colonial Office were becoming increasingly impatient with the Canadian attitude, they continued to support it as strongly as they could both through Tower in Washington and through Choate in London, dutifully forwarding proposals which they knew to be unacceptable and supporting them with arguments which they knew to be weak. At this time negotiations for a *modus vivendi* were still hanging fire because of the Canadian attitude. A Colonial Office letter noted that given an agreement to arbitrate there would probably be no difficulty in arranging a *modus*.[1] The methods by which Canada hoped to make Hay anxious for a *modus*, pressure from mining interests handicapped by Canadian regulations and the fear of armed violence between Canadians and Americans, have been discussed above. The Canadian plan, in fact, was to worry Hay and make him anxious to reach a *modus vivendi*, and then to tie the attainment of that to an arbitration agreement. In this they overreached themselves. They asked too much. Hay was far too subtle a diplomat, and too shrewd a man, to be flustered in this way. He was very ready to urge the danger of regrettable incidents as a reason for reaching a *modus*,[2] but not to modify terms which he regarded as already generous. And, at the proper moment, he was prepared to back American miners with force, as when he authorized the sending of a company of troops to Pyramid Harbour. In this way he handed the problem neatly back to the Canadian government, who were driven to protest that in their information there was no such danger of disturbances as Hay feared, giving up one of their own best arguments.[3]

Still more, Hay steadily refused to modify his demands for a final settlement in order to gain a temporary line. He was clearly able to see that time was at least as important to Canada as it was to the United States, and that the longer the fixing of the line was

---

Choate to Salisbury (private), 20 May, 1899; Salisbury to Tower, no. 119, same date: P.R.O., FO 5/2415.

[1] Colonial Office to Foreign Office (confidential), 22 May, 1899: P.R.O., FO 5/2415.

[2] Pauncefote to Salisbury (tel.), no. 43, 23 April, 1899: P.R.O., FO 5/2415.

[3] Minto to Pauncefote (private), 25 April, 1899; Minto to Chamberlain (tel.), 26 April, 1899: P.R.O., FO 5/2415.

delayed, the more favourable it would be to the United States. Once convinced that there was less cause for concern about the danger of conflict than the United States government had been led to suppose, Hay became noticeably less eager to reach a settlement. He had called the Canadian bluff.

The British Foreign Office had no illusions about the possibility of getting away with that bluff. At the beginning of June Joseph Chamberlain warned the Canadians that if their legal position was weak, their political position was weaker. 'The consequences of a delay in the settlement of the Boundary question appear to me more serious for Canada than for the United States who are in possession . . .' he wrote,[1] and a later telegram was still more emphatic:

> We desire to impress upon your Ministers that whatever arguments may be based on letter of Treaty of 1825, careful examination of United States case for possession of shores of Canal based on continuous uncontested jurisdiction since date of Treaty, and admissions of Hudson Bay Company, Imperial and Dominion governments, shews that it is unassailable.
>
> Delay in settlement highly prejudicial to Canadian interests. . . .[2]

Increasing conviction in London that the Canadian case was weak led to the trial of a new approach. On 12 July at an interview with Choate, Salisbury suggested that Canada might lease an area of land on the Lynn Canal as a port with right of way for a railway to the interior, citing as a precedent the terms on which Britain held land at the Chinde mouth of the Zambezi by treaty with Portugal. Though Choate noted that he thought this had already been suggested and found unacceptable in the Joint High Commission, he was willing to put it to his government.[3] In the event, the device proved acceptable neither to the United States nor to Canada. Though it would have given the Canadians the essence of what they had been demanding with so little realism,

---

[1] Chamberlain to Minto (tel.) (secret), 1 June, 1899: P.R.O., FO 5/2415.
[2] Same to same (tel.), 21 July, 1899: P.R.O., FO 5/2416.
[3] Salisbury to Tower, no. 147 (confidential), 12 July, 1899: P.R.O., FO 5/2416; Choate to Hay, 18 July, 1899, as cited in Hay to Senator Davis, 26 July, 1899: Hay Papers, L.B. I, p. 237. Substantially the same device *had* been rejected in the High Commission.

they rejected it, raising their demands to include jurisdiction over the port and a strip of land for the railway. The Canadians, in fact, by the curious psychology of politics, had begun by arguing a bad case till they came to believe it a good one, and then, when an opportunity arose of getting all the practical benefits for which they had been contending, declined it as not meeting their (manufactured) claims. The United States, on the other hand, which for the past month had been opposing legal argument with legal argument, now won its case and discovered that the solution ran counter to important West Coast interests. Hay welcomed the idea as involving recognition of United States sovereignty, and for the same reason it had been advocated by Lodge as early as January; but now that it was formally proposed, it became clear that despite the general support of the Cabinet and the experts a treaty embodying a lease would not get through the Senate.[1]

Hay's problem then became whether to introduce it and hope for the best, or to insist on arbitration.[2] Though at this time he felt that a lease would be better for the United States than any likely result of arbitration, and though McKinley would have supported him if he had introduced the treaty, Hay came to the conclusion that the Democrats might make use of it and be able to elect Bryan. That possibility was enough to decide Hay. Considerations of internal politics overrode those of diplomacy.[3] His mind would have been relieved had he known that the Canadian government were in process of rejecting the proposed lease for reasons of their own, but that came as a surprise even to the Colonial Office, who had sponsored the proposal only after consultation with the Canadian Minister of Public Works. Chamberlain cabled Minto in some irritation that if the American government accepted the idea of a lease, they would be making a substantial concession,

and we cannot but think that your Ministers will not wish to sacrifice only chance of obtaining an all British route to Yukon,

---

[1] Hay to Whitelaw Reid, 27 July; to President McKinley, 29 July; to Senator Davis, 4 August; to Choate, 18 August, 1899: Hay Papers, L.B. I, pp. 239, 246, 255, 268. H. C. Lodge to Henry White, 7 January, 1899. Quoted by Nevins, *Henry White*, pp. 189–90.

[2] Of course with reservations.

[3] Hay to Choate, 18 August, 1899: Hay Papers, L.B. I, p. 268.

and will acquiesce in action of Her Majesty's Government which was only taken after discussion with Mr. Tarte in full belief that it would be acceptable to Dominion Government. It is doubtful whether U.S. Government will accept in any case but we think it worth pressing.[1]

In Canada legalism overcame political interests; in the United States political interests outweighed legalism, and both parties rejected the idea of a lease.

They were better able to do so because actual conditions on the spot were becoming easier, and with the Canadians now willing to consider a *modus vivendi* without reference to the final settlement, attention reverted to the temporary line. After the reaching of a *modus vivendi*, interest in the final settlement of the boundary lapsed. Both parties were agreeably surprised by the smoothness with which the temporary arrangements worked; and the United States and Britain had more important matters to divert attention. The year 1900 saw Great Britain fully occupied by the Boer War and events in China, and the United States in the throes of a Presidential election.

Hay's readiness to let the matter drop is easy to understand. The United States was in possession of all the important ground, occupying all the Lynn Canal harbours. In Hay, strong pro-British sentiments, a realization that he would gain nothing by pressing his case and that it might be better in an election year to allow the public to forget Alaska, and the desire to negotiate a canal treaty without irrelevant reference to Alaska, all combined to incline him to let the matter rest. In this Salisbury and Chamberlain were very willing to acquiesce, both because their hands were full and because they were fully conscious of the weakness of their case.

At the end of October 1899 Choate sent home an article and editorial from *The Times* with the comment that he had reason to believe 'that these embody the present views and desires of the Canadian Government', material which A. A. Adee, the Nestor of

---

[1] Chamberlain to Minto (tel.), 21 July, 1899. On the draft of this telegram Villiers minuted: 'The reply to Lord Minto appears sufficient. The last paragraph but one conveys the view which I understand the Colonial Office now hold that the Americans have much the best case.' P.R.O., FO 5/2416.

the State Department, thought to show that Canada admitted
that she had no conventional rights and was basing her hopes in
arbitration on the equitable question of a natural right of ingress
and egress to and from the sea.[1] Whatever the views of the
Canadian government, those of the British government were
hardening. On 25 October, the Colonial Office sent to the Foreign
Office for Salisbury's approval, the most uncompromising despatch
they had yet written, urging Canada to modify her claims. It
reads as if the Colonial Office were convinced of the merits of the
American case, and argues that since no arbitrator could fail
to give the United States Dyea and Skagway, with or without an express clause reserving them, Canada can gain nothing
by holding out for concessions in return for such a clause. It
continues:

. . . Her Majesty's Government, as matters stand, entertain considerable doubt as to the expediency of continuing to press for arbitration on terms which would appear to raise doubt as to the position
of Dyea and Skagway, seeing that the facts above mentioned appear
to them already to have practically disposed of this question.

It is impossible to avoid the conviction that to do so, would have
the result of indefinitely postponing a settlement and most probably of throwing away whatever chance there may be of securing
Pyramid Harbour and the Chilkat Valley for Canada.

· · · · · · · ·

The claim of the United States moreover to the Islands command-
ing the entrance to Observatory Inlet, a claim which, however un-
founded it may be, is not likely to be withdrawn except on the
result of arbitration, seriously affects the military security of the
only practical route alternative to the Lynn Canal by which Canada
can secure an all British communication with the Yukon Territories. [So that Canada would lose both ways by declining arbitration.]

· · · · · · · ·

These considerations have forced Her Majesty's Government to
the conclusion that it would be desirable in the best interests of
Canada and the Empire to meet the objections of the United States

---

[1] Choate to Hay, no. 186, 25 October, 1899 and minute by A. A.
Adee: N.A., S.D., from London, Vol. 198.

to arbitration on the boundary dispute by offering to agree to an addition to the rules adopted in the Venezuelan Treaty. . . .

Salisbury concurred in the terms of this draft.[1]

These British views were sent to Canada for consideration together with those of Sir Louis Davies, then returning home after a visit to London for consultation. No reply was received from Canada, nor did the home government press for one. Meanwhile, as at intervals ever since the demise of the Joint High Commission, another formal note from Choate, long and closely reasoned, reached the Foreign Office. This argued the American case from the legal standpoint, its two chief points being to deny the Canadian claim that the interpretation of the treaty of 1825 had been open because undecided till 1898, and to demonstrate the differences between the present case and that of Venezuela, and so the inadequacy of the Venezuelan treaty without modification. It was sent to the Foreign Office on 22 January, 1900, but even as he sent it Choate knew that it was unlikely to get a rapid reply. In sending his draft back to Hay for approval he had written that the Foreign Office were in no greater hurry than Hay in the matter and expected 'a more favourable time for its final consideration will come by and by'.[2] In his forecast of British delay Choate was quite right. Nothing more was done for almost a year. By August the Canadians had still not made any observations on Choate's argument and the Colonial Office did not seem anxious to press them. 'An indefinite prolongation of the modus vivendi seems the probable result', said the Foreign Office,[3] and not till March 1901 was any acknowledgment received from Canada.

By that time Hay was already at work on a new arbitration scheme, which he outlined to Pauncefote on 24 April.[4] Most of the rest of the summer passed in urging Canada to agree. The Foreign

---

[1] Draft despatch, Chamberlain to Minto, n.d., enclosed in Colonial Office to Foreign Office (secret and confidential), 25 October, 1899; and Foreign Office to Colonial Office (immediate and secret), 30 October, 1899: P.R.O., FO 5/2417.

[2] Choate to Hay (private and unofficial), 29 December, 1899: Hay Papers, 19.

[3] Foreign Office minute, 1 August, 1900: P.R.O., FO 5/2479.

[4] Pauncefote to Lansdowne (private), 10 May, 1901: P.R.O., FO 5/2479; also Dennis, *Adventures*, p. 143.

Office at Chamberlain's insistence had been wearily drafting a
reply to Choate on the basis of the Canadian argument of March;[1]
now they gladly dropped it to concentrate on Hay's new offer.
Hay had receded from a specific reservation of Dyea and Skagway,
though, as the Colonial Office had earlier pointed out, this made
no practical difference to the fate of those towns. To silence objection from Pacific Coast interests who feared the results of a compromise, he had so drafted his terms of reference as to exclude
from the functions of the arbitrators anything but the strict interpretation of the treaty of 1825.[2] This new proposal was urged on
Canada with all the force at British disposal — even the advantages of connecting acceptance of the draft treaty with the
negotiation of the second Hay-Pauncefote Canal Treaty were
emphasized[3] — but in spite of increasingly emphatic telegrams
demanding a reply nothing was heard from Canada till the middle
of October, when a telegram stated their objections to Hay's
draft.[4] Some of these objections were well founded — Hay's draft
was not perfect, though it would have been better to accept it in
principle and modify it later — others less easy to understand,
but they proved in the event to be of minor interest. Lansdowne
instructed Pauncefote early in February to communicate the
Canadian views to Hay; in his reply Pauncefote indicated that
the situation had now changed and why. He wrote:

> When I delivered the Memorandum to Mr Hay and proceeded to
> explain to him briefly its purport with a view to further discussion
> I was surprised to observe a marked change of attitude on his part
> in relation to the question. He was quite despondent as to the
> prospect of any agreement for an arbitration. He gave me to under-
> stand that a strong opposition had arisen from an unexpected
> quarter to the mode of settlement proposed by him in May last.

---

[1] 'It appears that Mr Chamberlain is of opinion that the Canadian
Govt. should have their say & that a letter founded on the minute
should be addressed to Mr Choate. Matters will certainly not be advanced.
. . .' Minute by Villiers on a letter from the Colonial Office of 7 March,
1901: P.R.O., FO 5/2479.

[2] Minute by Pauncefote, in reply to a query by the Lord Chancellor,
15 July, 1901: P.R.O., FO 5/2479.

[3] Chamberlain to Minto (tel.) (most secret and urgent), 27 July, 1901;
same to same (tel.) (secret), 8 October, 1901: P.R.O., FO 5/2479.

[4] Minto to Chamberlain (tel.), 15 October, 1901: P.R.O., FO 5/2479.

He stated that the President disapproved of his Draft Convention and would not have sanctioned it had he been in power at the time. That the President considers the claim of the United States is so manifestly clear and unanswerable that he is not disposed to run the risk of sacrificing American territory under a compromise which is the almost certain result of an Arbitration.

This is a surprising change of sentiment considering his strenuous advocacy of arbitration in his Presidential Message.

It appears that the Senators whom he has consulted are in favour of letting the question stand over for the present, as all is going on smoothly under the 'Modus Vivendi'. I learn also from a private but reliable source that the President is anxious to postpone the question until after the termination of the War in South Africa.

I cannot but suspect that this sudden desire to postpone the question is due to political considerations of a domestic character such as pressure from the Western States and the agitation raised against England at the present time by the Pro-Boer and Irish Parties.[1]

The elevation of Theodore Roosevelt to the Presidency on the assassination of McKinley was the new feature which completely altered the situation. McKinley had been a mild, cautious man, one who knew little of foreign policy and who was prepared to entrust its conduct to Hay. Hay was a suave, worldly gentleman, very Anglophile in his views, subtle and shrewd, but more open to the charge of weakness than to that of excessive zeal. He belonged to the society of the eastern United States which was European in its sympathies, and he had small use for agitation about Alaska. Once reassured that there was no immediate danger he was reluctant to press Britain to settle, and very ready to wait. The settlement with Britain which he favoured would be unacceptable to West Coast interests. As a result he took refuge in inactivity.

Theodore Roosevelt was a man of very different stamp. His complex character has been often analysed and continues to fascinate scholars. One of his traits was a strong sense of the destiny of his country as the dominant and civilizing force of the western hemisphere. He overvalued the military virtues (which he did not analyse with any great subtlety), and had an exagger-

---

[1] Lansdowne to Pauncefote, no. 28, 5 February, 1902; Pauncefote to Lansdowne, no. 85 (confidential), 28 March, 1902: P.R.O., FO 5/2510.

ated fear of decadence, which he thought he detected in Europe. There was a reserve in his attitude even to men like Hay, good friends of his whose knowledge and judgment he respected, but whom he could not help feeling to be weak. Roosevelt had perhaps a shrewder sense of political power and the possibilities of its use than any other American politician of his day; but it was combined with a paranoic reaction to any opposition. It was not that he was ungenerous. In internal politics he was prepared, for instance, to support many pieces of progressive labour legislation, but he combined this with a much more violent reaction to the threat of a strike than many of his more conservative colleagues showed. Any concession gained by the workers, in fact, must be gained from an act of enlightened clemency by Roosevelt, and earned by a proper spirit of submission. To meet an opponent half-way seemed feebleness to Roosevelt, inexcusable when not necessary.[1]

In Alaska, as Roosevelt well knew, the United States was in a strong position. Therefore, she must get the utmost of her demands. The legal merits of either case now became unimportant. The American case was a strong one. Roosevelt thought it very strong, unassailable in fact; but then he always felt that way about any case he undertook to uphold. It was characteristic of Roosevelt that he was willing to make concessions to Canada in other areas. Arthur Lee[2] reported, on his return from a visit to the United States, that he would be willing to see some of the other questions at issue between Canada and the States settled in favour of Canada, to mitigate Canada's disappointment over Alaska. 'I understand that Lee intimates the President would even go so far as not to press the American case upon these other points to its full value . . .', noted Cranborne. Sir Michael Herbert promptly

---

[1] Morison (ed.), *Roosevelt Letters*, II, III, *passim*. For interesting interpretations of Roosevelt's personality see J. M. Blum, *The Republican Roosevelt* (Cambridge, Mass., 1954); R. Hofstadter, *The American Political Tradition* (New York, 1948), ch. ix; and H. K. Beale, *Theodore Roosevelt and the Rise of America to World Power* (Baltimore, 1956).

[2] Then Member of Parliament for Fareham. Earlier, however, while military attaché at Washington he had gained Roosevelt's friendship. He was not a man of distinguished ability.

made the obvious rejoinder that whatever the President's views
he could not act as suggested by Lee because all the other issues
affected local interests which would be just as vociferous as those
on the West Coast if they felt themselves sacrificed to gain a
victory over the Alaskan boundary.[1] Nevertheless, the suggestion,
which there is no reason to doubt, indicates the characteristics of
Roosevelt's thought. He was determined to take a stand on the
Alaska question, which he saw as a challenge to the supremacy of
the United States and of himself. That victory won, he was willing
to make concessions in matters of quite equal importance. It is
hardly too much to say that with the coming of Theodore Roosevelt to the Presidency, the maintenance of prestige became a
matter of principle in American foreign policy for the first time.
With his entry into the controversy, Britain was bound to give
way.

Though, as his character would suggest, the ultimate effect of
the coming of Roosevelt to the Presidency was to force the issue,
he was not unwilling to postpone the question for a few months,
as Pauncefote's despatch of March quoted above shows. The next
move in fact came from Lansdowne, who suggested to Choate at
the end of June that advantage should be taken of the presence in
London of both Minto and Laurier, as well as of 'one or two
Canadian Ministers' to discuss the boundary question. The suggestion seemed to surprise Choate, who pointed out that the
American mid-term elections were due in November and that the
time did not seem well chosen, a comment which confirms
Pauncefote's earlier analysis of Roosevelt's views.[2] Nevertheless,
Choate was very willing to meet Laurier and Minto, and a number of talks took place. Both Choate and Henry White, who also
took part, came away from these convinced that Lansdowne had
given up hope of getting any concession for Canada and was
anxious to settle, and that Laurier also was anxious for agreement, though to save his prestige he would be glad to have the

---

[1] Lansdowne to Sir Michael Herbert (tel.) (private), 10 December,
1902; Herbert to Lansdowne (tel.), 11 December, 1902: P.R.O.,
FO 5/2510. Herbert succeeded Pauncefote, who died in 1902, as
Ambassador in Washington.
[2] Lansdowne to Arthur Raikes, no. 134, 25 June, 1902: P.R.O.,
FO 5/2510. Raikes was then chargé d'affaires in Washington.

question settled against him by some kind of tribunal, rather than make the concession directly.[1]

The formal result of the conference in London was expressed by Lansdowne in a despatch to Raikes at the end of August. This was almost identical with the reply to Choate's long argument of two years before, the preparation of which had been interrupted by Hay's arbitration proposal in 1901, but which was now modified and sent. Only two points need be noted from this document, which recapitulated old arguments and which its authors hardly expected to produce any good results. The first is that in spite of the views of Roosevelt as reported by Pauncefote months before, the British government still held out for finality of arbitration, though they claimed to be prepared to consider any formula which would attain this end. The other is that the despatch was considerably weakened from the first draft which had been prepared more than a year before. Most of the modifications were made by Sir John Anderson of the Colonial Office, but some are in Villiers' hand and all were approved by Lansdowne. Each modification had the same object — to allow for withdrawal later. 'Impossible' is changed to 'difficult', 'must adhere to the view' to 'still consider'. The sentence 'To any such arrangement it would not be possible for His Majesty's Government to consent' was first weakened by Villiers to '. . . His Majesty's Government are not willing to consent' and then deleted altogether. The motive of the changes is explicit. Against one of them Anderson noted '? too strong if we contemplate giving way', and he explained his work in a minute: 'In the present mood of the Dominion Govt. the draft appears to be too emphatic in some points. I have made some marginal suggestions, but it is all flogging a dead horse and gets us no forrader.'[2] The care with which this despatch was worked over makes it certain that the insistence on the finality of decision was not merely a hangover from the draft written before

---

[1] Hay to Roosevelt, 7 July and 14 July, 1902: Hay Papers, L.B. II, pp. 299, 313. Both these letters are quoted in part by Dennis, *Adventures*, from the Roosevelt Papers. Henry White to Hay, 28 June, 1902, quoted by Nevins, *Henry White*, pp. 192–3. Lansdowne to Raikes, no. 146, 16 July, 1902: P.R.O., FO 5/2510.

[2] Drafts of Lansdowne to Raikes, no. 158, 18 August, 1902; Sir J. Anderson to Villiers, 18 July, 1902: P.R.O., FO 5/2510.

McKinley's death, but was deliberate; and if Great Britain intended to give way, as it is fairly clear she did, and if the impulse behind this came from Canada, as it did, the advantages are obvious. Laurier was now more anxious to avoid the full responsibility of giving way than to get his port — a merely advisory commission would throw the final negotiation back on himself. The home government had been advising Canada for long that her position was weak; a change of heart was something to be accepted readily.[1]

A good deal of discussion followed the receipt of this despatch, and Hay at first held out for a purely advisory tribunal. Herbert reported of an interview with him, that

> . . . he alluded to the question of the Alaska Boundary and took a very gloomy view with regard to the prospects of arbitration. Mr Hay inveighed bitterly against the Senate, who, he said, would not ratify any arrangement involving any concession by the United States at any point on the boundary line.

All Hay could do was to renew his proposal for a tribunal which would merely place its opinion on record, and though he admitted that this was unsatisfactory he still thought such a tribunal would facilitate settlement.[2]

The reference to the Senate, his dislike of which was perfectly genuine, was one of Hay's favourite diplomatic weapons. On this occasion, however, it need not be taken too seriously. The Canadians had agreed to a tribunal of six in July.[3] It must have been obvious to the Senate, as it was to everyone else, that a tribunal of three jurists on each side would reach a deadlock unless at least one voted against his own side. In case of such a deadlock the tribunal, whatever the terms under which it was set up, could not deliver an award, a fact which the British government had been stressing since 1899 and which meant that the United States could not possibly lose. In these circumstances, the opposi-

---

[1] Note White's talk with Minto summarized for Hay in White to Hay, 12 August, 1902, quoted by Nevins, *Henry White*, p. 193; also Choate's version of Laurier's views reported in Lansdowne to Raikes, no. 146, 16 July, 1902: P.R.O., FO 5/2510.

[2] Herbert to Lansdowne (tel.), no. 37 (secret), 17 October, 1902: P.R.O., FO 5/2510.

[3] Lansdowne to Raikes, no. 146, 16 July, 1902: P.R.O., FO 5/2510.

tion of the Senate was not likely to be serious, at least if due regard
were paid to the vanity of its members, and proper use made of
the arts of persuasion of which Hay was a master when he chose.
The opposition much more probably came from Roosevelt himself, convinced that the land in dispute was American, and well
aware that Canada had no means of wresting it from him. To a
man of Roosevelt's temperament it was an enormous concession
to provide an opponent with a means of retreating gracefully
from an untenable position, and Hay recorded in a letter to White
that he consented only with great reluctance.

> We have never had the slightest doubt of our right [Hay wrote].
> The President, at my earnest persuasion, consented to this tribunal,
> because I felt sure we could convince any great English lawyer, that
> our contention was just. He was not so sanguine, but agreed to try
> the experiment, to enable the British Government to get out of
> an absolutely untenable position, with dignity and honour. If the
> Tribunal should disagree he will feel he has done his utmost, and
> will make no further effort to settle the controversy. He will hold
> the territory, as we have held it since 1867, and will emphasize the
> assertion of our sovereignty, in a way which cannot but be dis-
> agreeable to Canadian amour propre. . . .
>   And this, after I have heard from Laurier, and Pauncefote,
> directly, *that they know they have no case.*
>   I will not believe it till the verdict is in.[1]

Roosevelt's attitude is confirmed by his own letters.[2] Pauncefote's
report, quoted above, that Roosevelt wanted to avoid the risk of
'compromise which is the almost certain result of an Arbitration'
is not to be taken literally. Hay, very conscious of the risk of compromise, had taken pains to meet just this objection in his form of
arbitration. Roosevelt's objection was not to compromise, but to
any arbitration, however formal.

Hay's assertion that he had it from both Laurier and Pauncefote that Canada had no case is much more doubtful. Coming
from so reliable a source as Hay, who repeated it several times, it

---

[1] Hay to Henry White, 20 September, 1903: Henry White Papers.
[2] Morison (ed.), *Roosevelt Letters*, III, to A. H. Lee, 18 March, 1901
(no. 1958); to same, 24 April, 1901 (no. 2028); to Hay, 10 July, 1902
(no. 2385); to same, 16 July, 1902 (no. 2392).

deserves respect,[1] but it is not confirmed, perhaps not surprisingly, by anything in the British documents. What *is* shown there is a growing conviction on the part of the Dominion government, a conviction reached much sooner by the Foreign Office, that they would not be allowed to win. This adequately accounts for their willingness to accept a dignified means of retreat, but it is not quite the same thing. In this matter it is impossible not to suspect Hay of self-deception. He protests too much. Can it really be true that Hay 'felt sure we could convince any great English lawyer that our contention was just'? If so, he had forgotten the complete failure of the United States Commissioners to convince Lord Herschell of just that.[2] It seems at least possible that Hay, bullied by Roosevelt into applying force to a country towards which he felt great personal sympathy about a boundary which he regarded as unimportant, and aware of his inability to stand up for his own more moderate policy, took refuge in the pretence that no one not obviously biased could dispute the American case. (Here it should be emphasized that the real merits or demerits of either case are no longer in question.)

Negotiations on the details of the arbitration dragged on till January 1903. In the middle of December 1902 Herbert reported Hay as willing that the decision of the judicial tribunal should be final if they reached agreement. He thought this preferable if the Senate would ratify such a treaty. By the 19th Herbert was able to report that Hay had consulted 'upwards of thirty Senators in regard to it, and he informed me this morning that, so far as he was able to judge, it would receive the approval of the Senate'.[3] The treaty was signed on 23 January, 1903, after considerable delay in Canada. It was now Hay who was urging haste, both because the Senate seemed amenable and Hay had well-founded doubts as to how long the mood would last — a number of

---

[1] Hay to White (absolutely confidential), 10 April, 1903; and same to same, 22 May, 1903: Hay Papers, L.B. II, pp. 411, 465.

[2] Ironically enough, the American complaint against Lord Herschell had been that he was too much of a lawyer, too insistent on the letter of his case, and not ready enough to compromise for the sake of agreement. Lodge to White (private), 3 December, 1898; Hay to White (confidential), same date: Henry White Papers.

[3] Herbert to Lansdowne, no. 347, 19 December, 1902: P.R.O., FO 5/2510.

influential Senators, including the redoubtable Morgan, was against the treaty — and because he was particularly anxious that the treaty should not hang over to be considered in the atmosphere of an election year.[1]

Even after the treaty had been signed, a major question remained to be settled, that of the nomination of the members of the panel. When the drafting of the treaty was in progress Hay expressed confidentially the hope that only one of the British jurists would be a Canadian. Herbert cabled this home, asking if *any* Canadian need be appointed. In return he urged that all the United States members should be Supreme Court justices. As reported by Herbert, one of Hay's arguments for his request was that it would be easier to get the treaty through the Senate if it were known that not all the members were to be Canadian. Lansdowne thought that one member should certainly be Canadian, but that one would be enough; the Colonial Office, however, thought that all the British members should be Canadian and were clear that Canada would not consent to having only one representative, still less none. In a letter to Villiers of mid-December their spokesman wrote that the treaty should allow for the appointment by each side of its members, without restriction for the benefit of the Senate, and that each party was to 'consider who is most likely to protect its interests'.[2]

This insistence on the part of the Colonial Office was a mere device to soothe Canadian public opinion, just as Hay's suggestion had been aimed at American, and more specifically Senate, opinion. It was already decided that one member of the tribunal should be an Englishman, and one Englishman was enough. If the tribunal was a judicial one designed to avoid compromise, as its terms of reference made clear, then any reference to protection of interests was out of place. On the other hand, the composition of the tribunal and the long process of argument by which it had been agreed made it difficult to feel that it was a genuine judicial

---

[1] 'I would rather have it rejected than go over till next year.' Hay to Senator Cullom (confidential), 11 February, 1903: Hay Papers, L.B. II, p. 390. Hay to Mrs Hay, 24 January, 1903. Quoted by Dennis, *Adventures*, Appendix VI E.

[2] Herbert to Lansdowne (tel.) (private), 8 December, 1902; Lansdowne to Herbert (tel.) (private), 10 December, 1902; Sir M. Ommaney (of the Colonial Office) to Villiers, 11 December, 1902: P.R.O., FO 5/2510.

process. At no point could any American be got to admit that the
American representatives were biased. Possibly they were not;
but neither would any American admit the possibility of disagreement among them. Then if the tribunal was to reach any
decision at least one of the British members must vote against his
side — and that unenviable task could much better be undertaken by an Englishman than by a Canadian.

On these lines the matter was arranged. Unfortunately, for the
later stages of the controversy no British official, or useful private,
sources are available. There is no cause, therefore, to modify the
generally accepted opinion that the tribunal did not act in a
strictly judicial manner, nor need its history be reproduced in any
detail.[1] Its members were to be 'six impartial jurists of repute'.[2]
Great Britain appointed, for Canada, Sir L. A. Jetté, then
Lieutenant-Governor of Quebec but formally a puisne judge of
the Superior Court of Quebec, and J. D. Armour, Chief Justice of
Ontario,[3] and for England, Lord Alverstone, Lord Chief Justice.
Roosevelt, on the other hand, in an excess of zeal which Hay
could not but deplore, appointed Elihu Root, Henry Cabot Lodge,
and George Turner. Root was then Secretary of War and Lodge
Senator from Massachusetts. Turner had recently retired at the
end of a term as Senator from the State of Washington. The
Canadians claimed, with justice, that these were neither impartial, nor jurists of repute. Turner was a highly competent
lawyer who had practised with distinction in the West and had

---

[1] For an excellent discussion of the appointment, work and decision of
the tribunal, see Gelber, *Anglo-American Friendship*, ch. vii. This is
necessarily based on other printed sources. The most important of these
are C. G. Washburn, 'Memoir of Henry Cabot Lodge' in the *Proceedings
of the Massachusetts Historical Society*, LVIII, 1924–5 (Boston, 1925)
for Lodge's own account of his work; Thayer, *Life and Letters of Hay*,
II, ch. xxv; Tyler Dennett, *John Hay: from Poetry to Politics* (New
York, 1933), ch. xix; Dennis, *Adventures*, ch. vi; Skelton, *Life and
Letters of Laurier*, II, ch. xii; J. W. Dafoe, *Clifford Sifton in Relation
to his Times* (Toronto, 1931), ch. viii. Morison (ed.), *Roosevelt Letters*
adds nothing.

[2] Convention signed at Washington, 24 January, 1903, for the Ad-
justment of the Boundary between the Dominion of Canada and the
Territory of Alaska, Article I. Printed in *Parliamentary Papers*, 1903,
LXXXVII, State Papers, United States. No. 1 (1903), (Cd. 1400).

[3] Armour died in London while the case was being heard, and was
succeeded by A. B. Aylesworth.

judicial experience. Lodge was a graduate of Harvard Law School but had never practised. Root had graduated in law from the University of the City of New York and had been a U.S. district attorney. He had at the time no judicial experience, though he later became a distinguished international lawyer and a member of the Permanent Court of Arbitration at The Hague. Lodge and Turner at least had already pronounced publicly on the merits of the dispute; and we have Lodge's own evidence that the appointments were political and that Hay disapproved.[1]

Hay defended the choice rather plaintively.

> The objections to Turner seem to me unreasonable [he wrote]. He stands at the head of the Bar of the Northwest, he is not now a member of the Senate, and he will have great weight in causing his judgment to be accepted by the people of the West. To say that our members of the tribunal have an opinion on the subject is simply to say that they are American citizens. There is not a man in the United States out of an idiot asylum, who has not an opinion on the subject. I believe in my heart of hearts that there is not an intelligent Englishman who does not know they have no case. Sir Wilfrid Laurier sent me a private messenger the other day to protest against the appointment of Lodge and Turner, and in the course of conversation his emissary said to me: 'Sir Wilfrid knows, and all of us know, that we have no case.' The whole machinery of the tribunal is got up with the expectation on our part that the British Government would see in it the means of receding from an absolutely untenable position, by appointing on the tribunal a man of open mind, who would see the case as we shall present it and vote with our members.[2]

The assumption in the last sentence, that any man of open mind would be bound to accept the American case, is interesting enough. It implies that the national prejudices of the Canadian lawyers would be not at all modified by professional ethics, while the American members would be reliably impartial. More important, however, is the inconsistency of the argument that Turner's presence on the tribunal would be of value in getting the judgment accepted in the North-west. The rest of the letter

---

[1] Washburn, 'Memoir of Lodge' in loc. cit., p. 340.
[2] Hay to Henry White (absolutely confidential), 10 April, 1903: Hay Papers, L.B. II, p. 411.

makes it clear that Hay confidently expected that judgment to be favourable and had no intention of accepting it if it were not. Why should the North-west find a favourable judgment difficult to accept? The appointment of Lodge was as offensive as that of Turner, without even so much excuse.

It is difficult to avoid the conclusion that Roosevelt was minimizing the effects of a treaty which he had accepted with reluctance, and was determined not only to emphasize the unwisdom of failing to reach a decision, and that in favour of the United States, but to make clear the extent of his diplomatic victory. In the conduct of politics, Roosevelt's failing was not that he carried a big stick, but that he was quite incapable of speaking softly.[1] At any rate, the appointments caused outcry in Canada and provoked the first sign of feeling on the subject in Britain. In the middle of August Choate conveyed to the British government Roosevelt's insistence that there should be no further delay, and though the exchanges between London and Ottawa are not available it is reasonable to suppose that this was decisive.[2]

The actual meetings of the Commission gave no more ground for supposing that it was really judicial. From the first it was noted that Lord Alverstone appeared to regard himself more as an arbitrator between two opposing factions than as one of six independent jurists. He conferred at least as frequently with Lodge as with his Canadian colleagues, and the Canadians complained that while there was the closest co-operation and private conference among the American members Alverstone declined to act similarly as a member of a Canadian-British team. Finally, of course, he gave his opinion in favour of the American view. Alverstone maintained in the face of all criticism that he had acted judicially and had been guided in his verdict only by the legal merits of the case. The weakness of the tribunal lay in the fact that no one could believe this of any of the other members, and that in those circumstances the result had been rigged against Canada. So the Canadians thought, and they were not ready to credit Lord Alverstone's probity.

---

[1] 'Speak softly and carry a big stick' was one of Roosevelt's favourite maxims.
[2] Roosevelt to Hay, 29 July, 1903; Choate to Hay (personal and confidential), 14 August, 1903: Hay Papers, 19.

In view of this the facts of the case become relatively un-important. It appears from the large mass of conflicting evidence cited, the earlier discussions in the Joint High Commission and opinions of the jurists in the final settlement, that there was a good deal to be said on both sides. The American case was a strong one, probably better than that of Canada. The terms of the treaty of 1825 which the jurists were to define were certainly ambiguous; the opinions of both Canadians and Americans were cogent and well reasoned. If the diplomatic exchanges which led to the signing of that treaty were considered, the Canadian claim was probably improved. It was in fact unchallenged American settlement during the seventy years since the signing of the treaty that weighed most heavily against Canada. Yet it was the American side that insisted that the terms of reference should be confined to the interpretation of the treaty, a remarkable position for them to take up had the interpretation not been decided in advance. They were anxious to avoid a compromise, always a sign of strength. The most that can be said with confidence is that the American case was not so overwhelmingly strong as Hay's writings suggest.

A sense of its strength did not play the leading part in deter-mining the American attitude. That attitude was determined by a consciousness of political power and a strong and aggressive nationalism. As Hay wrote,

> I see the Canadians are clamoring that he [Lord Alverstone] shall decide not according to the facts, but 'in view of the imperial interests involved'. Even in that view he should decide in our favor. For this is the last time we shall admit this question to any form of judicature. The land in question is ours. It was held by Russia in accordance with treaty from 1825 to 1867, and has been held by us ever since. We shall never think of giving it up. No administration could abandon it and live a minute.[1]

Lodge spoke still more strongly to the same effect and described the Canadian claim as one 'which no self-respecting nation could possibly admit'.[2] The adjective 'self-respecting' reveals how

---

[1] Hay to White, 20 September, 1903: Henry White Papers.
[2] Speech by Lodge in Boston, 27 September, 1902, as reported in the American Press. Enclosure in Raikes to Lansdowne, no. 257, 2 October, 1902: P.R.O., FO 5/2510.

emotional nationalism was used to darken the issue. Nowhere even in private American papers does there appear any attempt to estimate the importance of the interests involved, still less the value of good Anglo-American relations. The attitude of the Senate and of West Coast voters dictated American policy. A determination to safeguard the towns which American enterprise had built was only proper and to be expected; but any of a variety of arrangements suggested during the negotiations would have achieved that result. The contention that the territory was undoubtedly American was the result, not the cause, of American determination to keep it. When Whitelaw Reid spoke of a people 'who, a fortnight ago, were ready to break off their Joint Commission with Great Britain and take their chances, rather than give up a few square miles of worthless land, and a harbor of which a year ago they scarcely knew the name on the remote coast of Alaska' he spoke no more than the truth.[1]

If American public opinion felt strongly about Alaska, British opinion did not. The matter was kept before the public by the pronouncements of prominent men far more in the United States than in Britain. After the failure of the Joint High Commission the negotiations were unknown to the public until the appointment of the judicial tribunal was announced. Nearly all the Parliamentary references to the question were merely formal. Three questions were asked in the Commons in 1898, two by that notable Anglo-American imperialist, Sir Ellis Ashmead-Bartlett.[2] From the end of April 1898 to the end of February 1899 Alaska was not mentioned. Thereafter one question urged the need for a *modus vivendi*, but when Brodrick, then Parliamentary Under-Secretary of State for Foreign Affairs, denied any knowledge of disturbances in the disputed district the matter was dropped.[3] The adjournment of the High Commission led to enquiries as to what progress, if any, had been made. These questions, of which there were only four, were merely parried by the reply that negotiations were still proceeding and no statement could be made; but

[1] Address by Reid in New York, quoted in the New York *Tribune*, 16 June, 1899: P.R.O., FO 5/2416.
[2] *The Parliamentary Debates* (Fourth Series), 1898, LIII, p. 1052; LVI, pp. 950, 1401.
[3] ibid., 1899, LXIX, p. 146.

when on 24 October it was again asked whether any boundary agreement had been reached Balfour was able to reply that a provisional boundary *had* been fixed and that the text would be laid 'so soon as the terms of the notes recording it have been received from Washington'.[1]

The reaching of a *modus vivendi* apparently satisfied the Commons. Alaska was not even mentioned for three years. No less significant than the small number of questions asked is their form. None showed any ambition to embarrass the government. More were asked by Conservative than by Opposition members but no reliable conclusion can be drawn from party labels where foreign affairs are concerned. Some are obviously arranged questions from their timing, as when Mr Hogan, Anti-Parnellite, asked for news of a *modus vivendi* on the earliest day when the government could give it.[2] Others were used by the government to give information without appearing to do so. When, for example, Mr Norman, Liberal, asked on 12 December, 1902, whether any proposal for a judicial tribunal had been received from the United States government and, if so, what reply had been sent, he got the evasive reply that discussions had recently been renewed but that no useful purpose would be served by a statement at present. Nevertheless the House had been given a very clear indication of the line any settlement would follow.[3] None of the questions showed any hostility towards the United States. Their tenor suggested rather dissatisfaction with the Foreign Office for not making better speed in clearing up a very simple matter.

The formation of the judicial tribunal was announced in the King's Speech for 1903, and this apparently brought the matter to the notice of the Lords for the first time. The debate on the Speech is not likely to be revealing in either House; but certainly no attempt to criticize was made. The Duke of Roxburghe, opening the debate, perhaps revealed the unconscious inconsistency of British thinking. Speaking of the Anglo-German action in Venezuela he denied that it would jeopardize Anglo-American friendship, because

---

[1] ibid., LXVII, p. 298; LXXII, pp. 81, 299, 440, 1064; LXXIV, p. 1541; LXXVII, p. 578.
[2] ibid., LXXVII, p. 578.   [3] ibid., 1902, CXVI, p. 1027.

the friendship of a people so intelligent and so practical is not likely to be secured by an attitude which would appear to indicate on our part any desire to obtain it by unworthy concessions, or by any indifference to the just claims of our own people. . . .

and then went on to remark of Alaska that 'any steps towards the settlement of a question which might have involved us in serious difficulty with the United States must be welcomed by both countries'.[1] He made no attempt to examine those steps. Earl Spencer noted, in a significant turn of phrase, that this boundary question 'might raise great difficulty between ourselves and our American cousins'.[2] No more was said, then or later. For the Commons, Captain Greville, Conservative, could hardly have summed up the prevailing opinion better when he said:

It is not necessary to trace where the chief obstacles to a settlement have occurred, but it will probably be agreed that any English Government would do all within its power to come to an amicable settlement of this long standing controversy, consistent with the material interests of Canada, and the Government deserves our congratulations at having arrived at such an arrangement with the Government of the United States.[3]

The appointment of a judicial tribunal, though open to objections, was not itself offensive. When its composition had been accepted, and no serious protest was made against the American appointments, it was difficult not to accept its findings.[4] Any attack on the impartiality of the Americans would reflect on that of Lord Alverstone. Britain did not share Canadian anger at the result, and no attempt was made to question it when announced in the King's Speech for 1904. The King said:

The Tribunal appointed under the Convention concluded on the 3rd March last between My Government and that of the United States has given a decision on the points referred to it. On some of these the verdict has been favourable to British claims; on others it has been adverse. Much as this last circumstance is to be deplored, it must, nevertheless, be a matter of congratulation that the misunderstandings, in which ancient Boundary Treaties, made in ignorance of

---

[1] ibid., 1903, CXVIII, p. 6.   [2] ibid., p. 15.
[3] ibid., p. 63.
[4] See Gelber, *Anglo-American Friendship*, pp. 146–8 for the Canadian protest, which was unsuccessful.

geographical facts, are so fertile, have in this case been finally removed from the field of controversy.[1]

The three Lords and one member of the Commons who referred to the matter at all followed him in treating the controversy as one of 'misunderstanding'. They paid tribute to the Canadians for accepting the award calmly, and emphasized that Canadian interests were also those of Britain, though Lord Hylton had the grace to sound a little sheepish in doing so.[2] Lord Lansdowne himself defended the result, and his speech is worth quoting:

> Any serious clashing on the spot between the settlers belonging to Canada, on the one hand, or to the United States on the other, might at any moment have brought about an incident of the utmost gravity. It is therefore most fortunate that we should have been successful in removing that question from the path of our diplomacy. The result in the finding of the tribunal has no doubt not been entirely satisfactory to us, and in this respect I do not draw any distinction between the interests of the Dominion of Canada and our interests. The question at issue is a question of the position not merely of the frontier of Canada, but of the frontier of the British Empire, for the defence and the integrity of which we are responsible. But, my Lords, I do not think that any one seriously expected that we should obtain a favourable verdict on all points; and I am inclined to find some consolation in the fact that our military and naval advisers tell us confidently that the two islands in the Portland Channel which, under this award were given to the United States, are of no strategical value whatever.[3]

Even when allowance has been made for Lansdowne's position, this is an astonishing performance. The implication that if Britain lost some points she gained others of roughly equal importance was sheer dishonesty. Nor was it dignified to claim that islands for which he had thought it worth contending were valueless, or logical to find consolation in that when the islands had never been of the first importance.[4] But then Lansdowne had to find his

---

[1] *The Parliamentary Debates* (Fourth Series), 1904, CXXIX, p. 2.
[2] ibid., pp. 15, 23, 39, 107.   [3] ibid., pp. 39–40.
[4] 'He [Lord Lansdowne] made some reference to the merits of the question, to the vague expressions in the Treaty of 1825, which he

consolation where he could. The other speakers admitted that the verdict was heavily against Britain, but thought this of small importance when set against the fact that the controversy had been settled. They spoke and thought of a 'misunderstanding', when the controversy was the result of a genuine conflict of interests. True, it was the ambiguity of the treaty of 1825 which provided occasion for the dispute; but the legal character of the despatches in which it was discussed, and its final settlement by a judicial tribunal cannot conceal the fact that the interests of Britain and the United States clashed in Alaska, and Britain yielded to *force majeure*.

Such clash of interests, interests which were by no means vital but which any country concerned would defend to the utmost limit of diplomatic bluff, usually exacerbated relations between the antagonists. (Insistence on pushing small claims to the limit was the fatal weakness of German diplomacy.) Anglo-American relations seemed exempt from this law of nature. Parliament was not in session either when the tribunal was set up or when it announced its award. Parliamentary comment came too late to be useful. The Press, however, was placid on both occasions, and hailed the award with relief as marking the end of the last specific controversy between the two countries.

When the tribunal was set up the British Press declined to notice the central fact that it was so arranged as to make it impossible for the United States to lose. A Canadian correspondent wrote to *The Spectator* (which had welcomed the American appointments), citing the New York *Evening Post* to show that Lodge, Root and Turner were recognized in the United States itself as prejudiced and that 'it is understood that the actual appointments were dictated by political necessity, and as the price of ratification of the treaty by the Senate'. To this the editor replied, 'We print our correspondent's letter, but we hold that the

---

thought must be capable of various interpretations; to the doubt about line in Portland Channel, etc. [*sic*] I told him that I had not paid so much attention to that part of the case, and had thought that if there were nothing in dispute but the Portland Channel question it would be comparatively easy of adjustment in some way, although I had not studied that point carefully, that the great difficulty arose from the Canadian claim to get to the tide water at the inlets. . . .' Choate to Hay (private and confidential), 19 July, 1902: Hay Papers, 19.

known high character of the American Commissioners is a guarantee that they will apply their minds fairly and conscientiously
to the matter before them in spite of any previous *ex parte* statements they may have made.'[1]

When the award was announced, the dispute had been drag-
ging on for long, and for long it has been suspected that Britain
would lose. As at the time of the Venezuela crisis, the result was
reached by a series of stages which concealed the magnitude of the
defeat. Yet the quasi-judicial form of the defeat did make it possible to avoid acknowledging it. It was noted that if Lord Alverstone had voted only in accord with his view of the legal merits
of the case, and this was assumed, then it was very likely that the
impartial umpire originally demanded by Canada would have
voted the same way. So Canada, it followed, had lost nothing by
her concession on the composition of the tribunal; and that had
been offset when the United States gave up her reservation of
Dyea and Skagway. No one drew attention to the fact, made clear
in the American documents, that that reservation would not have
been given up had there been any chance of an issue hostile to the
United States.[2] The fiction of a judicial tribunal had still further
merits — it could be used as evidence of good relations between
Britain and the United States. What other two countries would
resort to this method of settling disputes and expect to reach a fair
conclusion? What better evidence that neither country wanted
anything not rightly hers? Britain's first concession was to treat
the dispute as judicial rather than as diplomatic; her second to go
on treating it as judicial long after this had become mere form.

The effect of the award on Canada was bad, of course, as everyone recognized. Too many Canadians thought that this was
another, 'almost a crowning instance, of the sacrifice of Canadian
interests by the British Government for the sake of obtaining
American goodwill'.[3] That was not admitted in Britain. A neat
twist was given to the debate by the suggestion that consideration
for the best interests of Canada was really behind British policy.

---

[1] New York *Evening Post*, 24 February, 1903. Quoted in a letter in
The Spectator, XC, 21 March, 1903, p. 452.

[2] See 'The Alaska Boundary Decision' in *The Economist*, LXI, 24
October, 1903, p. 1790.

[3] ibid., p. 1791.

'We may point out that it is in the interests of Canada that we desire to see a settlement effected. . . . It would . . . be Canada, and not these islands, that would suffer most if, owing to no settlement being found, the Empire and America drifted into a quarrel.'[1] A little pompous, perhaps, but the point was a good one. In later years Canada herself was to press strongly for good imperial-American relations as a major part of her policy. At the time, however, what Canadians saw most clearly was that their imperial connection was of small use. Independence would not help them against their powerful neighbour, but then, it appeared, neither would Britain. As *The Economist* put it, adding insult to injury, Canadians could 'regard it as a very real compensation that their chief ground of difference with the United States has been terminated in a manner entirely honourable to them'.[2] They got nothing more tangible.

The negotiations over the Venezuelan and the Alaskan boundaries present some interesting parallels, and some contrasts. Hay was a very different man from Olney, a cosmopolitan, experienced diplomat and known as a friend of Britain. Yet Olney's policy was considerably more moderate than Hay's. In the earlier dispute, of course, acceptance of United States intervention had itself been the major concession, while in Alaska she was directly concerned, defending her own interests rather than those of Venezuela; and American nationalism had developed in the intervening years. Hay, in fact, had no freedom of action. He was no laggard in defence of American interests nor, with a Congress so suspicious (and latterly a President so aggressive), could he afford to be. The best summary of his activity is his own lament: 'All I have ever done with England is to have wrung great concessions out of her with no compensation.'[3] Though he might regret the forces compelling him, he saw to it that the concessions were made. The only effect of his personality and views was to make him extraordinarily conscious of the malevolent force of his own public opinion. It irked him greatly, but he could do nothing to moderate it.

---

[1] *The Spectator*, XC, 21 March, 1903, p. 452. See also 'The Alaskan Award', ibid., XCI, 24 October, 1903, p. 637.

[2] 'The Alaska Boundary Decision' in LXI, 24 October, 1903, p. 1791.

[3] Hay to Foster, 23 June, 1900: quoted in Thayer, *Life and Letters of Hay*, II, pp. 234–5.

... behind us is the Senate [he wrote], thirty-one members of which can oppose a categorical veto to anything the Executive may determine upon. I have my doubts whether even our *modus vivendi*, in which we gained virtually everything, would pass the Senate if it required their sanction. The narrowness and prejudice of the men from the northwest is beyond any idea I had ever formed, though I have had occasion to know them pretty well.[1]

It is odd to find Laurier and Hay accusing each other of localism. Laurier complained that the American Commissioners were bounded by Seattle and Massachusetts interests,[2] while Hay wrote to Choate, 'The Dominion politicians care little for English interests. Their minds are completely occupied with their own party and factional disputes, and Sir Wilfrid Laurier is far more afraid of Sir Charles Tupper than he is of Lord Salisbury and President McKinley combined. . . .'[3] There was truth in both accusations.

The public opinion which made so moderate a man as Hay so extreme in his demands prevented him from granting any advantage in return. There is a plain implication in Hay's letter just quoted that British interests, larger British interests as opposed to those merely Canadian ones concerned with a sea outlet from the Yukon, were being sacrificed to Canadian stubbornness. Yet what were these interests? They are difficult to discover. It was already a commonplace that the concord with the United States was vital to Great Britain. Yet the same forces in American politics which made for friction when Britain and America came into contact not only prevented the goodwill of the United States from being particularly useful if gained, but equally would have prevented her from displaying effective hostility outside the hemisphere. Hay in fact leaned towards friendship with Britain; but had he favoured, say, Germany, similar forces would have come into play to prevent co-operation with her. Hay had the utmost difficulty in getting highly advantageous agreements through Congress, and was helpless to attempt anything more. If we grant him

---

[1] Hay to Choate (personal and confidential), 13 November, 1899: Hay Papers, L.B. I, p. 312.
[2] Skelton, *Life and Letters of Laurier*, II, p. 129.
[3] Hay to Choate (confidential and personal), 28 April, 1899: Hay Papers, L.B. I, p. 162.

and a handful of others an understanding of international politics, that only makes their helplessness more apparent.

The foreign policy of the United States, even under men who resented the fact, was then still governed by ignorance and provincialism. The local, and very minor, interests of the West Coast carrying trade were powerful enough to prevent the Joint High Commission with Canada from reaching agreement; Bryan made the first Hay-Pauncefote Treaty a campaign issue for reasons quite unconnected with its merits. This was symptomatic of a limitation which made for strength. The interests of the United States were concentrated in her own hemisphere and to opposition there she could react vigorously and from a strong strategic position. In America the sentiments of imperialism existed without the policy which would have given them purpose.

With varying degrees of consciousness and percipience this was recognized in Britain. If British concessions to the United States caused little stir and less resentment, this cannot be explained in terms of policy alone. Its explanation is rather to be found in a sympathy with the United States, neither accidental nor reasoned but a logical concomitant of the expansive impulses which brought the two countries into conflict. In Anglo-American relations, imperialism produced its own antidote.

CHAPTER FIVE

The Spanish-American War

BECAUSE Great Britain was not directly involved in a dispute between the United States and Spain, the evidence produced by the Spanish-American War on Anglo-American relations is necessarily indirect. It is no less interesting for that, though the official papers on the war are less bulky than those dealing with many minor matters. The war offers an opportunity for the analysis of British reactions to American policy where it did not directly affect Britain herself; and this in turn casts light on many of the assumptions, half considered but never wholly rejected, which lurked in the British mind when considering Anglo-American relations proper.

The Great Powers, and Britain among them, could not fail to watch the approach of the struggle with concern. It marked a new departure in the policy of the United States, it might be extended from Cuba to the Far East, and at the least there might be an opportunity of gain. The interest of the Powers was not the less because of the great difference in size and power between the combatants. Even had they wished to ignore the war they could hardly have done so in the face of repeated Spanish efforts to involve them. The Spaniards were eager for European intervention, in the hope that they could make concessions to a concert of the Powers such as pride forbade them to make to the United States. It was apparent, even to themselves, that they could not hope to win; opinion varied about what damage they could inflict or how long they could avoid defeat. To Spain the war, when it came, was a gesture, designed to save the dynasty rather than the empire, since it appeared that both could not be saved.

The efforts of Spain to secure the support of the Powers were, however, entirely unsuccessful. There is no evidence that any of them seriously considered carrying interference beyond the most cautious kind of protest, and attempts at international mediation of the dispute were late, hesitant and ineffective.[1] The reasons for abandoning neutrality were never strong enough to overcome an obvious determination to avoid useless and expensive enterprises, and that determination dominated European policy. Yet it was well recognized that, given the very great disparity in power between the United States and Spain, neutrality represented support, effective if not theoretical, for the United States.

Whatever the reasons for European neutrality, approval of American policy was not among them. The Spanish-American War, even more perhaps than most, induced moral judgments. The United States claimed to intervene in Cuba on moral grounds; Spain appealed for intervention on behalf of morality; the Powers, whatever the realities of interest, couched their notes in moral language. On the whole, Europe held the weight of morality to be with the Spaniards. The Spanish-American War was an aberration in American policy, leading to nothing, the result of a surge of expansionism which quickly died. It was the general opinion that it was unjustifiable.

The immediate and ostensible cause of American intervention was the failure of Spain to subdue the revolution against her rule in Cuba. Ultimately the United States, determined that the guerilla war which was ruining the island must be brought to an end, decided to end it herself. The justification of that position depends on the evidence about conditions in Cuba and their cause. This is conflicting, and almost all biased; but there is general agreement on the following points.

Spanish rule in Cuba was notably bad, opposed to any measure of autonomy, inefficient and corrupt; the island was regarded as a

---

[1] The view that German policy was hostile to the United States has long been discredited. See especially J. F. Rippy, *Latin America in World Politics* (New York, 1928), ch. x; and L. B. Shippee, 'Germany and the Spanish-American War' in the *American Historical Review*, XXX. July 1925. Both rely heavily on *Die Grosse Politik*. The evidence in Alfred Vagts, *Deutschland und die Vereinigten Staaten in der Weltpolitik* (London, 1935), Vol. II, ch. xii, does not alter the verdict.

good place for Spanish officials to make a fortune.[1] Further, since the revolt had begun, Spanish duplicity had made a settlement almost impossible. The Cuban insurgents distrusted all compromise and regarded any Spanish effort to negotiate, with some justice, as mere evidence of weakness. For their part, the insurgents were equally unable to maintain a government with which anyone could deal, and were little more than barbarous banditti. The bulk of the population remained apathetic and asked, unavailingly, only to be left alone. Increasingly they came to be harried by each side for compliance, real or alleged, with the demands of the other.[2]

The United States had large investments in Cuba, and bought nearly all the sugar which was the island's chief crop. As the persistent fighting desolated the island, not only were American financial losses heavy, but yellow fever was liable to spread from Cuba to the United States. Americans therefore had the keenest interest in the restoration of peace in Cuba, but they maintained till 1898 a proper neutrality. Their neutrality was, however, formal and official only. American sympathy was firmly with the Cubans, and President Cleveland's refusal to intervene was not popular.[3] Many Cubans fled to the United States and there collected money, arms and men. The shipping of money and supplies

---

[1] E. J. Benton, *International Law and Diplomacy of the Spanish-American War* (Baltimore, 1908), pp. 21–4. See also A. M. Low, 'The Month in America' in *The National Review*, XXXI, April 1898, pp. 254–5.

[2] Although one main reason for the refusal of the United States to recognize Cuban belligerency was the fact that recognition would benefit Spain more than Cuba, President Cleveland's words are worth quoting: '. . . the pretense that civil government exists on the island, except so far as Spain is able to maintain it, has been practically abandoned. . . . It is reported, indeed, on reliable authority that, at the demand of the commander in chief of the insurgent army, the putative Cuban government has now given up all attempt to exercise its functions, leaving that government confessedly (what there is the best reason for supposing it always to have been in fact) a government merely on paper.' Message of the President, 7 December, 1896 in *Foreign Relations*, 1896, pp. xxix–xxx.

[3] See Nevins, *Grover Cleveland*, pp. 713–19; J. W. Pratt, *Expansionists of 1898. The Acquisition of Hawaii and the Spanish Islands* (Baltimore, 1936), pp. 209–15; A. K. Weinberg, *Manifest Destiny* (Baltimore, 1935), p. 286 and *passim*. Expansion was an issue, though not the major one, in the election of 1896.

to Cuba could hardly be prevented, though the despatch of actual
filibustering expeditions was fairly effectively controlled.[1]

International law on the subject of insurgency was not clear
and some of the Spanish complaints were unreasonable, but the
Spaniards were exasperated by their knowledge that Cuban juntas
existed in the United States and that the insurrection was being
nourished there. They charged, probably rightly, that it would
quickly have collapsed, had the Cubans not been supported from
abroad, and had they not hoped to drive the United States to
intervene. Since, the Spaniards argued, there was at least a strong
body of American opinion anxious to acquire Cuba, the American
government was not discouraging the Cubans.[2]

When General Woodford took up his post as American Minister
at Madrid in September 1897, he brought with him instructions
to conduct a new and more active policy. He was to offer American
assistance in restoring peace to Cuba.[3] From about the middle of
February 1898, American activity and European interest both
increased. So did Spanish complaints against the United States,
and they were now against American policy, not against American
negligence. It was the Spanish charge that by the nature and
timing of their intervention Americans gave the lie to their

---

[1] Seventy-one expeditions were fitted out in the United States during
the insurrection. Twenty-seven successfully landed in Cuba. Of the
others thirty-three were stopped by the United States authorities and
five by the Spaniards. Many of the cases of ships stopped by American
revenue cutters never came to court, and the penalties in those that did
were very light. See Benton, *Spanish-American War*, pp. 41–64. For a
sound analysis of Spanish complaints, holding that they were justified,
see H. E. Flack, *Spanish-American Diplomatic Relations Preceding the
War of 1898* (Baltimore, 1906), pp. 15–31.

[2] For the complaints of Dupuy de Lome, Spanish Minister at Wash-
ington, and the Duque de Tetuan, Minister for Foreign Affairs, as
reported in the New York Press, see M. M. Wilkerson, *Public Opinion
and the Spanish-American War: A Study in War Propaganda* (Baton
Rouge, La., 1932), p. 72. See also G. W. Auxier, 'The Propaganda
Activities of the Cuban *Junta* in Precipitating the Spanish-American
War, 1895–1898' in *The Hispanic American Historical Review*, XIX,
August 1939. See also *The Times*, 29 March, 1898, p. 5b.

[3] Secretary of State Sherman to Woodford (then still in the United
States) no. 4, 16 July, 1897. Printed in *Foreign Relations*, 1898, pp.
558–61. This instruction is also quoted at length by F. E. Chadwick, *The
Relations of the United States and Spain. Diplomacy* (New York, 1909),
pp. 508–11.

repeated claim that it was dictated by humanity. War did not break out until Spain had made all the concessions asked for. One concession merely led to the demand for another, and the United States waited for the effect of none of them to become known.[1] Moreover, at no stage, either for the benefit of American opinion or to bring pressure on the Cubans, did the American government which was urging concessions on Spain urge their acceptance on the Cubans; though the activity of the American Minister at Madrid was such that American credit was staked on the success of these moves. Meanwhile, American correspondents in Cuba constantly inflamed public opinion against Spain.[2] The event which focused the whole conflict was the *Maine* disaster.

On 15 February, 1898, the American battleship *Maine* exploded in Havana harbour with heavy loss of life. The explosion has never been adequately explained. An American investigating commission reported that it was externally caused. A Spanish commission insisted equally firmly that it was internal. The *Maine* disaster was one of the most serious and most spectacular in modern naval history, and it happened at the worst possible time for Spanish-American relations. Incidental though it was to the real questions at issue it is important because of its effect on American opinion, because of the use made of it in American diplomacy, and because the investigations which followed it provided the first opportunity for foreign action.

One thing is clear. The Spanish authorities were not implicated in blowing up the *Maine*. Apart from the unlikelihood of their committing such a crime, they had everything to lose and nothing

---

[1] Gullon, Minister for Foreign Affairs (in succession to the Duque de Tetuan) to Woodford, 23 October, 1897, enclosed in Woodford to Sherman, no. 50, 26 October, 1897; same to same, 1 February, 1898, enclosed in Woodford to Sherman, no. 135, 9 February, 1898; Polo de Bernabe (Minister at Washington) to Sherman, 10 April, 1898. Printed in *Foreign Relations*, 1898, pp. 582–9, 658–64, 747–9. See also G. Barclay (at Madrid) to Salisbury, no. 59, 17 March, 1898; P.R.O., FO 72/2062; and Chadwick, op. cit., chs. xxv–xxvii, *passim*.

[2] For the activity of the American Press, see the pedestrian but useful study by J. E. Wisan, *The Cuban Crisis as reflected in the New York Press (1895–1898)* (New York, 1934), chs. xiii–xxv, *passim*; and, modifying some of Wisan's conclusions, G. W. Auxier, 'Middle Western Newspapers and the Spanish-American War, 1895–1898' in *The Mississippi Valley Historical Review*, XXVI, March 1940.

to gain from it. They left nothing undone that could be done to express regret without admitting liability. The American commission, while finding that a submarine mine was responsible for the explosion, did not charge the Spaniards with responsibility. When their own commission found that the explosion was an internal one, the Spaniards offered to submit the difference and the question of compensation due to arbitration, an offer which had good standing in international law. There was no reason why the incident should not have been peacefully settled.[1]

In the circumstances, however, the *Maine* incident made war all but inevitable. Even before the explosion, opinion in both Spain and the United States was becoming dangerously inflamed. The *Maine* explosion now drew attention to the state of Cuba in a more dramatic way than even the New York Press had been able to achieve. If the explosion was external — and no American doubted it for a moment — the Spanish authorities were responsible for their failure to protect a national ship of a friendly Power in a Spanish harbour. The background of hostility to Spain gave the *Maine* disaster its great importance. It has been argued — by Woodford among others — that had it not been for the explosion of the *Maine* war could have been avoided. Given the determination of the United States to get Spain out of Cuba and the determination of Spain not to go, that is unlikely. But the *Maine* incident was given immense importance in the report of the Senate Committee on Foreign Relations, which stated (absurdly) that the destruction was 'compassed either by the official act of the Spanish authorities or was made possible by a negligence on their part so willing and gross as to be equivalent in culpability to positive criminal action'.[2]

The immediate impact of the event was blunted by the delay

---

[1] It seems clear that the American commission made the more thorough investigation and reached the right conclusion. See the very judicious summary of the case in Chadwick, *United States and Spain*, p. 561*n*. Chadwick, then a captain in the United States Navy, was a member of the American commission.

[2] Quoted in Flack, *Spanish-American Diplomatic Relations*, p. 38. C. E. Chapman, *A History of the Cuban Republic* (New York, 1927), gives full weight to the *Maine* disaster but concludes, 'The blowing-up of the *Maine* is by no means to be considered the cause of the United States entry into the war.' (p. 85). 'The truth of the matter was, that war was inevitable.' (p. 89).

which the investigation imposed. President McKinley at once appointed his commission, rejecting the Spanish suggestion of a joint enquiry, but the commission did not report for six weeks. It placed its report, which was generally assumed to be adverse to Spain, in the President's hands on 21 March. Thereafter the threat that unless an agreement bringing peace to Cuba were reached in a few days the report would be sent to Congress, was used in an attempt to get further concessions from the Spanish government.[1]

The conduct of diplomacy was the responsibility of the President, but the issue of peace or war lay with Congress. Moreover, Congress was known to be hostile to Spain. To send the commission report to Congress, not for information but for action, would indicate that the President had given up hope of achieving anything by diplomacy. It was that fact which gave the American report on the *Maine* its importance, and that was why the Spanish government concentrated its first efforts on preventing the report from going to Congress.[2]

The Spanish government learned on 26 March that the President proposed to present the American report on the *Maine* to Congress without either giving it to the Spanish government or waiting for the independent Spanish report. Thereupon they asked the friendly offices of the British government to persuade the President to keep his report within executive jurisdiction for the present; and offered, if that were not possible, to ask for the advice of the Great Powers and to submit all questions, pending and future, to arbitration. The matter of the Spanish appeal was not well chosen. It enabled the British government to take refuge in the judgment that 'they cannot think that any useful end would be served by offering unasked advice to the United States government on a subject so obviously within its competence as the time and method of communicating a report of its own to Congress'.[3] This was in accord with normal diplomatic practice, and it

---

[1] Woodford to Sherman, no. 189, 25 March, 1898, printed in *Foreign Relations*, 1898, pp. 698–701, gives the first example of this.

[2] Memorandum of the Spanish Ministry of State, 25 March, 1898, enclosed in Woodford to Sherman, no. 192, 26 March, 1898. Printed in *Foreign Relations*, 1898, pp. 1038–9. See Chadwick, op. cit., pp. 554–6.

[3] Salisbury to Barclay (tel.), no. 5, 26 March, 1898, P.R.O., FO 185/863.

reflected the determination of the British government, already fully formed, to do nothing to offend the susceptibilities of the United States, but it concealed the fact that the *Maine* report was of secondary importance.

The real points at issue centred on the question of a Cuban armistice. The Spanish commander, General Weyler, whose methods had made him notorious, had recently been replaced, a change generally supposed to presage peace negotiations. The American government vigorously pressed its view of what the terms of the negotiations should be. Its demands were given to Spain in their final specific form on 27 March. Chief among them were these. An immediate armistice was to be proclaimed in Cuba till 1 October, during which time negotiations for a permanent peace would take place; Weyler's orders of concentration were to be immediately and completely revoked, and relief was to be provided for those in the camps; and the American Minister was instructed to gain Spanish acceptance of the President of the United States as arbitrator in case the terms of peace were not settled by 1 October.[1]

The last sentence of the Secretary of State's telegram giving these instructions reads: 'If Spain agrees, President will use friendly offices to get insurgents to accept plan.' It is difficult to see what that undertaking could mean in practice. There is no evidence that the United States had urged moderation on the Cubans in the past, or was in a position to do so effectively now. That is most clear in the question of the armistice itself. If the Spaniards announced an armistice at American request, American credit was staked on Cuban acceptance of it; yet it was quite clear that the Cubans would not accept it. On military grounds they could not do so. The rainy season was approaching, and till it was over the Spaniards would be at a disadvantage, and would be glad of an armistice, the last thing, therefore, that the Cubans would be willing to grant. They would grant it only as a preliminary to a more permanent peace, a condition of which would be that Spain should evacuate Cuba. A letter from Maximo Gomez, quoted in *The Times*, gave the insurgents' views:

---

[1] Secretary of State Day to Woodford (tel.), 27 March, 1898. Printed in *Foreign Relations*, 1898, pp. 711–12. See also Chadwick, op. cit., pp. 556–60.

The rainy season will soon be at hand and until it is over Spain and
her troops would like an armistice. We will not, however, throw
away the advantage. I am anxious that hostilities should cease, but
it must be for all time. If Spain agrees to evacuate Cuba, I am willing to agree to an armistice until October 1, when loyal Cubans
shall come into their own again. I am writing this at the direction
of the Cuban Provincial Government, with whom the Spaniards
may treat directly if they so desire.[1]

There are points of obscurity in this letter — what does Gomez
mean by loyal Cubans coming 'into their own' or by the evacua-
tion of Cuba? — and it strongly suggests that, as the Spaniards
alleged, the insurgents were raising their demands as their
confidence of American support grew; but the letter does bring
out clearly the point of divergence on which there could be no
compromise. Spain was willing to go a very long way towards
meeting American demands, in order to show good will and in the
hope that if all American demands were met, that would commit
the United States to support in restoring Spanish rule in Cuba.
She was not willing to negotiate the ending of that rule. The
Cubans were already unwilling to consider anything else.[2]

The Spaniards, in short, were reluctant to lose Cuba because of
its potential value; but they were quite determined to keep it for
reasons of pride. Their attitude meant that, if peace was the
object, American efforts to intervene did more harm than good.
American protests that all they desired was peace and order in
Cuba, under whatever circumstances, were promptly — and
rightly — discredited.

This unbridgeable gap between Spain and the United States
must be kept in mind when the policy of the Powers is considered. Clearly they recognized the Spanish dilemma, and the
Spanish eagerness to do anything at all to end Cuban hope of
American support. They also well understood the American
determination to get Spain out of Cuba. If, therefore, they did not
intervene, it was not out of sympathy with American policy nor,

---

[1] *The Times*, 12 April, 1898, p. 3c. Gomez was one of the insurgent
generals.

[2] Under Spanish law, Cuban independence was a matter for the
Cortes, not then in session. The Spanish government's powers of
negotiation were limited for constitutional as well as political reasons.

in all probability, because of the influence of Britain. As early as 1 April, Lascelles was reporting from Berlin Bülow's view:

> With regard to the application which Spain had addressed to Germany as well as to the other European Powers, Herr von Bülow said that the German Government would be ready to join with the other Powers if they proposed to mediate between the two parties, but that they were not prepared to take any initiative.
>
> With all the sympathy which the German Government entertained for the Queen Regent, and their desire for the maintenance of the monarchical principle in Spain, they could not neglect the vast commercial interests they had in the United States. There was moreover another point, which he found difficult to mention to the Spanish Ambassador, and that was that the Spanish Administration of Cuba had always been deplorably bad.[1]

The application to which Bülow referred had been made on 26 March. It was the Spanish reply to the failure — as they then thought — of their efforts to get the *Maine* report delayed, and it was a formal request to the Great Powers to advise Spain and the United States to accept arbitration.[2] The Powers, however, were in a dilemma of their own making. While they were determined to offer nothing more than good offices, which must be agreeable to both sides, the fiction of the pacific intentions of the United States had to be maintained. It was a fiction which became increasingly threadbare.

It was made easier to maintain by a secondary fiction. Though hostile to American policy in general, Barclay, the chargé d'affaires in Madrid, attributed a portion of the blame to General Woodford. Woodford, he suggested, was misleading the Spaniards. New to diplomacy and naturally anxious for the success of his mission, he was stressing a distinction, which the facts did not justify, between President McKinley and the jingoes who were urging him to war.[3] The distinction was real but not relevant. McKinley was not a jingo, but he was not the man to resist them

---

[1] Sir F. Lascelles to Salisbury, no. 99 (confidential), 1 April, 1898: P.R.O., FO 64/1437.

[2] Barclay to Salisbury (tel.), no. 16 (confidential), 26 March, 1898: P.R.O., FO 185/869.

[3] See especially Barclay to Salisbury, no. 95, 16 April, 1898 and no. 96 (secret), 17 April, 1898: both in P.R.O., FO 72/2062; and Barclay to Balfour (tel.), (private), 18 April, 1898: P.R.O., FO 185/869.

with any force of conviction; and though anxious to get Spain out
of Cuba by peaceful means if possible, he was not prepared to
defend a diplomatic defeat before his countrymen. Yet the distinction between the President, reputed to be pacific, and his
public opinion, was not confined to Woodford. It was expressed in
all the British official correspondence, and produced some curious
reasoning.

The Spanish request of 26 March had originally spoken of
'arbitration or some other means' of settling the question at issue;
but on the advice of the ambassadors at Madrid the reference to
other means was deleted. The next move came from the French,
who cautiously enquired in London whether a friendly representation was desirable, 'avoiding anything which might arouse
the susceptibilities of the United States.' In forwarding this
enquiry to Pauncefote, Salisbury added, 'We should be very much
guided in our answer by the view of the United States Government. You might confidentially enquire of President.'[1]

The private enquiry was made, and got the reply that any such
action would be premature. This sufficiently shows the close links
between the two countries, but a later message from Pauncefote
is more illuminating: 'The attitude of Congress is certainly
threatening to peace, but Mr Day thinks it will be restrained from
any immediate action as the critical moment for action by the
President is impending. . . .' Again the implication is that the
President wanted compromise, that if only he could be helped to
restrain Congress all would be well, and that the activity of the
Powers should be directed to strengthening his hand.[2]

The assumption was a natural one but it was based on a mis-
conception. The United States, President as well as Congress, had
already decided that Spain must leave Cuba; with the future of
the dynasty at stake, or thought to be so, no Spanish statesman
could grant anything more than autonomy — and even that was
an enormous concession for which the Spanish government was

---

[1] Barclay to Salisbury (tel.), no. 16 (confidential), 26 March, 1898 and
(tel.), no. 17 (confidential), 27 March, 1898: both in P.R.O., FO 185/869;
and Salisbury to Pauncefote (tel.), no. 36 (very confidential), 28 March,
1898: P.R.O., FO 115/1087.
[2] Pauncefote to Salisbury (tel.), no. 26, 28 March, 1898 and (tel.), no.
28, 30 March, 1898: P.R.O., FO 115/1088. The second of these also
indicates that intervention would be no more acceptable in the future.

K

eager to get the urging of the Pope and the Great Powers as a sop to Spanish pride. In these circumstances no concessions made by the Spaniards would have been adequate to meet American demands. The only effective action by the Powers would have been to bring pressure on the United States to reduce those demands. There was never the smallest chance of that. The good offices of Britain were declined because they 'would be of no assistance to Spain and might even increase popular irritation'.[1]

At this stage the United States was demanding that an armistice be granted pending further negotiations; Spain declined to grant it unless it were asked for by the insurgents. There was, however, Barclay reported, a chance that the Pope might use his influence to persuade the Spaniards to grant it unasked. The following day he added that 'at the instigation of the U.S. Minister' the Austrian and German Ambassadors had approached the Papal Nuncio to urge the mediation of the Pope; but that the Nuncio regarded the step as premature.[2]

On 2 April the Spanish government renewed their request for the good offices of Britain, and on the same day a joint *démarche* was urged by the Austrian Ambassador to Salisbury, who replied that in his judgment 'such an offer would do more harm than good unless the United States were desirous that it should be made'.[3]

Two days later a report from Barclay, who got it from Woodford, announced that the Pope had 'with the knowledge of the President' consented to ask Spain to proclaim an armistice, and that the Spanish government were ready to follow his advice — provided American warships were withdrawn from the vicinity of Cuba. The Spanish government asked for British assistance in obtaining this. Salisbury advised Pauncefote that he might join in any *démarche* agreed to by his colleagues *if* consultation with the President led him to suppose that it would be well received and useful.[4] At some stage the Spanish government became

---

[1] Salisbury to Barclay (tel.), no. 10, 1 April, 1898: P.R.O., FO 185/863.
[2] Barclay to Salisbury (tel.), no. 23, 1 April, 1898 and (tel.), no. 24 (confidential), 2 April, 1898: P.R.O., FO 185/869.
[3] Salisbury to Barclay (tel.), nos. 11 and 12, 2 April, 1898: P.R.O., FO 185/863.
[4] Barclay to Salisbury (tel.), no. 25 (confidential), 3 April, 1898: P.R.O., FO 185/869; Salisbury to Pauncefote (tel.), no. 44, 2 April, 1898, and (tel.), nos. 46 and 47, 4 April, 1898: P.R.O., FO 115/1087.

convinced that the Pope's mediation had been offered at the request of the United States. This was not so, and the confusion which resulted from the error, and especially the conditions which the Spaniards attached to their armistice when they supposed the United States to be weakening, held up the negotiations.[1]

The President's message to Congress accompanying the correspondence to date, which would, it was supposed, leave no room for further discussion, had been set for 5 April. At the last moment the American Minister secured a postponement of a day; but before this was known he had attempted to urge the Spanish government to instant concession by giving them the earlier date.[2] Throughout the whole crisis Woodford's actions showed extraordinarily little sensitivity to the Spanish temper. The Spanish reaction to pressure and demands for hasty action was always to procrastinate still further. It may be that Woodford and his government thought that, given the opportunity, the Spaniards would procrastinate indefinitely, but of that there is no evidence; nor does it appear that the Americans were being driven by their public opinion beyond the point at which they could delay. The real reason is probably confusion between Woodford and his government. When Woodford finally cabled his confidence that given time all would be well, he got the uncompromising answer, 'Would the peace you are so confident of securing mean the independence of Cuba?'[3]

The Spanish decision on an armistice was expected on the 6th. A Cabinet meeting was due and it was expected that the Pope would give his formal advice in favour of proclaiming an armistice. Even so it would be a considerable concession, it might easily be interpreted as a sign of weakness, and there was likely to be some controversy in the Cabinet; but Barclay recorded that opinion was hope-

---

[1] Barclay to Salisbury (tel.), no. 28 (confidential), 4 April, 1898 and (tel.), no. 32, 5 April, 1898: both in P.R.O., FO 185/869; Salisbury to Barclay, no. 48 (confidential), 6 April, 1898: P.R.O., FO 185/864.
[2] Barclay to Salisbury (tel.), no. 28 (confidential), 4 April, 1898 and (tel.), no. 30, 5 April, 1898: both in P.R.O., FO 185/869.
[3] Day to Woodford (tel.), 5 April, 1898. Printed in *Foreign Relations*, 1898, p. 733. Barclay was able to send a version of Day's telegram to Salisbury almost at once. Barclay to Salisbury (tel.), no. 32, 5 April, 1898: P.R.O., FO 185/869.

ful, and that the American legation appeared to share this hope.[1]

In part, according to Barclay, the hope was based on the knowledge that the President had decided not to recommend independence for Cuba in his message to Congress; and that knowledge led Woodford to a serious error. While the Cabinet was sitting and before any word had been received from the Pope, Gullon, the Foreign Minister, was called out to receive a note from Woodford giving him that information and expressing regret that no word had yet been received of the armistice. To that note the Spanish government returned a stiff answer.[2] Shortly thereafter the expected advice from the Pope arrived, and the Cabinet reconvened to consider it. They were given a little more time to do so because the President's message had been again postponed. Barclay's information was that the Cabinet had previously been agreed in principle that on the arrival of the Pope's advice they should declare an armistice. Their unconciliatory reply to Woodford had been dictated by the belief that he was trying to force their hand. Woodford's message had itself been the result of his ignorance of the latest postponement, and of his hope that a favourable message on the armistice might stop a warlike resolution in Congress. When he heard of the postponement, Woodford withdrew his note and the situation calmed down, yet leaving the Spanish government more convinced of American bad faith than before.[3]

Meanwhile the representatives of the Great Powers had finally agreed on the form of a collective representation in Washington. Pauncefote had taken the lead in drafting this, but had done so in consultation with the State Department and had ascertained that it would be well received and was likely to be useful in calming popular excitement. Instructions were slow to reach the Russian Ambassador, but the note was delivered on the 7th and well taken, both in the United States and in Spain.[4] With the

---

[1] Barclay to Salisbury (tel.), no. 34, 6 April, 1898: P.R.O., FO 185/869.

[2] Barclay to Salisbury (tel.), no. 35 (confidential), 6 April, 1898 and (tel.), no. 36, 7 April, 1898: both in P.R.O., FO 185/869.

[3] Barclay to Salisbury (tel.), nos. 39 (confidential) and 40, 7 April, 1898: P.R.O., FO 185/869.

[4] Pauncefote to Salisbury (tel.), no. 29, 5 April, 1898 and (tel.), no. 33, 7 April, 1898: both in P.R.O., FO 115/1088; Barclay to Salisbury (tel.), no. 41, 8 April, 1898: P.R.O., FO 185/869.

knowledge that the Powers were also urging their persuasions at Washington, the Queen Regent was enabled to ask that they should, individually or collectively, urge the Spanish government to proclaim an armistice.[1] Their advice, together with that of the Pope, proved adequate. While the American government staved off the action of the Powers as long as possible, the Spanish government were eager for it. But although the advice of the Powers was given at the request of Spain, the risks became apparent in the popular reaction. Many Spaniards felt that a concession denied to the Pope had been made to the Powers, and resented that. The attitude of the Spanish army especially gave cause for alarm.[2]

The Spanish concession having been made and the armistice pronounced, the Spanish government were eager that a *quid pro quo* should be obtained in the withdrawal of American ships from the vicinity of Cuba, where their presence annoyed the Spaniards and encouraged the rebels. To this end the Spanish government again circularized the Great Powers asking for a *démarche* at Washington; but it was perfectly well recognized that this step would in no sense be an equivalent of that taken at Madrid. The Spaniards wanted the European Powers involved in Cuban affairs — the Americans did not. 'We must leave any action on this request to Your Excellency's discretion', wrote Salisbury to Pauncefote.[3]

Though the Austrian Minister at Washington tried to organize a demonstration on the lines suggested by Spain, the other Powers were against it — Pauncefote opposed it vigorously.[4] By this time everything depended on what Congress saw fit to do with the President's message. On the 13th, by an overwhelming vote, the House of Representatives adopted a resolution directing the

---

[1] Barclay to Salisbury (tel.), no. 43 (very confidential), 8 April, 1898: P.R.O., FO 185/869.

[2] Barclay to Salisbury, no. 83 (very confidential), 10 April, 1898 and no. 85, 13 April, 1898: both in P.R.O., FO 72/2062.

[3] Salisbury to Barclay, no. 60 (confidential), 18 April, 1898, enclosing a communication from Count Rascon, the Spanish Ambassador in London, of 11 April: P.R.O., FO 185/864; Salisbury to Pauncefote (tel.), no. 63, 11 April, 1898: P.R.O., FO 115/1087.

[4] Salisbury to Pauncefote (tel.), no. 64, 11 April, 1898: P.R.O., FO 115/1087; Pauncefote to Salisbury (tel.), no. 34, same date: P.R.O., FO 115/1088.

President 'to intervene at once in Cuba to restore peace and secure to the people of the island by their free action a stable and independent government of their own'. He was authorized to use the land and naval forces of the United States to that end. That meant war if the President should sign the resolution.[1]

There was now opportunity for another European representation. The diplomatic corps in Washington telegraphed to their governments in terms very similar to those of Pauncefote to his:

> The attitude of Congress and the resolution voted yesterday in the House of Representatives by a large majority leave little hope for peace and the general opinion prevails that the warlike measures advocated have the approval of the Great Powers. The Memo of the Spanish Minister delivered on Sunday appears to offer a reasonable basis of arrangement and to remove all legitimate cause of war. If that view should be shared by the Great Powers the time has arrived to dispel the erroneous impression which prevails that the armed intervention of the U.S. in Cuba for the purpose of effecting the independence of the island commands, in the words of the Message, 'the support and approval of the civilized world'.
>
> Under these circumstances the representatives of the Great Powers at Washington consider that their respective governments might usefully call the attention of the U.S.G. to the above mentioned Memo of the Spanish Minister, and make it known that their approval cannot be given to an armed intervention which does not appear to them justified.
>
> The observation of the Powers might be in the form of a note delivered by the representatives at Washington to the Secretary of State but it seems to the representatives preferable that an identic Note should be delivered as soon as possible by each of the Foreign Ministers of the six Great Powers to the representative of the U.S. accredited to them respectively.
>
> The moral effect which would result from that course would be greater in the eyes of Europe and of the American people and would give to this intervention of the six Powers a character which would not expose their representatives to the appearance of having renewed their first representations which the Message of the President passes under silence.
>
> It appears to the representatives that the greatest publicity

---

[1] Pauncefote to Salisbury (tel.), no. 36, 14 April, 1898: P.R.O., FO 115/1088.

should be given to such a Note in order to relieve the moral responsibility of the civilized world for an act of aggression in support of which its authority is invoked.[1]

Arthur Balfour, deputizing for Salisbury, gave Pauncefote permission to join with his colleagues, but added:

> . . . it seems very doubtful whether we ought to commit ourselves to a judgment adverse to the United States and whether, in the interests of peace, such a step would be desirable.
>
> If your knowledge of the local situation suggests to you any observations we shall gladly receive them.[2]

Chamberlain thought even this cautious instruction too much, and was clear that Britain should do nothing to oppose, or even give the impression of opposing, the United States. Balfour's phrasing reflects the difficulty in which the British government found themselves. They already knew — had ample evidence from Madrid and other sources to make it clear — that war was inevitable unless the United States could be restrained from making demands which no Spanish government could grant.[3]

Given permission by Balfour to proceed with a joint protest which yet should not involve any moral judgment on the United States, Pauncefote temporized. He pointed out that there was, as usual, no agreement between the two houses of Congress as to the resolution to be passed, the Senate being anxious to declare the independence of Cuba, the House being less precipitate; and he suggested that it might be as well to wait till the result of a joint vote, if any, was known, and matters were once more in the hands of the President. To this suggestion Balfour joyfully agreed:

> I gather that the President is most anxious to avoid if possible a rupture with Spain. In these circumstances advice to the U.S. by other Powers can only be useful if it strengthens his hands, and of this he must be the best judge. Considering our present ignorance as

---

[1] Pauncefote to Salisbury (tel.), no. 37, 14 April, 1898: P.R.O., FO 115/1088.
[2] Balfour to Pauncefote (tel.), no. 72 (confidential), 15 April, 1898: P.R.O., FO 115/1087.
[3] Garvin, *Joseph Chamberlain*, III, pp. 298–300. Chamberlain was fully aware that the difference between Spain and the United States could not be settled without war.

to his views, the extreme improbability that unsought advice will do any good, and the inexpediency of adopting any course which may suggest that we take sides in the controversy we shall, at least for the moment, do nothing.

Please keep us informed of fresh developments.[1]

By this time, however, it was apparent to all that any further action implied a moral judgment on the activities of the United States, and the Austrian Minister at Washington reported his opinion that the time had come for such a judgment. This suggestion was taken to the British government for their opinion — would Britain join in a new representation 'which should no longer be simply a friendly appeal but which should express disapprobation of the aggressive attitude assumed at Washington'? The answer was evasive in form but definite in content. Her Majesty's Government 'think it very doubtful whether it would be wise to express any judgment on the attitude of the United States, or whether such a step would be conducive to the interests of peace'.[2]

This opinion was sound enough. It was not peculiar to Britain. Peace could be assured in only two ways — by forcing Spain to submit to the United States, or by forcing the United States to moderate her demands. The first was never in question, for the conciliatory temper of the Spaniards, born of weakness, was not in doubt. The second was hardly considered either, by any European Power. The principal conclusion to be drawn from the various suggestions for intervention described above is that, whatever their origin, they show the same hesitancy. All the Powers were willing to follow the others, none was willing to lead. When recriminations were exchanged later about the activity of the Powers, they arose out of an attempt to claim friendship for the United States. The German Ambassador tried to discredit Lord Pauncefote, as he had then become, by showing him as the leader in attempts to restrain the United States; but charge and countercharge concealed the fact that the most vigorous protest of which

---

[1] Pauncefote to Balfour (tel.), no. 39 (confidential), 16 April, 1898: P.R.O., FO 115/1088; Balfour to Pauncefote (tel.), no. 78, 17 April, 1898: P.R.O., FO 115/1087.

[2] Salisbury to Sir H. Rumbold (in Vienna), no. 32 (very confidential), 16 April, 1898: P.R.O., FO 5/2517.

Pauncefote or anyone else could be accused was extremely mild.[1]

The chief reason for European neutrality, apart from the inertia already mentioned, was the difficulty of organizing concerted action. No Power was able to act effectively alone; none was prepared to accept the risks involved in taking the lead. Whatever the outcome of a joint *démarche* to restrain the United States the resentment of that country and the opportunity offered for intrigue were risks too great to be faced. The implication of that attitude was that Cuba was of merely American importance. As the German Ambassador at Vienna early pointed out, unless Spain could convince the Powers to the contrary, there was no hope of intervention.[2] The Spaniards never ceased trying to do so, but with no success. Balfour, Hanotaux, the Kaiser, were all in agreement, to the distress of the Austrian Foreign Minister, Goluchowski.[3] All maintained the fiction of American desire for peace long past the point at which it should have been apparent that peace was incidental to the satisfaction of American demands — that was a necessary diplomatic convention. But it was also necessary because moral disapproval would have no effect on the policy of the United States, and it was undignified and unfair to the Spaniards to make protests on their behalf which the Powers had no intention of backing up.[4] The Powers agreed on a further point — it was quite impossible to say anything or use any influence at Madrid. The last word there had been spoken. War broke out on 21 April.

The attitude of the British government, then, did not differ substantially from that of other governments. The Spanish case, however, had great plausibility, and it was effective in Europe.

---

[1] The British file on these German allegations against Pauncefote and their denial is in P.R.O., FO 5/2517.

[2] Salisbury to Barclay, no. 49 (confidential), 6 April, 1898, enclosing a copy of Rumbold to Salisbury, no. 95 (confidential), 29 March, 1898: P.R.O., FO 185/864.

[3] Balfour to Pauncefote (tel.), no. 75A, 17 April, 1898, enclosing a telegram from Sir E. Monson in Paris; Salisbury to Pauncefote (tel.), no. 82, 19 April, 1898, enclosing a telegram from Rumbold: both in P.R.O., FO 115/1087; Lascelles to Salisbury, no. 116, 16 April, 1898: P.R.O., FO 64/1437.

[4] Salisbury to Barclay, no. 75, 30 April, 1898, enclosing a copy of Milbanke (British chargé d'affaires in Vienna) to Salisbury, no. 129 (confidential), 20 April, 1898: P.R.O., FO 185/864.

Public opinion there was almost uniformly hostile to the United States, and the hostility was towards what looked like land-grabbing by a powerful state at the expense of a weak one. If the reports sent home by British representatives abroad are to be trusted, the statesmen of Europe shared, in private conversation, that hostility.[1] The contrast between the formal neutrality of Europe and the hostility of the European Press towards the United States made a profound impression on Americans. They were correspondingly impressed to find it absent in Britain. Britain was credited in the United States with averting the very real danger of a coalition in favour of Spain, and that was chiefly because of the great difference in tone between the British Press and that of other countries. That difference gained for Great Britain the advantages for which all the Powers hoped, and the reasons for it are worth study.[2] Since neutrality was accepted almost without question as the proper British policy, newspaper comment on the war and the events leading up to it could take a more strictly moral line than it might have done if British interests had been involved, or if a policy had had to be formulated. In casting the issue in moral terms, the Press merely followed the lead of the parties in the dispute. Its space was largely devoted to judging claims and counter-claims.

One reason for the fact that British Press comment on Cuba did

---

[1] See L. M. Sears, 'French Opinion of the Spanish-American War' in *The Hispanic American Historical Review*, VII, February 1927; and Shippee, loc. cit.; Lascelles to Salisbury, no. 99 (confidential), 1 April, 1898: P.R.O., FO 64/1437; Salisbury to Barclay, nos. 35, 49, 52, 65 (all confidential), 16 March, 6 April, 7 April, 23 April, 1898, and no. 75, 30 April, 1898: P.R.O., FO 185/863 and 864. These enclose copies of reports from the European capitals. Salisbury to Pauncefote (tel.), no. 82, 19 April, 1898: P.R.O., FO 115/1087.

[2] B. A. Reuter, *Anglo-American Relations During the Spanish-American War* (New York, 1924), pp. 63–4; Wisan, op. cit., pp. 406–407; Nevins, *Henry White*, p. 133; Dennett, *John Hay*, ch. xvi, especially pp. 189–91; Thayer, *Life and Letters of Hay*, II, pp. 165–71; T. Roosevelt to A. H. Lee, 25 November, 1898, printed in Morison (ed.), *Roosevelt Letters*, II, no. 1091. For the subject of this chapter, parliamentary comment, for obvious reasons, is not enlightening. Some ninety or a hundred questions were asked during 1898 which had some reference to the war; all but five were concerned with neutrality or similar technical matters, and those five add nothing to Press comment. *The Parliamentary Debates* (Fourth Series), 1898, LIV to LXVI, *passim*, especially LVI and LVII.

not share European hostility to the United States is that it was more strongly affected by stories of Spanish atrocities. The Spaniards complained, and even the pro-American British Consul-General at Havana admitted, that British correspondents in Cuba, headed by the man from *The Times*, were sending home stories heavily slanted against Spain.[1] It was true that Spanish rule in Cuba was bad and its effects horrible; but it was also true that British observers expected Spanish rule to be bad, and held social theories which demanded that it should be bad and denied the possibility of improvement.

The analogy most usually drawn was with Turkish rule in Armenia or Bulgaria; and it was urged that had an Armenia lain as close to the shores of England as Cuba did to those of the United States, Britain would have had to intervene long since.[2] In the first instance the analogy was merely used to provide a vivid picture of just how bad the state of Cuba was; but its implications were adverse to Spain.

Turkey shared with China a peculiar position in the diplomacy of the day. They were sovereign states to which the Powers accredited ambassadors; but they were also regarded as inert bodies, fields for diplomatic activity rather than participants in the game, lacking in the power to take part and not to be relied upon to keep the rules, because either unable or unwilling to do so. To most Europeans the Armenians were the innocent victims of their barbarous rulers. Their religion and their political situation combined to bestow on them a moral quality which owed nothing to their own characteristics.[3] Though the conduct of British diplomacy was formally correct, British opinion on Cuba put Spain in the position, where the United States was concerned, of a smaller and less important Turkey. The Cuban situation was presented, not as that of a European Power attempting to restore order in a colony, but as that of a barbarous race oppressing its barbarous

---

[1] Private letter from Mr Gollan (British Consul-General at Havana) to Pauncefote, 8 April, 1898: P.R.O., FO 115/1087.

[2] A. M. Low, 'The Month in America' in *The National Review*, XXXI, April 1898, p. 255. For Bulgaria as an alternative parallel, see F. J. Matheson, 'The United States and Cuban Independence' in *The Fortnightly Review* (New Series), LXIII, May 1898, p. 831.

[3] See, for example, E. J. Dillon, 'The Fiasco in Armenia' in *The Fortnightly Review* (New Series), LIX, March 1896.

subjects. That was a situation to which the conscience of Europe
and especially of Britain reacted strongly, and one which it
became the duty of the United States, as the nearest Power, to
stop.[1]

The corollaries of this approach were all beneficial to Anglo-
American relations. The criticism, for example, that American
intervention took place just when Spain, at American urging, was
putting her house in order, could be refuted. Spanish rule was not
only bad, but must be expected to be bad. There was no reasonable likelihood of any improvement and so no point in waiting to
see what became of Spanish reforms. The misdeeds of any soldier or
administrator were merely representative of the general Spanish
traits of cruelty, callousness and inefficiency which made that
nation incompetent to govern dependencies. Or again, the
Spanish plea that it had taken the North longer to conquer the
South in the American Civil War, and yet the duration of the war
had not been made ground for interference, could be rejected. The
length of time involved became irrelevant, because it was axio-
matic that Spain was not a country that could govern dependencies. Similar arguments could be multiplied.[2]

If Spain was thus to be put on the wrong side of the line between civilization and the rest, it could plainly not be on grounds
of religion or of the lack of any European quality. It could only be
on grounds of race, and it was. The distinction was not between
Europeans (who would include for this purpose, of course, Americans) and others, but between Anglo-Saxons and others, between
calm, efficient, powerful but yet law-abiding Anglo-Saxons, and
cruel, corrupt, frenzied Latins. Again and again the theme recurs.
Even European papers, in expressing sympathy for Spain, drew
attention to this obvious bias and disclaimed a corresponding one
for themselves. As the *Journal des Débats* put it, 'Ce n'est pas

---

[1] This, from 'Spain and the United States' in *The Spectator*, LXXX,
19 March, 1898, is a not untypical comment. 'If our people once realised
what is the condition to which Cuba has been reduced by Spain, we
should have half England calling the Americans hard names because
they had not intervened earlier to stop the cruelty and bloodshed that
were being perpetrated at their very doors.' (p. 398).
[2] Leading article in *The Times*, 16 April, 1898, p. 11*b*; 'England's
Attitude and the War' in *The Spectator*, LXXX, 23 April, 1898, p. 566;
'The Anglo-Saxon Alliance,' ibid., 21 May, 1898, p. 718.

comme Latins que nous sommes sympathiques à l'Espagne.'[1]

This attitude hardly involved any hostility to Spain. Almost everyone felt sympathy for Spain, and especially for the Queen Regent. The very obvious difference in power between the combatants precluded anything else. Nor was friendship for the United States universal. The important emotion was something less conscious. The fact that the United States was a party in the quarrel, and the stronger party, influenced the British reaction to the questions in debate even before they were consciously considered. A conflict between Spain and the United States was taken to be a stage in an inevitable process, the increase of the power of the Anglo-Saxon race, increase which it was to achieve by double right, racial characteristics fitting it for rule, and political institutions which would impose themselves by sheer merit on the rest of the world. In describing such a process hostility to Spain was out of place.[2]

It is not necessary to draw on these ideas to explain British neutrality — which was, after all, the most comfortable and least expensive policy. But they underlay both the immediacy with which it was accepted that neutrality was the proper British policy, and the moral terms of the discussion which neutrality made possible. American expansion was assumed to be Anglo-Saxon expansion, and so could not be disadvantageous to Britain. Even the few dissentient voices in the discussion, which deplored American policy, largely accepted the assumptions of their opponents, much as they claimed to dislike having to do so.[3] The Press refused to see in the activities of the United States any cause for alarm. As significant as the various attitudes towards the Spanish-American conflict when it broke out, was the general indifference to its coming.[4] If the United States could settle with Spain without

---

[1] *Journal des Débats*, 22 April, 1898. Quoted in Sears, loc. cit., p. 28.

[2] 'Are the Americans Anglo-Saxons?' in *The Spectator*, LXXX, 30 April, 1898, p. 614.

[3] The views of *The Spectator* and *The Saturday Review* make an interesting contrast on this point.

[4] References to the state of Cuba and to the progress of the insurrection were fairly frequent during the early months of 1898. But there was a remarkable reticence about the part played by the United States, at least till the beginning of April — although the *Maine* disaster, naturally, produced a good deal of comment.

war, excellent; if not, why worry? The important thing to the British mind was not any change in the position of the United States, but that no European country should be allowed to make mischief from it. Those who approved the action of the United States and those who did not agreed in this, that it would not be prejudicial to Great Britain.

As an example of this, *The Saturday Review* is interesting. Somewhat erratic in its approach, it hardly referred to Cuba till 9 April, when it suddenly leapt into action with a series of leading articles whose contents are indicated by such titles as 'America the Bully' and 'The Blatant American'.

> Spain [said *The Saturday Review*], is, no doubt, a decaying nation, and America is an expanding nation, and, therefore, by the laws that govern the practice of land-grabbing, the stronger is entitled to despoil the weaker; but in the name of common honesty let us have no cant about it.

> We have done something in that line ourselves [land-grabbing], and have no wish to pose as censors. But when we find the bulk of the English newspapers calling on us to admire the attitude of the United States and to accord our moral support to the Washington Government, it is time to protest.[1]

The protest owed, of course, a good deal to the notion that the Cuban rebellion was being maintained from the United States. Equally, it was very far both from British official opinion and from the great bulk of British newspaper comment — as *The Saturday Review* itself admitted, not without pride.[2] But even in this indictment Britain and the United States are by implication bracketed together. The appeal for less cant was not a realistic one. As *The Saturday Review* would readily have allowed, it was just because they had indulged in the same kind of cant, swallowed the same kind of excuse for British activities in the past, that British newspapers were now prepared to make them for those of the United States. Cant no less than expansion was common to both countries, and was accepted in both, by the men who wrote it and believed it, as yet further evidence of

---

[1] 'American Morality' in *The Saturday Review*, LXXXV, 9 April, 1898, p. 479.

[2] 'The Blatant American' in LXXXV, 23 April, 1898, p. 546.

their similarity and the gulf between Anglo-Saxon Powers and others.[1]

The bulk of the British Press, then, supported the American intervention as both inevitable and moral; but even those who challenged its morality did not doubt that it was inevitable. America would attack Spain, America would defeat Spain, America would take Spain's colonies. It was all very sad, but that was the present state of the world.

> Our sympathies are frankly with the weaker power, which has surrendered everything but the national honour in its endeavour to avert the calculated wrath of its powerful opponent. In healthier times, before Teutonic brutality had dulled the senses of European public opinion, the aggression would have been resented by every State having interests in the Western Hemisphere. But there is no longer a conscience of Europe, and so the annexation will no doubt in the long run be completed . . . of course the resources of America must in the long run wear out those of Spain, as surely as the Northern States wore out the Southern thirty years ago. Cuba will be over-run and 'civilisation' will be able to boast of a further illustration of the maxim that might makes right.[2]

It is noteworthy that the senses of public opinion were held to have been dulled by 'Teutonic brutality'. To *The Saturday Review*, hardly less than to the papers it criticized, moral attitudes were a function of race.

The debate on the conduct of the United States, in short, could be and was conducted as an exercise in manners and morals. The appeal, however, was to two different moralities. One was based on a narrow interpretation of international obligation between European Powers, which the United States was held to have outraged; the other thought, or claimed to think, in terms of the spread of civilization and its requirements. Both made it easy to ignore any implications of power politics in the situation. The United States might be attacked as a vulgar bully,

---

[1] Almost any comment on the subject demonstrates this, but see especially three leaders in *The Times* on 16 April, 1898, p. 11*b*; 21 April, 1898, p. 9*c*; and 22 April, 1898, p. 9*f*.

[2] 'American Morality' in *The Saturday Review*, LXXXV, 9 April, 1898, p. 480.

but there was no attempt to suggest any large menace in her activities.[1]

That was understandable at the beginning of the war, when the general supposition, in the rest of the world as in the United States, was that the war was being fought over Cuba. The test came with the possibility that the United States would annex the Philippines. That was a possibility admittedly of concern to all Powers with interests in the Far East. The pro-American Press, which had been somewhat muted in its comment, became more explicit, but its moral tone was hardly modified. 'We rejoice in the efficiency of the American representative of our race [Dewey at Manila], because we believe that, failing the Anglo-Saxon, the wronged of the world will find no defender. . . .' said *The Spectator* simply, and went on to explain its hope for the future:

> We think America will keep the Philippines, and we heartily hope i t. She will govern them well enough, much better than any Power except ourselves, and we have more of the world's surface than we can well manage. . . . The envy we excite is already too great. . . . It would be a relief if another English-speaking Power would take up a portion of our task, and in taking it, perform the duty of repaying something to the world which yields her such advantages. The 'weary Titan', in fact, needs an ally while traversing 'the too vast orb of his fate', and the only ally whose aspirations, ideas, and language are like his own is the great American people. The Frenchman is too fickle, the Russian too full of guile, and the German too harsh in his treatment of all who do not think that to be drilled is the first, if not the only, duty of man.[2]

There was a shift here from the argument that the war was a matter of no importance to the argument that the rise of the United States could only be beneficial to Britain, but it went unremarked, because both arguments depended, in slightly different ways, on the concept of race. Only by concentrating attention on the race rather than the nation state as the agent in international affairs could the logical gap between the first and the second be

---

[1] Contrast 'The "Moral Sense" of America' in *The Saturday Review*, LXXXV, 23 April, 1898, p. 545 with 'The Anglo-Saxon Alliance' in *The Spectator*, LXXX, 21 May, 1898, p. 718.

[2] 'The Capture of Manila' and 'The Fate of the Philippines' in LXXX, 7 May, 1898, pp. 645, 646.

concealed. When Britain's need of an ally was mentioned, the context was not that of power. The American annexation of the Philippines in fact made no change in the power position in the Far East. German, Japanese and Russian readiness to accept it was largely based on the calculation that it would not. Though this calculation was incompatible with British hopes, it was hardly mentioned in the British Press. It was not so much challenged as ignored.

Two corollaries of the British attitude are of particular interest. The first is that it required that the United States be treated as a single-minded agent, not only when policy was finally being implemented but even before. The Spanish-American War split the United States in much the same way, though not so seriously, as the Boer War was to split Great Britain. It became intimately connected with the domestic discontent reflected in the Progressive movement.[1] Many of those who objected to the war — as of those who supported it — were to be found in just those groups whose social and political views were coming to be admired in Britain. The British Press at that time was of a remarkably high standard; and in general it was interested in and well-informed about the United States. Yet the divisions in that country went unnoticed. If the United States was to be seen as one branch of an expansive race in action, there was no relevance in a domestic debate which related the war to entirely different considerations.

Second, the persistent feeling was expressed that from the British point of view the war could only do good (as it did) by revealing the 'real' sentiments of Europe towards the United States. In the past, the argument ran, when America and Britain had come into conflict, France, Germany and Russia had been able to display a spurious friendship to the United States which was really no more than hostility to Britain moulded by circumstances. Now Continental hostility to America would show itself, and Britain's real friendship shine the brighter by contrast. This in fact is just what happened; and to such an extent that it was easy for hostile journalists to mock at the speed and thoroughness

---

[1] See especially W. E. Leuchtenburg, 'Progressivism and Imperialism. The Progressive Movement and American Foreign Policy, 1898–1916' in *The Mississippi Valley Historical Review*, XXXIX, December 1952.

of the change in American sentiment towards Britain.[1] The change was caused solely by the contrast between British and other opinion. Correct though the policy of their governments was, the peoples of Europe appeared to disapprove almost universally of the action of the United States in Cuba; and that fact was made known in America at a time when opinion there was exceptionally sensitive, so sensitive that one gets the impression that Americans themselves may have been suspicious of their own motives. At that time they found to their surprise that in Britain, of all places, their assertions were taken at face value and their cry of moral indignation endorsed. This inexpensive support gained a richer dividend of good will than many more tangible offerings.

That kind of sentiment is not a thing that lasts. It had some immediate and excellent effects. Congress was induced — largely by Henry Cabot Lodge — to vote the money for the payment of an arbitration award to Canadian sealers, which it had declined to do for some years.[2] But on the whole it gained Britain very little in her dealings with the United States. Equally, it did not have to be bought with any real concessions. Once the issue of non-intervention was settled, the British consideration of neutrality was entirely technical. The rules governing the conduct of neutrals in a maritime war were obviously of intimate concern to Britain. It was therefore important for her to gain acceptance of the rules which she would wish applied were she involved in a war with a maritime power. Much the most important of these rules was that dealing with the definition of contraband of war, and in the British consideration of this, possible future British interests played a much greater part than any desire to sway neutrality in the direction of the United States. Certain gestures of friendship there were; but few and reluctantly made. Chamberlain urged the desire of the Governor-General of Canada to

[1] *The Spectator*, LXXX, 16 April, 1898, p. 530, and 23 April, 1898, pp. 561–2; Sears, loc. cit., pp. 34, 37–8, 40–1; Wisan, op. cit., pp. 406–7; Nevins, *Henry White*, p. 133; Reuter, op. cit., ch. iv, *passim*; Thayer, *Life and Letters of Hay*, II, pp. 168–9; memorandum by Mr Tower enclosed in Pauncefote to Salisbury, no. 182, 27 May, 1898: P.R.O., FO 5/2362.
[2] Henry White to Mrs White, n.d. Quoted in Nevins, *Henry White*, p. 133.

gain goodwill by allowing American warships, armed, to pass through Canadian waters on their way from the Great Lakes to the Atlantic. The law officers of the Crown compromised, but declined to let fully armed ships proceed. The requirements of the Foreign Enlistment Act were perfectly properly enforced against both countries; and in spite of protests the American squadron under Dewey at Hong Kong was instructed to leave on the outbreak of war before it was fully ready for sea.[1]

It was an axiom of Salisbury's that to attempt to gain the goodwill of a foreign country by anything more than ordinary diplomatic courtesy was a waste of time — that goodwill would disappear as soon as conflicts of interest arose. The Alaska boundary controversy was to prove him right. The goodwill which British support for the United States engendered could not, it appeared, be drawn upon in a dispute between the two countries themselves. Yet realism of Salisbury's kind was almost confined to him. The Alaskan dispute did not undo the good which the Spanish-American War had brought about. It was not related in the British Press to that war. These two American diplomatic activities were treated as quite different; and that is yet further evidence that there was on the British side an important irrational element in the *rapprochement*. The good understanding between the two countries was held to be not the result of goodwill and good management, but something mystic and inevitable, a law of nature. Therefore, it was not to be destroyed by arguments between the two countries; their falling out had no relevance to the great unity which set both apart from any other nation. Only by some such irrational thought process can the continued improvement of Anglo-American relations at the end of last century be explained. The British attitude to the Spanish-American War shows just that process in action.

---

[1] Nevins, *Henry White*, p. 131; *The Parliamentary Debates* (Fourth Series), 1898, LVI and LVII, *passim*; John Macdonell, 'England's Duties as a Neutral' in *The Nineteenth Century*, XLIII, May 1898; P.R.O., FO 72/2091 and 2092; N.A., S.D. Post Records, C8.4/49 and C8.5/49, *passim*.

CHAPTER SIX

The Far East

ONE important reason for the readiness with which Great Britain gave way to the United States when their interests conflicted was, that the two countries were supposed to have some mystic community of interest which overrode any conflicts, and made them of no importance. Often the argument, if so it may be called, rested there, and it was merely asserted that 'in the last resort' the Anglo-Saxon nations would be found on the same side — not a prospect of much concern to the practising diplomatist. Sometimes, however, it was implied that the United States was on the brink of a great burst of international energy, which would, as a result of the similarity of race, ideology and tradition, be exerted in directions which the British would find good. 'The weary Titan', in fact, would find his ally.[1]

If the Anglo-American concord were to be effective anywhere, it must be in the Far East. There was a long history of American commercial and missionary enterprise in the Far East. Expansion to Americans had always meant expansion to the west; and their dream did not stop at the Pacific. An important part of the myth of manifest destiny was the vision of the United States seated between East and West, a country uniquely fitted to be the centre of their trade. Another was the idea that civilization moved ever westward as empires rose and fell, till only North America was left to become the home of the last and greatest. These did not conflict with the withdrawal from Europe so fundamental in the American mind. Trade and missionary work in the Far East could

---

[1] Above, p. 152. See, for example, 'The Anglo-Saxon Alliance' in *The Spectator*, LXXX, 21 May, 1898, p. 718; and 'Alliances', ibid., LXXXI, 17 December, 1898, p. 897.

even emphasize that withdrawal. Such ideas had been advanced long before the conquest of the continent made it necessary to consider their implications for foreign policy.[1] When the time came to reconsider American policy, the minds of Americans were conditioned by two generations of myth-making. It was in the Far East that they first attempted a policy not confined by the traditions of diplomatic thought epitomized in the Monroe Doctrine.

American theorists of race expansion and the race struggle gave great importance to the future of China. '. . . on the decision of the fate of China', wrote Brooks Adams, 'may, perhaps, hinge the economic supremacy of the next century.'[2] But American concentration on the Far East was not determined by American history only. It was accidental but important that the late nineteenth century, which saw Turner's frontier close, saw also the imperialist struggle for the Far East reach its height. The China question became important in international politics very suddenly, and it lost importance with equal suddenness. It held attention only from the Sino-Japanese War to the Russo-Japanese War, only for ten years; but during that period China was a centre of international rivalry and the relations of the Powers were of great complexity. Did Britain and the United States, in these circumstances, effectively support each other, either in formal co-operation or by working independently towards the same end?

The first part of the question can be answered at once. There was almost no joint action. It was not expected by British exponents of the Anglo-Saxon alliance. Their confidence was that British and American policies would automatically be in alignment. In considering how far they were justified two problems arise. Both Britain and the United States had policies — of a sort — and in both the Far East got a good deal of public attention. In the absence of formal co-operation Anglo-American relations,

---

[1] See H. N. Smith, *Virgin Land: the American West as Symbol and Myth* (Cambridge, Mass., 1950), chs. i–iv; and Weinberg, *Manifest Destiny*.

[2] *America's Economic Supremacy* (New York, 1900), p. 196. See also A. T. Mahan, *The Problem of Asia and its Effect upon International Policies* (London, 1900).

as they affected Far Eastern policy, must be deduced from a vast mass of material most of which is only marginally relevant. The documentary problem only reflects a larger one. American policy in China, effective or not, was fairly single-minded. British policy in China was only one facet, and not the most important, of British world policy. Anglo-American relations must be dissected from the whole complex of international rivalries in China and of British diplomacy. Fortunately many of the documents on the China question have been available for some time. New documentary evidence has filled in detail rather than changing the outlines; and a great deal of recent monograph work has made analysis easier.

To none of the Powers of the time was China anything more than an object of policy, an enormous expanse of territory and a huge population to be exploited commercially and if possible politically. We look in vain in their policy for any understanding of China, any sympathy for her aspirations or problems, any realization of the line which her future development would take. The men who dealt with Far Eastern policy, whether as traders, journalists, diplomats or politicians, had on the whole remarkably little interest in China and the Chinese. It is with something of a shock, for instance, that we find Lord Lansdowne in 1901 urging the merits of a scheme by which the indemnity demanded from China for the outrages of the Boxer rising should be finally paid in 1944.[1] To Western statesmen, even after the Boxer rising, it appeared that China, like Turkey, could only move as dictated by the external forces acting on her. Their object was to gain the paramount influence at Peking or to prevent their rivals gaining it, to partition China to their own advantage or to prevent for their own ends her partition.[2] In their manoeuvres two main policies were possible — those which were usually known as maintaining the 'open door' and taking a 'sphere of influence'. With some important qualifications it can be said that both Britain and the United States favoured the 'open door' policy, though the United States was more consistent and fervent in support

---

[1] Memorandum by Lansdowne for Joseph Choate, American Ambassador in London, 18 July, 1901: N.A.S.D., C8.4/52.

[2] For a great deal of evidence and a full bibliography see Langer, *Diplomacy of Imperialism*, chs. vi, xii, xiv, xv, xxi, xxiii.

of it.[1] Here surely was a real community of interest such as alone can produce any useful co-operation in policy. Yet, often though it was invoked, the Anglo-American concord was ineffective.

Although China became a centre of international rivalry briefly and late, British traders there had been urging a more active policy on the Foreign Office for many years.[2] Their objects were twofold. The first was to get from the Chinese government relaxation of the internal restrictions on trade, and in particular the abandonment of internal customs duties. That was a purely commercial problem. The obstacle was the corruption and backwardness of Chinese officials, and the general hostility of the Chinese to foreigners. As late as 1896 Valentine Chirol was writing, 'Whether the maintenance of the Chinese Empire itself continues to be in the future, as in the past, a matter of British interest is a question to which China must be left to furnish the answer by her own acts.'[3] '. . . the trade of China', remarked the Shanghai Committee of the China Association in the same year, 'remains at this date under the control and to a great extent hampered by tradal conventions unsuitable to the existing requirements of a commerce capable of vast extension if proper means are adopted for its enfranchisement.'[4]

The second policy of the traders was the result of some success in reaching the first. Treaty concessions might be wrung from the reluctant Chinese central government at Peking; but there was no assurance that they would be honoured by local officials. As the China Association said, 'the complaints of residents here are not directed against the Treaties, but against the gross and scandalous disregard of them by every Chinese official.'[5] While

---

[1] See A. W. Griswold, *The Far Eastern Policy of the United States* (New York, 1938), ch. ii.

[2] The section of this chapter dealing with the demands of British traders in China draws heavily on the admirable work of N. A. Pelcovits, *Old China Hands and the Foreign Office* (New York, 1948), especially chs. vi–ix.

[3] *The Far Eastern Question* (London, 1896), p. 180. Chirol wrote for *The Times* on Far Eastern matters. He was both popular with the China traders and influential with the public.

[4] Letter to the General Committee of the Association, 10 July, 1896. Quoted in Pelcovits, op. cit., p. 197.

[5] Memorandum by the Shanghai Committee, 23 January, 1899. Quoted in Pelcovits, op. cit., p. 247.

China remained under Chinese control, the vexations of foreign traders were endless; and the old China hands, convinced of their right to trade, demanded that China should be put in tutelage under British officials. That demand the Foreign Office always rejected. They were not prepared to turn China into another India, and felt that they were doing all they could or should to help trade.[1]

The traditional British policy had been devised by importers and exporters of consumer goods. China was regarded as a market. 'We look upon it [China] as the most hopeful place of the future for the commerce of our country', said Sir Michael Hicks Beach, and his speech was typical.[2] In the 1890s the nature of commercial enterprise in China began to change. The new competition was in securing railway concessions, and in financing the Chinese government. These two things were closely connected. Any railway concession had to be financed by a loan, since the efforts of the Chinese government to raise funds of their own were a complete failure. A loan offered an opportunity for demanding guarantees, and the building of a railway, often linking China with the territory of another country, was itself a means of bringing pressure to bear on the Chinese government. In the building of railways and the raising of loans a success was, by its nature, exclusive; it offered no scope for competition, but could only be matched by an equivalent concession elsewhere.[3]

This change in the nature of commerce coincided with the growing interest of the other Powers in China — and was in part responsible for it — producing the China problem as the 1890s knew it. Both the Foreign Office and the China merchants found it difficult to adjust their ideas. The indemnity which Japan asked

---

[1] See especially Pelcovits, op. cit., chs. vi, vii.

[2] Speech at Swansea, 17 January as reported in *The Times*, 18 January, 1898, p. 6d.

[3] A point made most explicitly by Balfour on 10 August, 1898, in answer to an attack by Sir William Harcourt in the House of Commons. *The Parliamentary Debates* (Fourth Series), 1898, LXIV, p. 829. In spite of Balfour's skill, his speech was widely taken to imply the abandonment of the 'open door' policy. For Salisbury's account of Anglo-German rivalry over one railway concession see G. S. Papadopoulos, 'Lord Salisbury and the Projected Anglo-German Alliance of 1898' in the *Bulletin of the Institute of Historical Research*, XXVI, November 1953, pp. 216–18.

for the retrocession of Liaotung after the Sino-Japanese War was a heavy burden on China, and the foreign loans with which it was paid gave the European Powers a grip on the country. But although the penetration of other Powers into China began very quickly after the rescue of the Liaotung peninsula from the Japanese, British merchants were slow to divert their attention to the new menace. (So, *a fortiori*, was the Foreign Office. The demand for action always came from the merchants.) The activity of other Powers first made itself felt commercially, as in the Franco-Chinese agreement of 20 June, 1895, and it could be answered commercially, with the Anglo-Chinese agreement of 4 February, 1897.[1] There was no debate on China in the House of Commons in 1896 or 1897, and only five questions on China were asked.[2]

Though slow to meet new conditions, the complaints of the China Association grew louder. They saw, or thought they saw, other Powers obtaining from the Chinese government just those reforms which they had been urging the Foreign Office to obtain, and they suspected — correctly — that these reforms would not benefit everyone. In addition to their other diplomatic activities, the foreign Ministers at Peking were pressing the claims of specific firms. That the British government had always been unwilling to do. As Sir Claude MacDonald, Minister in Peking and not unsympathetic to merchants' complaints, remarked, 'British enterprise in China must be independent, individual, and self-reliant. The moment it ceases to be this and leans too much on State assistance, it ceases to be enterprise, indeed I may say it ceases to be British.'[3] Now, however, in a market which had long been British, the nationals of other countries were being given support by their governments such as the British government would not give. That gave them an advantage that called for counter-measures.

Most of those interested in the China trade continued to regard

---

[1] These agreements are to be found in J. V. A. MacMurray (ed.), *Treaties and Agreements with and concerning China, 1894–1919* (New York, 1921), Vol. I, pp. 28–30 and 94–8.

[2] *The Parliamentary Debates* (Fourth Series), 1896 and 1897, XXXVII to LII.

[3] Speech, 28 September, 1899. Quoted in Pelcovits, op. cit., p. 257. He was, of course, speaking of trade rather than concessions.

the 'open door', the largest possible market, as the proper aim.
The concessionaires and financiers, however, whose profits came
from loans to the Chinese government, preferred exclusive rights
in part of China. The Yangtze valley became accepted as the
British 'sphere of interest'. The two policies reflected two essentially different interests; and when traders supported a 'sphere of
interest' they did so because convinced that the 'open door' was
unattainable. To them, the 'open door' was the more vigorous
policy. But whatever the policy they advocated, British business
men in China never got nearly the support they wanted. The
Foreign Office interpreted the 'open door' policy differently, as
one of self-denial similar to that favoured by the United States. All
Powers would refrain from making exclusive demands, and British
trade would prosper on its own merits. The reform of China,
against the opposition of both Chinese and foreigners, they declined more firmly than ever to undertake. There were two 'open
door' policies, not one, and that was a source of confusion.[1]

The difference between traders and the Foreign Office is no
more than that between those to whom their trade was of the
first importance, and those with many other things to think of.
The views of the traders are worth analysing for two reasons.
First, they make it clear that the politicians' 'open door' policy,
developed in opposition to traders' demands, was necessarily weak.
Its character as a negative policy was too firmly established for it
to be modified into an effective defence of Chinese integrity.
Second, the traders' views now became effective enough, through
the writings of men like Chirol and Curzon[2] and Beresford,[3] to
shape the public, and to some extent the official, notion of what
the problem was. Britain's primary interest in China continued
to be commercial. The object of concern was still the Chinese
market. For a brief period, during which nations were thought to
be in inevitable competition, commercial as well as imperial, the
anxiety of China traders for their profits found support among the

---

[1] Though he never makes the point explicit, this seems to me to follow
from the long analysis given by Pelcovits, op. cit., as well as from a study
of contemporary debates and periodicals.

[2] G. N. Curzon, *Problems of the Far East* (revised ed., London, 1896);
see also *The History of 'The Times'*, Vol. III (London, 1947), pp. 186–7.

[3] Lord Charles Beresford, *The Break-up of China* (London, 1899).

British public; the China market came to be regarded as more important than it was, and even as vital. Estimates of British policy suffered as a result. It was apt to be regarded as weak because British traders were not being given what they had been denied for thirty years, support which the size of their trade did not warrant. The change was less in policy than in public excitement.

There was, of course, an occasion for the excitement. It was primarily the activity of Russia that made the Chinese question a political one. Russia was perennially short of cash; her activities in China were largely financed by the French; and much of the material for the construction of the trans-Siberian railway had to be imported. There could be no question of a Russian need for markets. There were two parties in the Russian Cabinet when China policy was discussed. One held that expansion into Manchuria should be by commercial, the other by political, means. Both agreed that, whatever the answer, not commerce but the control of North China was the object.[1]

The event which focused attention on the new problem was not the Sino-Japanese War, but the German demand for Kiaochow. That followed directly from the war, which established China in the European mind as a country not only backward but ripe for dissolution; but it did not take place till 1897. It made the China question one of diplomacy proper, that of preventing the partition of China, if it took place, from damaging British interests. Much of the debate on British policy turned on different assessments of the likelihood of the break-up of China.[2]

The situation was complicated by the officials of the Manchu Empire, who had, weak though their position was, ideas of their own about the best way of preserving the empire. The most obvious was to maintain a suitable balance of power, especially in North China. The gratitude which the Chinese had felt for Russia after Shimonoseki had been short lived. Even before the

---

[1] Witte led the commercial, Muraviev the political, faction. See E. H. Zabriskie, *American-Russian Rivalry in the Far East, 1895–1914* (Philadelphia, 1946), pp. 30–44; Langer, op. cit., pp. 454–8.

[2] Those who favoured an arrangement with Russia were apt to argue that China would not break up. See, for example, 'The Fate of China' in *The Spectator*, LXXX, 19 March, 1898, p. 400; and 'The Dry Bones Stirring in China', ibid., LXXXI, 24 September, 1898, p. 395.

Germans took Kiaochow and the Russians Port Arthur, there was
a strong faction in the Chinese government which argued that
Russia was a more immediate menace than Japan, and that it
would be quite agreeable to have Japan stay in Weihaiwei for a
time. That would, of course, have the added advantage that the
Sino-Japanese War indemnity, for which Weihaiwei was the
security, need not be paid at once. Only one thing hampered this
plan. The Japanese then wanted money, not Weihaiwei.[1]

Meanwhile Salisbury decided with reluctance that Britain must
make some gesture towards getting compensation for the taking
of Kiaochow. 'It will not be useful,' he wrote, 'and will be expensive; but as a matter of pure sentiment, we shall have to do it.'[2]
Hence the taking of Weihaiwei. The British request for the port,
cleared with the Japanese, could hardly have been denied; but
it was actually welcome to the Chinese. Their objection was not
that the British wanted to move in, but that the Japanese were
moving out. The British were second best to the Japanese as a
counterweight to Russia. Significantly, however, the leader of the
Chinese faction which urged the lease of Weihaiwei to Britain was
strongly opposed to the British loan which enabled the Chinese
indemnity to be paid. He saw the first as a means of achieving the
balance of power through which alone China could hope to
survive. He saw the second as only another means of dominating
China. The first was directed against Russia, the second against
China.[3]

What the Western Powers saw as inoffensive trade measures
might, then, be seen by the Chinese as directed against China;
while what the Western Powers regarded as an attack on the
integrity of China might be welcome to the Chinese. Because of
this Chinese attitude as well as for other reasons, the 'open door'

---

[1] See Langer, op. cit., pp. 460, 474–5; G. P. Gooch and H. Temperley
(eds.), *British Documents on the Origins of the War, 1898–1914* (London,
1927), Vol. I, nos. 30, 40, 46; E-tu Zen Sun, 'The Lease of Wei-hai
Wei' in *The Pacific Historical Review*, XIX, August, 1950, which
modifies the judgment of Langer, op. cit., p. 463; and Sir E. Satow (in
Tokyo) to Salisbury, 24 February, 1898: Salisbury Papers, Bound
Volume, Private — Japan (from and to) 1895–1900.

[2] To Chamberlain, 30 December, 1897. Quoted in Garvin, *Joseph
Chamberlain*, III, p. 249.

[3] Sun, loc. cit.; Langer, op. cit., p. 473.

policy — the politicians' 'open door' — had no practical chance of success. Political and commercial matters were too closely inter-woven to be separated. The Japanese pointed this out when they were approached by Chamberlain, hopeful of a joint resistance to the Russian acquisition of Port Arthur. England's policy, said the Japanese Minister, seemed to be based on purely commercial considerations, but how did England expect to keep her com-mercial position intact if she lost her political influence in China?[1]

In another connection the link between commerce and politics was made even clearer. It was suggested that the best way of stopping the decay of the Chinese Empire was to offer a large loan at a rate so low as to undercut any possible foreign competition. (The British money market could still, it was held, do this.) Naturally, to make such a loan acceptable to investors would require a government guarantee. *The Spectator* laid claim to moral scruples about using a loan in this way as a political weapon, but went on to argue that it might be the least of possible evils if it averted the partition of China. That was still the great disaster, for if China broke up, Britain would be 'compelled' to take a slice.[2]

The struggle for China thus became a struggle to gain con-cessions, or alternatively to prevent rivals from gaining them. As a result it became clear how closely affairs in China were linked with those of Europe. Russian policy benefited from two advan-tages. The first was proximity. The distances in Siberia were enormous, and the trans-Siberian railway not yet built; but, when it was, a system of branch lines into Manchuria from the basis of a trans-Siberian line could both give Russian manufacturers a great advantage over those of other Powers, and bring northern China ever more firmly under Russian control. The other advantage was strategic. Russia was the only country in Europe which could actually hope to gain strength from adventures in China.[3] The policy of all the other Powers came to be dominated by the need to make some response to Russian policy.

---

[1] Langer, op. cit., p. 472, following Baron Kato's memoirs.
[2] 'Lord Salisbury in China' in LXXX, 8 January, 1898, pp. 38–9. *The Spectator*'s views on this point are of particular interest as those of a leading pro-Russian journal.
[3] Zabriskie, op. cit., pp. 25–33, 35–44; Langer, op. cit., pp. 397–404.

For the French, the first concessionaires in China, extending
into Yunnan and Kuangsi from their base in Indo-China, the Far
East was never a problem. The Russian need of funds to finance
Far Eastern expansion offered the French a means of fostering
the Franco-Russian Alliance. France in the south of China and
Russia in the north did not come into conflict. Italy and Austria-
Hungary were hardly interested in China; for Austria-Hungary,
Russian interest in the Far East was welcome in so far as it
took Russian attention away from the Balkans, as for a decade it
did.

The problem was much more complicated for Germany and
Great Britain. They were the two Powers most concerned in the
struggle for markets, and so most concerned for their trade with
China. Two policies were worth consideration. One was to co-
operate in opposition to Russia, the policy that underlay Chamberlain's attempt at an Anglo-German alliance.[1] It received classic
expression in Balfour's statement to the House that

> within China . . . British interests and German interests are abso-
> lutely identical. Jealousy, I suppose, there may be between indi-
> vidual traders, individual concessionaires, and individual producers.
> But fundamentally the interests of the two countries are the same
> and must be the same, and I certainly believe we shall be able
> without difficulty to work hand in hand towards carrying out these
> general commercial objects. . . .[2]

Commercial rivalries then as now involved the governments of
the countries concerned and could not be regarded as producing
an identity of interest; but even setting that aside, commercial
interests were not an adequate basis for effective Anglo-German
co-operation. Germany, centrally placed in Europe, might try to
play Russia against Britain, but there was no chance that she
would abandon her position between them to align herself with
either. The free hand was fundamental to her policy.[3] 'Alliances',
as A. J. P. Taylor has recently reminded us, 'are not made by
purchase; they spring from a community of vital interests. . . .

---

[1] See Langer, op. cit., pp. 492–6; Garvin, op. cit., III, ch. lviii.
[2] 5 April, 1898. *The Parliamentary Debates* (Fourth Series), 1898,
LVI, p. 232.
[3] See Langer, op. cit., pp. 496–503; Taylor, op. cit., pp. 373–7.

Germany had no such vital interests in China; therefore all talk of alliance was vain.'[1]

The alternative policy for Germany, as for Great Britain, would have been to regard commercial rivalry as of the first importance, and to try to get commercial concessions out of Russia in the Far East by a recognition of her dominant political interests there. That was never really possible. It was not possible because not acceptable to Russia. It interfered with the Russian determination to have a free hand in their sphere of interest. Any attempt at *rapprochement* broke on that rock. The German dilemma was the fairly obvious one that her new world policy was coming into conflict with her European situation. The Chamberlain attempt at alliance with Germany was a reaction to the menace of Russia; but it was also a recognition that the most effective way of inducing Russia to modify her policy in China was to bring pressure to bear on her in Europe. The European implications of an Anglo-German alliance, not its strength in China, would give Russia pause.[2]

The British position was still more complex than that of Germany. Chamberlain's efforts were probably personal to himself; certainly they did not have the support of Salisbury, still dominant in the Cabinet.[3] Salisbury placed the Far East low on his list of priorities in British policy. He was prepared to defend British trade there only so far as it could be done without sacrificing interests he regarded as more important.[4] In China, Russia was undoubtedly the Power whose advance was most dangerous. Germany, in spite of Anglo-German rivalry, was not a serious menace.[5] But Salisbury was always acutely aware that policies in

[1] ibid., p. 377. The Chamberlain-Hatzfeldt negotiations of 1898 need not, therefore, be taken too seriously.

[2] German policy is shrewdly analysed by J. D. Hargreaves, 'Lord Salisbury, British Isolation and the Yangtze valley, June–September, 1900' in the *Bulletin of the Institute of Historical Research*, XXX, May 1957, pp. 71–4.

[3] See Papadopoulos, loc. cit.

[4] He was also much less worried than most of his colleagues by the cries of alarmists about the state of British trade. See his speech at the Albert Hall reported in *The Times*, 18 January, 1898, p. 9.

[5] German rivalry was real enough. See Kazuo Kawai, 'Anglo-German Rivalry in the Yangtze Region, 1895–1902' in *The Pacific Historical Review*, VIII, December 1939. But the successes of Germany were

all parts of the world were closely interrelated, and British interests elsewhere made it impossible to oppose Russia with any force.
The possibility of Franco-British conflict in Africa was enough to
incline him to an agreement with Russia. Combined with his distrust of German intentions, it precluded a vigorous policy in
China.[1]

It is in this context of European commercial and political
rivalry that American policy must be seen. All the various British
policies which were advocated at the time, whether reaching
agreement with Russia, or joint action with the United States or
Germany or Japan; all were designed to check Russian expansion
or minimize its ill effects, without taking the lead in opposing her.
That Britain, for reasons of European policy, could not do. It is
clear that a firm defence of the 'open door' by the United States
would have been ideal from the British point of view. The
'Anglo-Saxon Alliance' owed much to the hopeful conviction that
the defence would be made.

At the end of the nineteenth century, American trade with
China was very small; and it was virtually confined to a few
staple products.[2] There was nothing in the state of trade to make
China of much interest to the United States. Those business men
active in China had long tried, like their British counterparts, to
get more active support from their government, but with even
less success. What American interest there was in China was far
more the result of missionary activity. American missionaries in
China numbered about fifteen hundred and their influence was
considerable.[3]

---

successes for that standard — and fatal — tactic of German policy, making capital out of extraneous difficulties. Remove the difficulties and
German policy would become ineffective.

[1] A. L. Kennedy, *Salisbury, 1830–1903* (London, 1953), pp. 275–6;
and see Langer, op. cit., pp. 460–2; Chung-fu Chang, *The Anglo-
Japanese Alliance* (Baltimore, 1931), pp. 49–70; and Hargreaves, loc.
cit., pp. 62, 74. I am indebted to Mr F. H. Hinsley for the use of his
chapter, then unpublished, on 'British Foreign Policy and Colonial
Questions, 1895–1904' from *The Cambridge History of the British
Empire*, Vol. III (Cambridge, 1959).

[2] Rounsevelle Wildman (U.S. Consul-General at Hong Kong) to Hay,
6 January, 1899: Hay Papers, General Correspondence, 1899.

[3] Griswold, op. cit., pp. 16, 61 and n. This section owes much to the
excellent study by C. S. Campbell, Jr., *Special Business Interests and the
Open Door Policy* (New Haven, 1951).

American business men came to be haunted in the 1890s by an industrial problem to which they saw no solution — that of overproduction. A sudden export surplus which developed very quickly between 1893 and 1898 argued not only an impressive volume of production, but a saturated home market. If the United States came to produce more than she could consume, disaster, it was held, could be avoided only by finding new export markets. For various reasons, Europe, the Empire, Africa, even South America, all seemed to offer little hope. Only China remained, and to American business men as to Europeans, it came to have an importance beyond the reality of the trade involved. The magic figure of four hundred million customers enchanted the industrialists of the West.[1]

Before the Spanish-American War the China lobby had been notably unsuccessful in persuading the government to take action in China, alone or in co-operation. Cleveland was hopeless. Even after McKinley's election, the war and the feebleness of Sherman delayed the growth of American policy. In March 1898, Pauncefote had approached President McKinley with an informal enquiry as to what could be done by the two countries working together in the Far East. The United States, replied McKinley, had a well-defined tradition of declining joint action. His answer was a courteous rebuff.[2] At the time, the Cuban crisis was near its height, and the United States was not free to pursue an active policy in the East. But it was confidently hoped in London that American co-operation had only been postponed. 'American interest in the question of open ports and free markets in China may seem less keen amid agitations nearer home. But it is permanent and is not forgotten at Washington.'[3] When Hay became Secretary of State, the China merchants had a spokesman after

---

[1] Campbell, op. cit., ch. ii. 'The belief in the great potentialities of the Chinese market . . . had little rational basis.' (p. 10).

[2] Gelber, *Anglo-American Friendship*, p. 13; Dennis, *Adventures*, pp. 170–1; Henry White to Hay, 12 and 18 March, 1898: Henry White Papers.

[3] *The Times*, 14 March, 1898, p. 5a. It is fair to say that this may be special pleading by the New York correspondent of *The Times*, a pro-British American, designed (needlessly) to gain British sympathy for the United States.

their own desire. The influence of men like Beresford and Rock-hill became important.[1]

The men with business interests in China were not, on the whole, imperialists. What evidence there is suggests that in general they opposed the Spanish-American War, and that imperial expansion was the work more of publicists and politicians than of business men.[2] Nevertheless, trade with the East was the ostensible object of the expansionists. They connected it with the need of a nation to expand or go under, but it was one of their most potent arguments, and they used it to the full. It was the destiny of the United States to dominate Pacific trade, but destiny must be given a helping hand. The need to defend trade routes across the Pacific was given as the excuse for the building of a large navy, the acquisition of Hawaii, the control of the isthmian canal.[3] On the other hand, business men with interests in the East opposed the Spanish-American War on the ground that it would divert energies better spent in protecting the China trade.[4] It was therefore ironical that the first American adventure in the Far East was the decision to keep the Philippines. Once the decision was taken, however, the business lobby realized how valuable the new American interest in the Far East could be, and redoubled their propaganda. They saw, and were prepared to help others see, the connection between the Philippines and China.[5]

The decision to keep the Philippines was welcomed in Britain and viewed with disfavour in Russia, and for the same reason. It was disapproved by the Russians, not for itself so much as because it had to be connected with the growth of Anglo-American friendship. 'We could . . . console ourselves with the

---

[1] Campbell, op. cit., pp. 46–8, 51; Griswold, op. cit., pp. 47–63. Some letters from Beresford to Hay are in the Hay Papers, General Correspondence, 1898.

[2] See J. W. Pratt, 'The "Large Policy" of 1898' in *The Mississippi Valley Historical Review*, XIX, September 1932; same author, *Expansionists of 1898*, ch. vii.

[3] See F. R. Dulles, *America's Rise to World Power, 1898–1954* (London, 1955), chs. ii and iii, which summarizes a great deal of evidence.

[4] ibid., p. 46; Griswold, op. cit., p. 8.

[5] Campbell, op. cit., pp. 40–1 and ch. vii.

passing of the Philippines into the hands of our friends, the Americans, whom we love and value. But the transfer of these islands to the United States, friends and possible allies in the future of Great Britain, should give us pause to think things over.' And again, if the United States were to conclude that the Philippines 'were suitable as a point of departure in the Far East', Russia would then have to recognize a new factor of importance in the Far Eastern situation. So wrote Count Cassini, Russian Minister in Washington.[1]

The quotations selected exaggerate Cassini's fears. He also pointed out that the friendship between Britain and the United States 'is not destined to go beyond the limits of mutual kindness and friendly assertions, and it will hardly reach the dangerous condition of an alliance'.[2] In this his judgment was sound. The 'large policy' had already spent most of its force. It is true that one main argument for keeping the Philippines was that they would be the base for American commercial expansion. The United States would be able to operate from Manila as Britain did from Hong Kong. The argument is a doubtful one, and it gained in force and became vocal only after Dewey's victory in Manila Bay. After that victory the United States had the Philippines, and the embarrassing question of what to do with them was most easily solved by keeping them. To allow any other country to acquire them would cause international complications, and the martial pride of the United States, roused by victory, made it difficult to return them to Spain. Enthusiasm roused in such circumstances was not likely to last.[3]

The taking of the Philippines meant, says one authority, that 'for better or worse the American Republic became a part of the network of Far Eastern power politics'.[4] That statement is difficult to maintain. Whatever the reasons for it, annexation did not of itself necessarily involve the United States in the Far East, and the emphasis on commerce as the basis of interest is suspect. In the late nineteenth century it was seldom an adequate basis. It

---

[1] Cassini, to Muraviev, 22 June, 1898; Cassini to Lamsdorf, 23 June, 1898. Quoted by Zabriskie, op. cit., pp. 48–9.

[2] ibid. See also p. 185n.

[3] See Dulles, op. cit., pp. 46–8; Griswold, op. cit., pp. 23–35.

[4] Zabriskie, op. cit., p. 51.

soon became clear that the United States had no policy. 'If it were
not for the Philippines the United States because of remoteness
from China, would have been compelled to have been satisfied
with a passive relationship to all the disorders in China. Now, the
interference of America is spreading in ever wider circles.' That
was the verdict of a Russian diplomat in 1900, but even then it
was not so.[1] The mere ownership of a base in the Far East was not
enough to give the United States power. The intention of using
it was also needed.

That intention, even under Theodore Roosevelt, was hardly
formed. In spite of his efforts and those of propagandists for the
navy, the United States did not have an effective base in the
Philippines. As late as 1902 Congress had not been persuaded to
vote the money necessary for defence and facilities.[2] Nor was that
all. The United States was not an Asiatic Power, as both Japan
and Russia might claim to be. Her policy in the Far East, whatever it was, had to be conducted under great disadvantages of
time and distance. As a commercial base the Philippines were
doubtless of some value.[3] As a centre for penetration they were,
for a country some thousands of miles away, useless. Political
competition, not commercial competition, was what Russia
feared. Since the United States was not an Asiatic Power, she
suffered in China from the same disadvantages as the European
Powers, and could not conduct an effective policy without co-
operation. But Chinese politics were too closely interwoven with
European to be treated as a thing apart. Involvement in China
meant involvement in Europe, the one thing the United States
was not yet prepared to face.

---

[1] De Wollant, First Secretary of the Russian Embassy in Washington,
to the Russian Foreign Office, 7 June, 1900. Quoted by Zabriskie, op.
cit., pp. 51–2. As will appear below, it *was* during the joint action of the
Powers in the summer of 1900 that the United States was diplomatically
most active.

[2] See W. R. Braisted, 'The Philippine Naval Base Problem, 1898–
1909' in *The Mississippi Valley Historical Review*, XLI, June 1954; and
S. W. Livermore, 'American Naval-Base Policy in the Far East, 1850–
1914' in *The Pacific Historical Review*, XIII, June 1944.

[3] It should be remembered that the Panama Canal was not yet built.
American goods had to be protected by a preferential tariff even in the
Philippines themselves. Wildman (at Hong Kong) to Hay, 6 January,
1899: Hay Papers, General Correspondence, 1899.

For all these reasons, American acquisition of the Philippines was of small moment in Far Eastern policy. It was regarded by the Russians with distrust; the Germans made an effort to get at least part of the group for themselves; but in general the United States decision was inoffensive to the Powers. If they could not have the Philippines themselves, all the Powers preferred the United States to have them.[1] That was not a vote of confidence but a tribute to inertia. When the British Press welcomed the taking of the Philippines, it did so in terms that had extraordinarily little to do with the conduct of foreign policy. Even when some evidence against that statement can be found, it is not convincing. Take this from *The Spectator*:

> They [the Americans] will, we believe, from the first hesitate to give up the Philippines, partly because the islands will provide admirable stations for their fleet, but chiefly because they are determined that China, which is their biggest natural foreign market, shall not be closed to their trade. They must be ready to strike, if need be, on the Chinese coast, and to strike hard, and seeing that, they will not give up islands which offer them impregnable defences for their dock-yards, their coal-vaults, and their arsenals. To retain them is, of course, to give up their traditional policy of non-interference in the politics of the world; but we confess we have not much faith in self-denying policies of that kind.[2]

That is, no doubt, a fair statement both of what Britain hoped for from American involvement in the East, and of what American navalists and China traders thought. But only two weeks later *The Spectator* reversed itself.

> The Anglo-Saxon Alliance [it admitted] is founded not on political convenience, but on identity of sentiment and identity of the higher political interests. It would not . . . help us, except indirectly, in a struggle with Russia, for America, like ourselves, is a non-military Power, and could only give what we can ourselves supply, ships and money.[3]

These two attitudes to American policy in the Far East run

---

[1] See Griswold, op. cit., pp. 18–23; Gelber, op. cit., pp. 30–4; Shippee, loc. cit.; J. K. Eyre, Jr., 'Japan and the American Annexation of the Philippines' in *The Pacific Historical Review*, XI, March 1942.

[2] 'The Fate of the Philippines' in LXXX, 7 May, 1898, p. 646.

[3] 'Mr Chamberlain and Russia', ibid., 21 May, 1898, p. 717.

together through British writing on the subject, neither giving
way to the other. The hope that the United States would take a
strong line in the Far East to gain for both countries what Britain
was not prepared to achieve for herself struggled with the realization that the United States would not act firmly in the Far
East, though not for quite the reasons that motivated Britain.
Certainly the second was nearer the truth.

> Commerce and civilization in those lands and seas [the Far East]
> mean far more to the English and the Americans, who were the
> first to open them up to Western intercourse, than they can possibly
> mean to Powers which look immediately and chiefly for political
> domination and which do not understand the policy of the open
> door. There never was a time when it was more clearly necessary
> for all countries that are interested in keeping the trade of the Far
> East, with all its boundless possibilities of future development, from
> being fettered by the policy of Continental tariffs to stand firmly
> together.

So spoke *The Times*, and its tone is highly significant.[1] It would
be stretching criticism to complain that *The Times* used vague
phrases without considering what they meant in terms of action,
but it is clear that when it spoke of commerce and civilization
'meaning more' to the virtuous Powers than to those that sought
dominion, it was speaking of emotions and not of political action.
Britain and the United States shared not only the same interests,
but the same reluctance to defend them.

The unity of the two Powers was, indeed, in inaction. Enterprise by the one was suspect to the other. It was after they had
enquired, with no great hope of success, whether the United
States was ready to support them in Asia, that the British took
Weihaiwei. That seemed to Americans to indicate that Britain
had given up hope of maintaining the 'open door'. Their sus-
picions were reinforced by the speeches of British statesmen later
in 1898,[2] and still further by the so-called Scott-Muraviev Con-

---

[1] Leading article, 29 March, 1898, p. 9e.
[2] See especially the influential speeches of Balfour in the House of
Commons, 10 August, 1898, in *The Parliamentary Debates* (Fourth
Series), 1898, LXIV, pp. 820–36, reported in *The Times*, 11 August,
1898, pp. 7f, 8a, b, c; and of Chamberlain at Wakefield, 8 December,
1898, reported in *The Times*, 9 December, 1898, p. 7a, b.

vention of April 1899.[1] By that agreement Great Britain undertook to seek no railway concessions north of the Great Wall in
return for a similar Russian undertaking south of it. American
interests welcomed a limitation of Russian expansion, but the
seeming acceptance by Britain of the principle of spheres of
interest, even if only for railway concessions, outweighed that
benefit. It looked certain to lead to spheres for commerce as well,
and that would mean the final closing of the door. John Barrett,
formerly American Minister in Siam, summed up American
opinion. 'The move that England has recently made', he said,
'. . . has placed her irrevocably in the category of nations that
recognize "spheres of influence" . . . which are synonyms of
"areas of actual sovereignty".'[2]

That reaction was at least partly due to the different American
situation in China. American trade was chiefly with the north;
the area reserved for Russia under the Scott-Muraviev agreement
was the principal market for American cotton goods.[3] The United
States had no such region of domination as the Yangtze valley on
which to fall back — Russian advance was directly threatening.
For that reason, the occasional British resort of demanding
counter-concessions was not open to the United States, and its use
by Britain was resented there. Even Rockhill remarked that
'Great Britain is as great an offender in China as Russia itself'.[4]
It was essential to American interests that the Powers refrain
from demanding any new privileges.

When the Spanish-American War was won and the Philippines
were American, the United States did give some attention to the
Far East. The result was Hay's famous 'open door' note, the
genesis of which is now well known.[5] On 6 September, 1899,
Hay sent virtually identic notes to Russia, Great Britain and
Germany, the Powers most immediately concerned in the leasing

---

[1] Printed in MacMurray, *Treaties*, I, pp. 204–5.

[2] Speech to the New York Chamber of Commerce, 1 June, 1899.
Quoted by Campbell, op. cit., p. 52.

[3] ibid.

[4] Rockhill to Hay, 28 August, 1899: Hay Papers, 22 (from Rockhill).

[5] See Griswold, op. cit., ch. ii; Dennis, op. cit., ch. viii; Gelber, op.
cit., pp. 75–80; P. A. Varg, *Open Door Diplomat — the Life of W. W.
Rockhill* (Urbana, Ill., 1952), ch. iv.

of territory, and in November similar notes were sent to France, Italy and Japan.[1] This note was greeted with mixed feelings by most of the Powers. None welcomed it, all accepted it conditionally on its acceptance by the others. Britain raised some difficulty over the status of leased territory (a difficulty easily overcome),[2] the answers of the other Powers could perhaps be taken as satisfactory, but that of Russia was so equivocal as to constitute a rejection.[3] Hay contrived to express himself as satisfied, but the Japanese government complained that

> . . . the replies of the three Governments [Germany, Russia and France] are no more than assurances for the application of the most favored nation treatment to all nations and cannot be construed as to [*sic*] correspond with . . . non-interference with the existing treaties with China and non-discrimination in treatment between the subjects and citizens of the Powers interested and those of all other nations.[4]

That was fair comment, even on the wording of the replies, but the conduct of the Powers was to show even more clearly how little attention they were disposed to pay to the desires of the United States.

The weakness of the 'open door' policy has often been recognized, but the nature of the weakness has usually been misunderstood. It was not that the United States, 'which possessed no leasehold and claimed no sphere of interest, sought to secure a self-denying declaration from those Powers which did'.[5] That was important, but it had been argued that it was this very fact that

---

[1] Printed in *Foreign Relations*, 1899. The earlier drafts of the note are conveniently to be found in P. H. Clyde (ed.), *United States Policy towards China. Diplomatic and Public Documents, 1839–1939* (Durham, N.C., 1940), ch. xxx.

[2] For the Anglo-American exchanges on this, see P.R.O., FO 5/2408, and N.A., S.D., C8.4/50, C8.4/51, C8.5/50, C8.5/51. The changes made for publication are not important.

[3] Printed in *Parliamentary Papers* (1900), CV, State Papers, China. No. 2 (1900), (Cd. 94), enclosure no. 6 in no. 5.

[4] Enclosed in Buck (American Minister in Tokyo) to Hay, no. 434, 1 June, 1900. Quoted by P. J. Treat, *Diplomatic Relations between the United States and Japan, 1895–1905* (Stanford, 1938), p. 87.

[5] Treat, op. cit., p. 88. As he also points out, 'the United States at this very time set up a closed-door policy in its recent Asiatic acquisitions, the Philippine Islands'. (ibid.)

enabled the United States to make the request.[1] It was not even that, for all the Powers, the policy was an essentially negative one. Though the United States had nothing to offer in exchange she would not have gained anything beyond equality from her proposals. The point of importance is that there was a causal connection between the self-denying policy which the United States was urging and the vigour, or lack of vigour, with which she was prepared to back it.

The 'open door' note was clearly an appeal to international public opinion, a device to get the Powers to commit themselves in public. The history of the process by which the note came to be written makes it clear that it was Russian expansion in North China which worried American business men and which worried Hay.[2] Though it was ostensibly a circular note, the Russian reluctance to subscribe indicated that they well realized that it was chiefly directed against Russia.[3] In those circumstances, the note was an admission that the United States was unwilling to deploy any force in opposing Russia. If she had intended energetic opposition, a circular note would not have been the means employed. The Russian reply was designed to avoid unfavourable publicity, but it did not imply that the Russians intended to modify their policy, since they realized that the note could not be backed up.

The United States was not prepared to back it. In spite of the work of navalists and the China lobby, public opinion in the country would not have countenanced an active policy in the Far East, or even the spending of money on preparations.[4] Russia was still generally held to be friendly, intervention alone would be expensive, and it could be opposed as that interference with the affairs of Europe which it was still necessary to avoid. Joint intervention, though more effective and less costly, would be open to even stronger objection on the last ground.[5] Such success as the

---

[1] Zabriskie, op. cit., p. 54; A. E. Hippisley to Rockhill, 21 August, 1899. Quoted in Griswold, op. cit., pp. 70–2.

[2] See Zabriskie, op. cit., pp. 52–4; Griswold, op. cit., pp. 65–76; Campbell, op. cit., pp. 54–5.

[3] A point curiously underemphasized by Zabriskie, op. cit., pp. 55–60.

[4] See Braisted, loc. cit.

[5] See Hay to Foster (confidential), 23 June, 1900: Hay Papers, L.B. I, p. 455 (quoted below, p. 182).

note had came from the suspicion that the United States might be
roused by an attempt to repudiate it, once accepted. Where the
United States would not oppose a hostile policy, she might oppose
a broken commitment. A certain legal caution can be detected in
the policies of the Powers after the 'open door' note, and was its
only result.

The failure of the note was concealed for a time by the outbreak of the Boxer rebellion three months after Hay announced
his acceptance of the European replies, on 20 March, 1900. The
rebels entered Peking on 13 June, and, the legations in Peking
cut off and under fire, the German Minister and the Secretary of
the Japanese Embassy murdered, and foreign nationals in much
of North China dead or in danger, the Powers were, with great
reluctance, forced to co-operate. Chaos in China produced a situation so out of the ordinary that no Power could object to any step
that another might take to protect its nationals. In such a state
policies altered, but they altered in recognizable patterns and
continued to reflect the interests and strengths of the different
Powers. There were two main groups as before, those with
expansive intentions and those without. It was apparent to the
first group that the presence of the others was a danger. While
their resolution was high and their troops on the spot, they
might easily be moved to a more active policy than they would
employ at any other time. It was important to damp down the
crisis.

Japanese policy has been studied in some detail. Bold both
before and after the Boxer crisis, during that crisis it was one of
collaboration designed to prevent the partition of the Manchu
Empire. Its object was to find out what the other Powers were
likely to accept and to support that, supporting, where there was a
difference of opinion, the least onerous demands. Japan was in
favour of scaling down reparations, worked to modify German
demands on the occupation of Peking and on the death penalty
for guilty leaders, and supported the moderate American position
on tariffs.[1] That was not altruistic. While Japan was pursuing a

---

[1] P. A. Varg, 'The Foreign Policy of Japan and the Boxer Revolt' in
The Pacific Historical Review, XV, September 1946. See also Whitehead
(in Tokyo) to Salisbury (tel.), (private and confidential), 25 June, 1900:
Salisbury Papers, Bound Volume, Private — Japan (from and to) 1895–

policy of careful moderation in north China, she was planning an
— abortive — *coup d'état* in the south.[1] The same kind of motives
affected the policies of the other Powers. The policy of Germany,
which had admittedly suffered most heavily from Boxer activity,
appears to have been vindictive rather than anything more
sinister. Her demands may have been justified, but are an argument against rather than for any German designs for expansion
in China.[2] Russia, on the other hand, which had been the leader
in making demands on China, was now the first to urge that
troops should be withdrawn, and to withdraw her own to Tient-
sin. No doubt the Russians argued that they could lose nothing
and that their troops could usefully be employed in Manchuria.[3]
In the Yangtze valley, where British interest was concentrated,
the Viceroys were still in control; but the British residents had no
confidence in them and, backed by the acting Consul-General and
later by General Gaselee, commander of the British contingent
for Peking, demanded protection from British troops. Salisbury's
reluctance to meet this demand was based partly on the belief that
it would do more harm than good, but also on the conviction that
a British landing would stimulate other Powers to send forces of
their own. He finally had to give way, but his view was proved
correct. French, German and Japanese contingents followed the
British, and British influence over the Yangtze Viceroys was
weakened — a result for which, ironically, Salisbury was blamed.[4]

In all this the United States played the expected part. On 10
June, Hay telegraphed Conger, the American Minister at Peking,

---

1900, which reports an analysis of the situation by the Japanese Foreign
Minister.
    [1] M. B. Jensen, 'Opportunists in South China During the Boxer
Rebellion' in *The Pacific Historical Review*, XX, August 1951.
    [2] See Langer, op. cit., ch. xxi; also the immense amount of material
in *Parliamentary Papers* (1900), CV, State Papers, China. No. 1 (1900),
(Cd. 93) and No. 3 (1900), (Cd. 257). I have checked these publications
against the copies of correspondence sent to Pauncefote in Washington
at the time, and nothing of importance seems to have been omitted —
further evidence of an unusual situation.
    [3] ibid.; Varg, loc. cit., p. 282; Hardinge, Secretary at St Petersburg,
to Bertie, 20 September, 1900; to Sanderson, 4 October, 1900: both in
the Cambridge University Library, Hardinge of Penshurst Papers,
Bound Volume, 1898–1903.
    [4] Hargreaves, loc. cit.

'We have no policy in China except to protect American citizens and the Legation. . . . There must be no alliances.'[1] When it became clear how serious the situation was, Hay was willing to approve joint action. He made his intention known in the famous circular note of 3 July, 1900, which stated that the United States would 'act concurrently with the other Powers . . . in opening up communications with Peking . . . in acting to prevent a spread of the disorders . . . and in protecting American nationals and all legitimate American interests'. That was not startling, but the following passage described American policy as being

> to seek a solution which may bring about permanent safety and peace to China, preserve Chinese territorial and administrative entity, protect all rights guaranteed to friendly powers by treaty and international law, and safeguard for the world the principle of equal and impartial trade with all parts of the Chinese empire.[2]

This sentence has often been taken to initiate an American determination to defend the integrity of China.[3] In fact it implied nothing of the kind. It was, of course, an advance on the 'open door' note, which had left it to be inferred that equality of commercial opportunity depended on the maintenance of the Chinese Empire. That was now made explicit; it had always been assumed. Secretary Sherman had once ventured the opinion that if the partition of China came about, 'the powers would gladly seize the opportunity to trade with us. Our commercial interests would not suffer, as far as I can see, in the least — quite the contrary.' His view got no support. It was ridiculed as 'quaint and dangerous', and as yet another proof of Sherman's 'serious intellectual limitations'.[4] No one supposed that it was held by the author of the 'open door' note.

More important, the note of 3 July has sometimes been interpreted as meaning that the United States herself was determined 'to . . . preserve Chinese territorial and administrative entity . . .'. That does not follow from its wording, but if the United States had adopted a vigorous policy the wording would have been un-

---

[1] Hay to Conger (tel.), 10 June, 1900. Printed in *Foreign Relations*, 1900, p. 143.

[2] Printed in Clyde, op. cit., ch. xxx.

[3] See Griswold, op. cit., p. 81; Zabriskie, op. cit., pp. 61–2.

[4] Campbell, op. cit., p. 30.

important. In fact American policy was as cautious as before. For a time it appeared that the objectives of American policy were being reached, and that gave an illusion of effectiveness. During the Boxer period even Russia and the United States seemed to be pursuing similar policies in Chinese affairs, but that did not mean that they were in genuine agreement. Hay remarked that Russian vows were 'as false as dicers' oaths when treachery is profitable', adding, 'In this case it is for us to take care that treachery shall not be profitable.'[1] He never made clear how that was to be done. Technically, Hay conducted his policy with skill. On at least one issue his instructions were misinterpreted by Conger; but the essence of the crisis is revealed by the fact that a mistake which ruined a month's work did not matter.[2] All the Powers, except perhaps Germany, were prepared, temporarily, to be moderate, whether in order to end the negotiations and free their hands, or in order to strengthen the Chinese government. There was general agreement on preserving the integrity of China and the concert of the Powers. They were regarded as going together. That agreement concealed both fundamental differences among the Powers and the weakness of American policy.

During the negotiations Britain and the United States worked closely together, and did seem to be reaching the sort of working partnership advocated by the apostles of Anglo-Saxondom. They achieved considerable success, but against no opposition. Only under some such stress as that of the Boxer rising, however, could the United States act in concert with other Powers — and certainly with Britain — even in defence of her own interests. At other times, insistence on avoiding entangling alliances prevented not only common action but often any policy that another Power happened to be pursuing. American policy in this period has been summed up as follows:

Realizing the necessity of strengthening its position to meet the growing menace of Russia in Manchuria, the United States attempted: first, to create a common front of the powers as a counter-

---

[1] Quoted by Dennett, *John Hay*, p. 317.
[2] Hay to White, 23 December, 1900: Henry White Papers, and Hay Papers, L.B. II, p. 76; also the official correspondence between Hay and Choate: N.A., S.D., from London, Vol. 201.

weight to the separate designs of Russia and, second, to render
treaty relations between China and the other powers more effective.[1]

Both policies were an indication of weakness, and hard as Hay
tried to conceal the fact, he almost certainly recognized it. The
'common front' was never a real possibility. As Hay remarked,

> . . . anything we should now do in China to take care of our im-
> perilled interests, would be set down to 'subservience to Great
> Britain'. France is Russia's harlot — to her own grievous damage.
> Germany we could probably get on our side by sufficient concessions
> and perhaps with England, Germany and Japan we might manage
> to save our skins. But such a proceeding would make all our fools
> throw fits in the market place — and the fools are numerous.[2]

The object of each Power, in short, was to get the other to do
the work in preventing the break-up of China. Hay was very
conscious of a rising sentiment against Britain in the United
States, which he felt tied his hands. China politics were increasingly complicated by conflicts over Alaska and the isthmian canal.
But the real obstacle to effective co-operation was the determination of the United States not to become involved in European
politics. It was difficult to translate an understanding which
existed only on the level of emotional sympathy into effective
terms. It may be that it was only possible to speak in terms of a
natural concord between Britain and the United States so long as
two conditions were fulfilled. The first was the activity of Russia.
As long as Russia was aggressive in the Far East, the notion of
community of interest had some reality in the common desire to
check her. But another condition was required. Neither Britain
nor the United States must adopt a strong policy. If either had,
Russian aggression might have been effectively checked, but the
idea of a natural community of interest could not have been
maintained.

The political virtue to which publicists in Britain and the
United States laid claim was, not surprisingly, political indifference. The interests of both countries in the Far East were commercial; if those of Britain were more, she had other interests

---

[1] Zabriskie, op. cit., p. 65.
[2] Hay to Foster (confidential), 23 June, 1900: Hay Papers, L.B. I,
p. 455.

elsewhere which were of greater importance. In the 1890s it seemed for a time just possible that commercial interests might be interpreted as also strategic interests — that was the importance of the doctrines of necessary competition between nations that achieved popularity then. In the event, however, those doctrines did not become sufficiently dominant to produce real political action. Probably they could only be maintained as long as they were never put to the test. The community of Britain and the United States was a passive one.

Britain then had to turn to other Powers for support. The agreement of 16 October, 1900, with Germany, proved useless. When the time came to make use of it the Germans insisted that it did not refer to Manchuria.[1] Their European position again prevented them from opposing Russia. It is probable that Salisbury knew as much when he made it, and quite certain that Hay knew it. Hay's objections were on the ground that it would be useless, not that it would be disadvantageous to the United States.[2] Equally, the Anglo-Japanese Alliance was not unwelcome to the United States while Russia was still the threat. As Lodge wrote, 'The Anglo-Japanese Treaty was, of course, very good for us, for it is in the direction of the policy for which we have been working, and it was well received here.'[3] The Japanese alone had interests to defend that were not merely commercial; as a result their opposition to Russia was effective, and as a further result they proved as antipathetic to the trade ambitions of the United States as Russia had ever been. That was not, however, obvious till after the Russo-Japanese War. By that time, Anglo-Saxondom as a political cry was already dead, and international attention had turned away from the Far East.

Two letters from Hay to Roosevelt as late as April 1903 sum up

---

[1] See Langer, op. cit., pp. 700–3, 717–23. British efforts to get German support continued. See J. A. S. Grenville, 'Lansdowne's Abortive Project of 12 March, 1901 for a Secret Agreement with Germany' in the *Bulletin of the Institute of Historical Research*, XXVII, November 1954.

[2] Sanderson to Hardinge, 24 October, 1900: Hardinge Papers, 1898–1903; White to Hay, 27 October, 1900: Henry White Papers; Hay to President McKinley, 26 October, 1900: Hay Papers, L.B. II, p. 46; Choate to Hay (personal and confidential), 31 October, 1900: Hay Papers, 19.

[3] To White, 10 March, 1902: Henry White Papers. See Griswold, op. cit., p. 89; Zabriskie, op. cit., p. 81.

American policy in the Far East, as it affected Britain. Rumours of a new Russian-Chinese banking agreement which seemed to infringe American rights had reached Washington, and Hay had been moved to protest, or at least to invite an explanation.

> The Russian Secretary, speaking in behalf of Cassini [he wrote], explained to me that the power aimed at was England and not ourselves, but the first two clauses of the [Russian-Chinese] convention are apparently injurious to us. . . .
>
> I am sure you will think it is out of the question that we should adopt any scheme of concerted action with England and Japan which would seem openly hostile to Russia. Public opinion in this country would not support such a course, nor do I think it would be to our permanent advantage. Russia is trying to impress us by the most fervent protestations that, whatever happens in Manchuria, our national interests shall not suffer. This is an object which I have been striving for for four years, and if worse comes to the worst, I think we can gain it; but there is something due to self-respect also, and it is pretty hard to stand by and see an act of spoliation accomplished under our eyes.
>
> I am hurrying these cables off today before any of the Powers approach us on the subject, so that the record may show we acted without concert.

Three days later he was writing,

> I had an hour's serious talk with Cassini on Sunday. . . . He did not admit a shadow of a doubt as to the right and the determination of Russia to insist on her demands, and I was equally frank in telling him that I considered them inadmissible, and in the highest degree disadvantageous to Russia herself.
>
> I have as yet got no replies from Conger or from McCormick. I take it for granted that Russia knows as well as we do that we will not fight over Manchuria, for the simple reason that we cannot. . . . If our rights and our interests in opposition to Russia in the Far East were as clear as noonday, we could never get a treaty through the Senate the object of which was to check Russian aggression.[1]

The hopeful feature, concluded Hay, was that Russia was really afraid of Japan, and aware that Japan might fight on slight encouragement from Britain or the United States. Ultimately, of

---

[1] Hay to President Roosevelt, 25 and 28 April, 1903: Hay Papers, L.B. II, pp. 425, 428.

course, Russian fears proved to be well-founded, and Japan accomplished the object for which Britain and America had both been unwilling to combine.[1]

As a basis for effective political action, then, the idea that the Anglo-Saxon nations had interests in common proved useless. In the Western hemisphere it derived from the willingness of Britain to withdraw and her inability to do anything else; it was used to cover her withdrawal. In the Far East it concealed the fact that neither Britain nor the United States had interests that she was prepared or able adequately to protect. The exponents of race expansion, influential in both countries for a brief decade, exaggerated the importance of China; but they were able to avoid the implications of their own assessment by relating it to the inevitable expansion of a race, not to national policy. When the time came to demonstrate its cohesiveness and vigour, the Anglo-Saxon race proved a fiction.

---

[1] We still do not know just how seriously the Russians took the possibility of a more vigorous American policy in the Far East between 1898 and the Russo-Japanese War. For a recent discussion of some Russian evidence, see E. R. May, 'The Far Eastern Policy of the United States in the Period of the Russo-Japanese War: a Russian View' in the *American Historical Review*, LXII, January 1957. Neither the Russian historians whose work May discusses nor the Russian statesmen on whose writings they base it are completely reliable witnesses. The verdict must be open, but it remains unlikely that the Russians were seriously alarmed by American policy and certain that, if they were, their fears were unrealistic.

CHAPTER SEVEN

The Nature of the 'Rapprochement'

WHEN Britain and the United States came into conflict at the end of the nineteenth century it was as a result of new demands, of larger ambitions, on the part of the United States. Those demands, however, were related, as such demands usually are, to accepted American traditions. The United States had developed in relative isolation from Europe, isolation which had come to be taken for granted. That America developed behind the guns of the British fleet is a commonplace of present day historiography. It was by no means so obvious to the Americans of fifty years ago, though Mahan, Brooks Adams, and a handful of others were beginning to take the point. As George Kennan has reminded their descendants,

> those Americans had forgotten a great deal that had been known to their forefathers of a hundred years before. They had become so accustomed to their security that they had forgotten that it had any foundations at all outside our continent. They mistook our sheltered position behind the British fleet and British Continental diplomacy for the results of superior American wisdom and virtue in refraining from interfering in the sordid differences of the Old World. And they were oblivious to the first portents of the changes that were destined to shatter that pattern of security in the course of the ensuing half-century.[1]

The shift in viewpoint has, however, been overdone. American security till the 1890s *was* based at least as much on her policy of remaining aloof from events outside her own continent as on British protection. The first, indeed, was a necessary precondition

---

[1] G. F. Kennan, *American Diplomacy, 1900–1950* (London, 1952), p. 5.

of the second. True, the United States before the Civil War could not have protected the continent against a serious European attempt at encroachment. But then, between the Spanish loss of her South American colonies and the growth of the new colonialism at the end of the century there was no serious European attempt to establish political dominion in the western hemisphere. The characteristic event of those years is Russia, not only willing but eager to get rid of Alaska, selling it to the United States in 1867 for some seven million dollars, a ridiculous sum whose size can be judged by comparison with the fifteen odd million dollars paid by Great Britain at about the same time in settlement of the *Alabama* claims. Throughout most of the century the British fleet protected the United States at a time when she needed little protection. No wonder the Americans of 1898 thought they were the architects of their own security.

When, at the end of the century, conditions changed, the British fleet was of little use to the United States, and was quickly seen to be of little use by the generation that fell under the spell of Mahan. That was not because in some new and rash enthusiasm the European Powers were casting greedy eyes on the Americas, and the British fleet was inadequate to protect them, but because the United States herself could not long avoid being caught up in the wave of imperialist fantasy which surged over Europe. The same causes which might have made the British fleet useful prevented the United States from continuing in her placid acceptance of its presence. Nothing is more futile than to attempt to understand the Spanish-American War in terms of any rational calculation of self-interest. Americans were swept off their feet in a wave of unreasoning emotion against which the few voices that attempted to stem it resembled nothing so much as the woman with the mop immortalized by Sydney Smith.

During the Spanish-American War British policy, and still more the support of British opinion, won for Britain a considerable harvest of uncritical American gratitude. Yet the British attitude was possible, and was effective, for two reasons neither of which was long to continue. The first was that the war was begun, and chiefly fought, in a region contiguous to the United States and subject to much the same strategic considerations as if it had been on the continent itself. (Chichester's gesture in Manila harbour has gained by its dramatic quality an importance it did not possess.) The second and more important reason was that the Americans themselves carried over into their new expansiveness traditional attitudes and preconceptions. For years the foundation stone of American foreign policy, both as reiterated in orotund oratory and as expressed in practice, had been just the virtuous abstention from the sordid quarrels of Europe noted by Kennan. The extent of their new ambitions was only slowly realized. The language of Congress and the Executive in the discussion which preceded the Spanish-American War owes, for the most part, far more to such well-established American ideals as concern for liberty and self-government than to any enlarged notion of the American part in world politics. Nor was this hypocritical. If we can now look back and see in that discussion a classic example of self-deception by a whole people, if historians point out now, as the Spaniards pointed out then, that Spanish concessions were more than adequate to meet the demands Americans thought they were making, the important thing for the present argument is just that self-deception. Others were deceived too.

A tradition to which such constant reference was made had obviously considerable vitality. In the Far East, the first area of American interest,

> up to 1898 — indeed to 1900 — the American policy of respect for the territorial integrity of the Far Eastern nations had the effect of a purely self-denying ordinance. It did not enjoin on the United States the obligation of defending this territorial integrity from others. The U.S. was then able to keep free of serious involvement in the politics of Eastern Asia.[1]

Even long after 1900 American intervention in world affairs was often ineffective because half-hearted. The new ideas of expansion, economic imperialism, strategic interests on the other side of the globe, the importance of sea power, fought a long battle with the older conception of the United States as a nation apart, fortifying on the North American continent a shining citadel for free men, a nation with only the most secondary interests abroad. Both survive today; but there can be no doubt how much the second has modified the first.

---

[1] Griswold, *Far Eastern Policy of the United States*, p. 7.

The two conceptions did not, of course, necessarily come into direct conflict. Sometimes, as during the Spanish-American War, they mingled and strengthened each other. It was plainly in the western hemisphere that they conflicted least. There the idea of manifest destiny, that the future of the United States necessarily included domination over North America, or even the Americas, had been a commonplace for a generation. It had often been suggested, in many tones of voice, that it was only a matter of time before Canada was acquired. When the United States began to extend her claims Britain, having been at some pains to keep other European Powers out of the western hemisphere, was now the Power with which she came most obviously and forcibly into conflict. The British position was challenged and strongly, not to say rudely, challenged. As the three occasions of conflict — Venezuela, Panama, Alaska — were all in the Americas, so there was very little doubt or self-criticism in the American challenge. The expressions of American politicians and public opinion on those issues (and sometimes those of responsible statesmen too) were marked by the loudest kind of self-assertion. British resistance would have been, whatever its outcome, more protracted and effective than that of Spain. The British government and public hardly considered it.

What, then, was the British attitude towards the new pretensions of the United States? First, surprise that any conflict should have arisen, a refusal to believe that after at least thirty years during which the United States and Britain had had no cause for disagreement of major importance to either, any could now arise. A habit of regarding the western hemisphere as an area which could be ignored had developed and was not lightly broken. Since Canning's day Britain had accepted, and had helped to make others accept, the idea that the *status quo* there should not be disturbed. When in the 1890s she came into conflict with the United States, it was natural to suppose that there must be some mistake. No one in Britain could suppose for a moment that there had been any change in British policy, that Britain was making any new demands. Her resources were fully engaged elsewhere. Therefore, if there had been no cause for disagreement with the United States before, there could be no valid cause now.

Yet it might be supposed that British consciousness of British virtue would lead to the obvious conclusion that the United States must be making some new and revolutionary claim, some outrageous aggression. That was not so. There was an assumption of goodwill, a readiness to believe that there must have been some mistake, which is not to be found in British dealings with the European Powers. A number of elements can be analysed in this attitude. First is the simple fact that the United States was the newest factor in the equation, and that men's habits of thought change slowly. Britain had been concerned for centuries to match the shifts in power and prestige of European states by new stratagems of her own. The points at issue might range from the Channel to China but the underlying preconception remained the same. The growth of imperialism enlarged the scope of European competition and stretched British resources further than before, but the tendency was to see it as an extension of the old problem. Increasingly difficulties which, whatever their setting, had their origin in Europe, were fully engaging British attention and energy. The British were the less ready to debate the exact significance of new American pretensions because it was highly inconvenient for them to do so.

The newest, the least known, factor in the equation was the easiest to cancel out. A concession to the United States was the least possible concession, the least revolutionary, the one that involved least analysis and least reorganization of Britain's world position. Such an attitude, useful as it was, meant that most British statesmen were underestimating the effect of the rise of the United States. It was not only a new phenomenon, but by far the most important in generations, for Britain as for other countries, and they were slow to take proper account of it. In part, this was no more than the conservatism induced by the conduct of foreign policy; and it was doubly excusable at that time. British statesmen might have been more ready to make fundamental assessments of policy had their attention not been directed elsewhere. But more important, American expositions of American policy made underestimation of its importance easy. British analysts could follow American in carrying over into the new era the mental conventions of the old.

In minimizing the importance of American ambitions, the

British could point to the fact that, initially, American claims were confined to the western hemisphere. Americans themselves went to a good deal of trouble to insist that their aggressions were not new, but no more than a logical extension of traditional claims, an extension which nature itself would limit. It was easy to maintain that the Monroe Doctrine, offensive as its immediate expression might be to Britain, was really a limitation on the activities of the United States. This argument was used on both sides of the Atlantic. As Andrew Carnegie protested, Britain could not 'fairly grudge her race here one continent when she has freedom to roam over three'.[1] From this it was only a short step to the idea that if the United States could be induced to take charge of the Americas, it would be a positive advantage for Britain. Once allow other European Powers to become involved there, and the results for Britain would be unpredictable but probably expensive. An enhanced determination by the United States to prevent that was welcome even if it reacted on Britain. If Americans themselves were so slow to admit their new pretensions, so eager to identify them with the old, British acceptance of their arguments is understandable.

Anglo-American relations did not, of course, deal in abstractions like these. The disputes were real and immediate, but their confinement to the western hemisphere had other consequences. It had long been established British policy that the western hemisphere was not an area open to European expansion. When Canning initiated it he had trade chiefly in mind; the policy now paid a different dividend. Europe had, on the whole, accepted the injunction laid down in the Monroe Doctrine. Though Germany was now suspected of cherishing designs on Brazil — the British Press was generous in warnings to our American cousins that they must keep an eye on the Kaiser[2] — there was in the event no European activity in the Americas. The United States would have opposed attempted expansion by any other Power quite as vigorously as she opposed Great Britain; but American antipathy was

---

[1] 'The Venezuelan Question' in the *North American Review*, CLXII, February 1896, p. 142.

[2] A favourite line with *The Spectator*. To select one article from many, see 'The Meaning of the Venezuelan Settlement' in LXXVII, 14 November, 1896, p. 665.

to any involvement of Europe in the western hemisphere, and not merely to expansion. The same Monroe Doctrine which was invoked against Great Britain forbade the United States to get support from Britain's rivals. The same American traditions which until the Spanish-American War were against adventures outside the Americas led the United States to play a lone hand in diplomacy. When the expansionists had won their first success this tradition of operating alone remained, and decreased both the immediate effectiveness and the larger impact of American foreign policy.

Outside the Americas the refusal to enter into joint action was undoubtedly a weakness in American policy, since it often implied a reluctance to act at all. Long after 1900, and even in those regions such as the Far East in which the United States claimed consideration, American policy could be discounted, and was, by the European Powers. This inevitable weakness was hardly felt when the arena was Venezuela or Panama. There, indeed, the United States actually gained from having no commitments elsewhere or to any other Power, gained, in short, from concentration of strength. The tradition of isolation did, however, mean that a conflict with the United States could be treated as a thing apart, unaffected by European politics except in so far as these modified the resources Britain could spare. Not because of the unimportance of the matter in dispute, but because of American determination to avoid commitments, a concession made to the United States involved no weakening of the British power position in Europe.

These considerations did not prevent real friction between the two countries. They came into play at a later stage, when a crisis had arisen, and helped to moderate its effects. Surprise that there could be any dispute — always about matters which most Englishmen had hardly heard of — was inevitably followed by annoyance at the brusquerie of the United States and a firm resolution to defend an old position against unwarranted American expansion. American braggadocio caused great irritation, and outspoken assertions that the United States must have her way, however unimportant the issues and whatever the cost in offence, were treated firmly. 'It is not the custom of this country', snapped *The Times* on one occasion, 'to conclude treaties of surrender with

any nation — even with those whose friendship we value most —
and that is a custom from which we have no mind to depart.'[1]
Even this, however, was not quite the reaction that was felt towards the activity of other nations. It was modified by the unwillingness already noted to suppose that there could be any real
ground of difference, and for that and other reasons it was easily
assuaged. In fact Great Britain signed what *were* virtually treaties
of surrender on a number of occasions, but a very small amount of
diplomatic camouflage apparently sufficed to conceal the fact.

The idiosyncrasies of United States diplomacy helped, in a way,
in achieving this result. The very brusquerie which did so much
to annoy made it difficult, somehow, to take Americans quite
seriously. When an American President decided to settle himself
a dispute between two independent states, one of them a Great
Power, or the American Senate spoke as if it had the right, of its
own action, to abrogate a valid treaty with a Great Power, the
magnitude of the affront to the established standards of diplomatic conduct distracted attention from the real question at issue.
The first reaction was resentment — how dare the President or
the Senate adopt this tone with Great Britain? — but it called up
its own antidote of amusement. No man or body of men so innocent of the ways of the world, so ignorant of the proper way to
behave, could be regarded as a serious menace to Britain or as
cherishing any deep designs against her. The very different
British reaction to the Kruger telegram is paradoxical. His breach
of diplomatic manners did not lessen the Kaiser's offence. In part
at least the explanation is that the Kruger telegram was out of
character. The Germans did not normally behave like that. They
knew better, and must be presumed to have some deep and
hostile reason for breaking the rule — even if it was the Kaiser's
doing. With Cleveland it was not the manner that startled, so
much as the evidence that the United States felt strongly about
Venezuela — not that he was rude, but that there was anything
to be rude about.

The important characteristic of American diplomacy, of which
brusquerie was no more than a symptom, was its obvious lack of
calculation, its rash spontaneity. That was noted and held unto the

[1] Leading article, 19 December, 1900, p. 9*e*.

United States for virtue, though its most obvious implication was enormous confidence. Americans themselves paid so little regard to the effect of any action of theirs on the international scene, that it was natural for men of other nations to ignore those effects too. There was a concentration in their diplomacy on the immediate and ostensible object that was unique. When the United States undertook to settle the boundary dispute between British Guiana and Venezuela, most Americans thought of themselves as dealing even-handed justice and protecting a small state from oppression. Their action was devoid of any desire either to score a diplomatic victory at the expense of Britain, or to obtain advantages for themselves in South America, though it had both these results. When the United States decided to take Cuba — for whatever reason — very little regard was paid to the larger implications of a war with Spain. Americans really wanted Cuba, or the control of the Panama Canal, or a given boundary in Alaska; and they were able to convince themselves that it was mere justice that they should have these things.

An attitude so direct had both advantages and disadvantages for a country in conflict with the United States. In the American discussion of, say, the canal issue, there was necessarily plenty of reference to American interests — and even strategic interests — but extraordinarily little calculation. Once established that American interests demanded an American canal, the next stage in the argument was that no country of goodwill would oppose the demand. Opponents of the United States were not ill-advised or merely furthering their own interests, but malevolent — since the demands of the United States were reasonable — and their opposition proved that the initial demands had been justified. This made Americans extraordinarily tenacious in dispute and impervious to compromise, but it meant also that they were not engaged in the constant battle for compensation and prestige which was the essence of European diplomacy. The American insistence on a canal treaty of American dictation had nothing in common with, for instance, the British demand for Weihaiwei because other Powers had just acquired ports. American diplomacy in those days competed with none, and Britain was relieved of the need to compete. Both these characteristics of American foreign policy can be found long before the 1890s. They were survivals from an earlier age. The objects of American policy changed more rapidly than habitual methods of conducting it.

These arguments suggest that the instinctive British feeling, that the United States was unique and could be treated differently from any other country, was sound. But they were not the arguments used at the time. The British attitude had other roots. A great part of the explanation of British willingness to withdraw came from a sense of kinship with Americans felt towards the people of no other country. When *The Economist*, though grumbling that the upshot of the Venezuela crisis was something of a defeat for Britain, nevertheless continued that 'we may congratulate ourselves on the avoidance, though at some cost, of a quarrel which our own people regarded with disgust as a kind of civil war',[1] it was voicing no more than the general opinion. The British took a pride in the achievements of the United States, in its growing strength and wealth and population, as one takes pride in the achievements of one's descendants, and gave the credit to the Anglo-Saxon stock which had first settled the country. America was an English-speaking nation, flourishing by British virtues, owning British institutions, a daughter country in whose self-assertiveness even there was cause of a sort for satisfaction, though the immediate victim might be Britain herself.

The notion of identity of race was central in British thinking about America. The United States was regarded as an Anglo-Saxon country, and little attention was paid to the other diverse strains which went to make up its population. The United States, in fact, was treated as a branch of the British Empire which, owing to a regrettable misunderstanding, had broken away and achieved political independence in the past. This fact naturally seemed of smaller and smaller importance at a time when the imperial trend was towards increasing political autonomy. The links holding the Empire together were far from merely political. Canada controlled her own internal affairs. In external affairs she was a considerable nuisance. The problem of giving what support they could to the (often unreasonable) demands of Canada, at a time when imperial feeling was very strong, without earning the hostility of the United States, was one which bedevilled British

---

[1] 'The New Horizon' in LIV, 14 November, 1896, p. 1488.

statesmen all through these years. Yet despite all that, imperial
ties were strong enough to bring Canada unasked into the Boer
War. It was natural to regard the United States as another
example, though perhaps a deviation from the classic pattern, of
the British tendency to spread over the globe, something not to
be opposed but to be applauded.

Only this view can explain both the endless references to 'our
American cousins' and 'the trans-Atlantic branch of our race'
which can be quoted from the writings of the time, and the
readiness with which qualities infuriating in anyone else were
explained and excused in Americans. Were Americans brusque
and discourteous in speech? Plain blunt-spoken Englishmen had
never had the subtle — and by implication double-dealing —
suavity of French and Italians. Were Americans aggressive and
domineering? They were only displaying the same drive and
energy that had made Britain great. Always the question that was
never adequately faced was why this expansive energy should be
unexceptionable in Americans, and not in, say, Russians. The
answer was not that they were good democrats, but that they
were British. The acceptance of kinship was not, indeed, new.
One can find references to 'Brother Jonathan' in the British Press
much earlier than the 1890s. But such phrases were then used in
scorn as often as in friendship. What was new was the assumption,
implicit in the use of phrases like 'the trans-Atlantic branch of our
race', that ties of race created ties of sympathy, and that civilization itself depended on the strength of the ties.

As the United States was rose-tinted, so also was the relationship between the two countries. Salisbury's speech at the Guildhall
announcing the satisfactory conclusion of the Venezuelan dispute
was a masterly example of how to display a defeat, not as a victory
— victory over the United States was never what British opinion
wanted — but as an honourable compromise, a triumph for
Anglo-Saxon common sense and fair play. Salisbury, of course, had
the most obvious reasons for trying to give this impression, but the
readiness with which it was accepted — had indeed been accepted
in essence many months before—is remarkable and characteristic.[1]

---

[1] See ch. ii. Salisbury's speech was fully reported in *The Times*,
10 November, 1896, p. 4e, and discussed in all the reviews.

The British sense of kinship with Americans owed, indeed, surprisingly little to any similarity of political tradition or theory. At few times have ideological considerations been less effective in the determination of European foreign policies than at this. The division between the liberal and the autocratic powers of Europe which had had some reality following the Napoleonic War had almost disappeared. Britain found it no easier to come to terms with the Third Republic than with Imperial Germany or Russia, and owned a tenuous tradition of friendship with Austria-Hungary. Among the Powers of Europe at least, no differences of ideology important enough to modify the calculations of shifting alignments were to be found. The fear of revolutionary doctrines had died down with revolutionary enthusiasm; the increasing competition among the states of Europe, competition outside the continent, meant that one found allies where one could. In comparison with the 'lesser breeds without the law' whom they were concerned to exploit or to civilize, the differences among themselves diminished in importance. The world was divided into states which came within the operation of the public law of Europe, the Powers and the small nations which existed among them, and the rest.

The pattern of British thinking was most clearly shown at the time of the Spanish-American War. There was in Britain as elsewhere in Europe a good deal of sympathy for Spain, sympathy for gallantry in decline. In Europe the feeling went further, and there was a strong sentiment for intervention on behalf of Spain. The difficulty of forming a European concert, and the danger of acting without one, together with the known temper of the United States, were strong arguments against action, and even the Germans confined themselves to fishing in troubled waters. The British position was a crucial one, if only by virtue of sea power, and it is plain that both British official policy and the bulk of British opinion was friendly to the United States. There was calculation in this, of course, but also much uncritical enthusiasm for Anglo-Saxon advance. Latins were inefficient colonizers — far better to let the United States take over Cuba and the Philippines. Indeed the two elements went together — the calculation assumed the advance. If Spain lost the Philippines, Britain was anxious for the United States to keep them, as the least awkward of possible owners, but also on the assumption that American involvement in the Far East would be profitable to Britain.

It is doubtful if this feeling of kinship was reciprocated to any great extent. The American population was already largely of other origin than British, a fact the British Press was apt to ignore. The assumption in Britain of sympathy between her and the United States caused a good deal of irritation there even among those who were not of German or Irish stock. As for these latter, they were always ready to see the hand of Britain in American policy, and their loud objections were a constant source of embarrassment to the Executive. British statesmen were aware of the extraordinary sensitivity of the United States to anything that might be considered interference in her domestic affairs, or to any suggestion that she was tied to Britain. They were apt to regard this sensitivity as springing more from the Revolution and republicanism than from the real differences between the two countries — and indeed these elements were also present, important in the Anglophobia of a man like Henry Cabot Lodge. They saw it as a kind of neurosis rather than anything more, anything that need shake their sense of kinship. Nevertheless, they remembered well the uproar caused by Sir Lionel Sackville West's innocent incursion into American politics when Minister in Washington, and were not disposed to underestimate American sensitivity. 'They are deeply interested in it here,' wrote Henry White of the prospect of McKinley's re-election in 1900, 'and quite understand that they must not let this feeling be known.'[1] Chamberlain's speeches almost certainly did more harm than good — his speech at Leicester on 30 November, 1899, produced a storm of American dissent — but even Chamberlain usually confined himself to generalities and was careful not to assume too much.

These are valid reservations, but the British feeling was not absurd. There was a real concord between the two countries; the reservations imply only that in the United States it did not have the same narrowly racial base. Americans could not avoid sharing the ideas current in Europe. There was plenty of race sentiment in the United States, but the history of the country and the com-

---

[1] To John Hay, 26 May, 1900: Henry White Papers.

position of its population made the expression of that sentiment so various and complex that it was ineffective in directing policy.

The hostility to Britain of Irish and German Americans was of limited effectiveness. The dominant groups in the United States were still of English or Scots-Irish stock, and, though prepared on occasion to adopt a defiant American policy in opposition to Britain, still felt more sympathy for her than for any other country. The non-English stock in America, when most politically effective, made its effect by acting as a racial opposition, and principally in state or local politics. Just as the Irish vote in England could on occasion bring parliamentary business to a standstill but could not direct it to any more constructive end, so the racial minorities in America were limited. They could elect Senators, they could hamper Executive policy, but, if only because the constitutional role of the Senate is to prevent activity, not to further it, they could do little more. They either remained detached minorities with comparatively little effect on policy or merged in the general population.

When the latter alternative happened, it was remarkable how fully they adopted the whole outlook of the earlier settlers. As Nathan Glazer has pointed out,

> everywhere the first-comers were Anglo-Saxons . . . the economic prosperity attendant on the superior technique of the immigrants did not give them the power to mold the cultural and political life of the state. Again and again it can be seen how the first few thousand settlers in an area had far more weight in this respect than hundreds of thousands who came later. They set up the school system; the legal system; they wrote the state constitution; they had the most political experience; they had the prestige which led the later coming majority — or at least their children — to conform to *their* standards, rather than vice versa.[1]

In so far, in fact, as Americans were primarily Americans, and not displaced Germans or Irish, they accepted the attitudes and prejudices of the dominant Anglo-Saxon stock.

These attitudes and prejudices, however, were themselves far from simple; and they were not, as American diplomacy shows,

---

[1] Nathan Glazer, 'America's Ethnic Pattern' in *Perspectives*, IX, Autumn 1954 (reprinted from *Commentary*, April 1953), pp. 141–2.

so wholly well-disposed towards Great Britain as were those of the British towards America. Pride of race among Americans of British ancestry there was, and a growing suspicion of newcomers of other stocks. The Progressive movement expressed a good deal of resentment against the immigrants from south and east Europe whose ready obedience to party machines was ruining American politics. The demand for immigration control was already under way. The lamp had hardly been lifted beside the golden door before men were urging that its welcome was too indiscriminate. Yet in the most Anglo-Saxon of Americans pride of race struggled with an inherited, republican distrust of Britain as the old — and the perfidious because the related — enemy, a distrust which was not so much a prejudice as an article of faith, and to which they clung the more because they could not use against Britain the weapons which were so effective against the rest of Europe. In an extreme example like Henry Cabot Lodge, cultured, conservative, arrogant, this struggle fatally warped his political judgment.

American sympathy for Britain, then, could not have a simple racial basis. Successful political leaders threaded their way through a complex of emotions, their own and their followers'. A consideration of the views of Theodore Roosevelt may throw some light on the problem; he was the most successful and one of the most articulate if not quite a typical specimen of the group. Roosevelt was a remarkable figure, open to the gibes of cartoonists and humorists even in his day, and his ideas were not general; but he would never have gained his huge popularity had they not made a large appeal, and in a cruder and less original form they were widely shared.

It was one source of Roosevelt's strength and one of the best qualities about him that, where individuals were concerned, he had remarkably little racial feeling. He could meet a Japanese, a Samoan, an Indian, and assess them as men; and many of his judgments of events were modified by his friendship with some representative of the nationality concerned. Nevertheless, he could not avoid the general characteristic of his time of judging races and nations as a whole. He could not help regarding some races as inferior to others. Thus most of the brown, black and yellow races he found inferior, with perhaps a mental reservation in favour of the Japanese; but their day was not yet. The Germans he approved, for their efficiency, their masterful qualities, their militarism and their energy. (The British, he thought, were not sufficiently aware of the potential of the Germans.) The Russians, too, he respected. They were handicapped by backwardness, they were barbarians, but tough, thrusting barbarians who might yet have to be opposed by force. The Latin races on the whole he despised as effete, and cruel through fear and weakness. With these views Roosevelt combined, though in a complex form, most of those ideas that have commonly gone with racism — respect for the fighting man, a primitive code of chivalry, emphasis on the family as a unit (with its tendency to nepotism), and so on.

Two elements can be isolated from Roosevelt's philosophy as relevant to this study, the first shared with Britain, the second unique to the United States. The first was the general extension of biological thinking and biological analogies into political thought until even many who were unconscious of the influence came under it. It was a commonplace that nations like species competed for survival, that by a kind of political evolution a race held a dominant position till its natural vigour faded or its power to adapt to new circumstances declined, when some new power would drive it out and take its place. The weakest would go to the wall, on this theory, not because of malevolence on the part of the strong, but because it was in the natural order of things for the strong to prey on the weak.

The natural order was ethical as well. It would be immoral as well as impracticable to interfere with the process, since it was to result in the survival of the physically and mentally fitter race on which the whole progress of mankind depended. 'This dependence of progress on the survival of the fitter race,' said Professor Karl Pearson speaking for many others, 'terribly black as it may seem to some of you, gives the struggle for existence its redeeming features; it is the fiery crucible out of which comes the finer metal.'[1] The struggle for existence was assumed. It was taken as a fact. What was needed was to prove it moral. Neither *Machtpolitik* nor doctrines of race conflict strictly depended on Darwin's work or involved the idea of natural selection. But the theories of

---

[1] *National Life from the Standpoint of Science* (London, 1901), p. 24.

the racists gave a moral basis — of a kind — to national conflicts, and affected the choice of an opponent which they did so much to make necessary.

The idea that strife was necessary to the health of nations probably flourished more strongly in Britain than anywhere in Europe except Germany. It did not, however, exclude a strong sense of trusteeship towards peoples so backward as to be outside immediate competition. This is not the place to discuss at length the complex of ideas summed up in the phrase 'the white man's burden' or its connection with social Darwinism; both were strong in Britain. The political tradition of the United States modified greatly there any sense of a duty to lift less fortunate peoples towards the light, though Americans could not altogether avoid ideas so current in the western world. But to the notion of a necessary struggle among advancing aggressive nations they were particularly prone. Nor were the two ideas unconnected. Incompetence in colonial government was one of the first symptoms of decadence. The well-being of dependencies could be invoked as a reason for removing them from weaker rulers.

While these ideas might be held to foster sabre rattling in diplomacy, each nation striving to assure itself and others of its virility, nothing in them demanded that tests of strength should be sought. The emphasis was on disposing of the weak rather than on challenging the strong. Spain was feeble; better for all if the United States took over her tasks — to condense the half-spoken argument. Arguments like this could readily lead to a kind of accommodation among the Powers. The idea of a preventive war was at a discount. Britain, like the United States, was obviously strong, a force for the furtherance of civilization. In the circumstances the United States, like Britain, came strongly to feel that there was a kind of larger alliance, overriding differences in policy, between nations so plainly bound to the same task of furthering the advance of man, and sharing so many of the same qualities. The obvious solution to conflict was a division of the spoil.

So far Britain and the United States could agree. They differed in that no American conscious of the diverse origin of his people could hold the narrow racial view of Anglo-American affinity taken in Britain. By a minor adaptation, however, racism could be incorporated into the American philosophy. A distinction could be drawn between the individual and the group, and in the United States, with its tradition of welcoming men of all stocks and forging them into a new nation, the distinction was an easy one. That there was excellent stuff in individual Spaniards or Frenchmen, that they had something to give to the new race, need not as yet be denied — the theory of the 'melting pot' had not yet been effectively challenged — even while it was maintained that as a group on their native soil they were decadent. Yet if not race, there was need for some other cohesive principle to hold the new nation together. No country was better fitted to provide it than the United States, the outstanding example of a state founded on a political theory. The United States was a nation endowed with both the vigour and the opportunity to propagate those principles of liberty and equality established by the Founding Fathers.

The Boer War provided an excellent test. There arose in the United States a considerable outcry against what appeared to many an open aggression by Great Britain for the crassest material gain against two innocuous small republics battling for existence. Not only was there considerable racial sympathy among German Americans for the Boers, but the magic of the word 'republic' (together with the discrepancy in size between the contestants and the gallantry of the Boers) blinded many Americans to the real questions at issue. As at the time of the Venezuela crisis they tended to assume virtue in a republic and vice in a monarchy, especially that against which they had won their own independence. Nevertheless, the United States government firmly refused to take any action, however formal, in favour of the Boers. It would have been difficult for them to do anything effective, but the studied friendliness to Great Britain of Roosevelt and Hay went far beyond the strict demands of neutrality. A considerable body of opinion could be found in the States to uphold the view that, monarchy or no monarchy, the Anglo-Saxon tradition of political freedom and social equality flourished in Britain as in the United States and could not survive in the racist republic of Oom Paul. Roosevelt himself, who felt a strong emotional sympathy for the Boers, hardy open-air individualists good with horse and rifle such as he admired, felt bound to admit that they were a small and backward group, and that the advance of civilization in South Africa demanded a British victory.[1]

This suggests that similarities of ideology which were then of secondary importance in Europe were of the first importance in the United States. British emphasis was on qualities of the race which peculiarly fitted it for rule. American emphasis was on the possession of those sacred principles which marked the highest point yet reached by mankind — to make no less modest claim. Americans not only recognized the real similarity of institutions and political outlook between the two countries, but were even prepared to deduce from them alignments of economic interest. At a time when the United States tariff was steadily rising, Britain and the United States were held to share a unique concern for free trade in other parts of the world. Principle was not absent from the British position. The possession of a civilizing mission, after all, involves having something to impart and the British, without conscious hypocrisy often though they were accused of it, regarded themselves as spreading the blessings of Christianity, parliamentary democracy and British fair play. But principle played a still larger part in American imperialism. Because it had to overcome a living tradition of isolation it was more articulate, more theoretical, than the British variety. Anglo-American sympathies, where they existed, were based, in Britain on a sense of racial community, in America on a sense of ideological community.

The difference is not a minor one of emphasis. It is fundamental and of wide importance. Clearly the American analysis was more rational and more in accord with the facts. The two countries *did* share important political principles and practices. Racial community was a far more dubious basis for concord. It would have been stronger if 'Anglo-Saxon' had been used merely as a shorthand description of a whole complex of qualities essentially cul-

---

[1] Morison (ed.), *Roosevelt Letters*, II, to J. St L. Strachey, 27 January, 1900 (no. 1460); to C. A. Spring Rice, same date (no. 1461); to F. C. Selous, 7 February, 1900 (no. 1496); to A. J. Sage, 9 March, 1900 (no. 1550); III, to A. H. Lee, 18 March, 1901 (no. 1958). H. H. Bowen, 'American Public Opinion of the War' in the *Nineteenth Century*, XLVII, May 1900; and E. J. Hodgson, 'An American View of the Boer War' in loc. cit., XLVIII, August 1900. Both these emphasize pro-British opinion. For American policy see J. H. Ferguson, *American Diplomacy and the Boer War* (Philadelphia, 1939).

tural which Britain and the United States had in common. Sometimes the word was used in just this way — the British attitude was not entirely unreasonable — but the choice of a racial term, loosely used, to sum up cultural attributes is suspicious. The American analysis of Anglo-American relations could be checked against the facts. It was relevant to political action. The British analysis could not be used in the same way. It was one thing to argue that countries with the same political beliefs have something important in common, and that they should co-operate in spreading their advantages. It was quite another to deduce some mystic sympathy from a common origin, a sympathy whose major characteristic was that it need never, and could never, be tested.

The important difference between Britain and the United States, then, lay not so much in what they said about each other, as in the political philosophy on which their opinion about each other was based. In the United States similarities with Britain were emphasized, and differences from Britain minimized, under the influence of a new concept that was generally applied. For some influential political leaders a traditional hostility to Britain was modified, for others a sympathy for Britain which had other origins was strengthened, by racial thinking. But British activities — and sometimes American — could be tested by Americans against the principles to which both countries laid claim. In Britain, on the other hand, racial thinking supported an attitude to the United States which could have no other foundation, and which differed in kind from that to any other country.

The distinction made in Britain between the United States and other countries is striking. It was not reciprocated in America, but it owed what realism it had to a more fundamental peculiarity of American foreign policy. The American approach to foreign policy may have been rational, but it was also unique. However imperfectly, it treated the domestic politics of other states as relevant in the discussion of American policy towards them. In this it differed from the general practice of the Great Powers at that time. The American sense of mission had not weakened, even if the image of America was losing its effectiveness in the radical mythology of Europe. Americans still did not think of themselves as like other peoples, as members of a nation state like other nation states. How was this possible? The answer is in the stage which American emergence from isolation had reached.

It is not too fanciful to draw a parallel between this period of American foreign policy and Jackson's tenure in the development of the American Presidency. Jackson was dictatorial by temperament, a man who liked to exercise power. He was extraordinarily conscious of the dignity and importance of his office. As a result he was extraordinarily sensitive to anything that might be considered an affront to the Presidency, and met any challenge with exaggerated vigour. These traits might have damaged American government far more than they did. If Jackson had given them free rein, his activities would certainly have roused more opposition; but they were held in check by his Jeffersonian distrust of government, all government. Jackson resented limits set to his power, but the limits he set for himself were narrow. American foreign policy in the 1890s might be described as Jacksonian. There is the same confidence of power. There is the same enlarged sense of dignity. There is the same sensitivity to anything that might be considered an affront, however unimportant. And there is the same sort of check on all these traits, a distrust of international relations and a reluctance to engage in them.

The phenomenon was a temporary one, and necessarily temporary. Paradoxically, the limits set by tradition to the exercise of American power enabled Americans to exaggerate that power, and to ignore the context in which it would have to be exercised. It was already supposed that the United States would shortly play an important part in world affairs, but she was not yet playing that part. It was therefore still possible to maintain old notions of the nature of foreign policy which could not survive the test of practice. (They have proved remarkably durable, but they have steadily been forced to give way.) Isolation had bred enormous confidence, which survived after the end of isolation. American ideas were incompatible with the exercise of power, but not with a sense of power. This was hardly understood in Britain. American aggressiveness was ascribed to other causes, and judged by other standards. The judgment was faulty, but it made for good relations.

It is not difficult to expose inconsistencies in British thinking about the United States. The inconsistencies were there, and any attempt to summarize British opinion is more apt to reveal them than to account for them. Britain was undoubtedly taking the brunt of the new American energy and interest in foreign affairs. It might have been that it was worth while to put up with this in the expectation of future gain, to encourage the United States to foreign adventure in the belief that a strong America with a strong foreign policy could only be of advantage to Britain. This belief was indeed present in British thought. But American activity in the western hemisphere provided little basis for it. There was no need to postulate hostility to Britain in order to reach the conclusion that American interests might conflict with British elsewhere than in the Americas. The assumption that they would not do so was logically unsound. Another British argument did nothing to strengthen it. For British opinion tended, when convenient, to minimize the importance of American activity by regarding it as limited in area and not related to any consistent world policy. Britain need not take American activity in the western hemisphere too seriously, since it would go no further. Not weakness, of course, but the American political tradition would prevent it. On this hypothesis any benefit to Britain from American policy was unlikely to be great.

The second argument was the better of the two. The United States gained half her strength in Venezuela or Alaska from the fact that she could neither be threatened nor be bribed in other parts of the world. More, the very ideas which made the United States strong on her own ground weakened her elsewhere. (Theodore Roosevelt may have introduced some real understanding of the implications of *Weltpolitik*, but he was a political accident.) American policy during the Boer War was friendly, and the friendliness was of considerable benefit to Britain; but it was entirely negative, it consisted in avoiding effective sympathy for the Boers and in looking after British interests in Pretoria. Since it was clear that there was no likelihood of American intervention it was not necessary to bid very high for American support, and British treatment of American shipping, though reparation was made later, was severe. American policy in China has been recognized as feeble, the 'open door' note notwithstanding. It is true that any American policy in the Far East was likely to profit Britain, and what logical content there was in British policy towards the United States had this as its origin. But on their own assumptions the British might have seen that American policy would have very little effect.

There is a third point. If American activity, when the two countries clashed, was not based on anti-British feeling — and the British Press insisted that it was not — then presumably it would be very difficult for any British action to make that policy pro-British. Either American interests would lead the United States to pursue a policy favourable to Britain, in which case there was no need to buy the favour, or to one unfavourable to Britain, in which case nothing could be done. This is over-simplifying the logic, but there is no evidence that this line of reasoning occurred to anyone but Salisbury. In general, a determination not to conflict with the United States was concealed behind an assumption that no conflict would arise.

The simplest explanation of British policy is that Britain gave way to the United States at the end of the century merely because she could do nothing else, because the demands of imperialism had stretched her resources too far to meet a new challenge. It is probably impossible to say whether external circumstances or the special elements described in this book were more important in Britain's American policy, but certainly those elements were very important. It is impossible to imagine the Englishmen of Palmerston's day, for instance, whatever the circumstances, reacting in the same way to the activities of the United States. Palmerston foresaw American expansion, but he did not suppose that it would necessarily benefit Britain, and he thought it should be opposed as far as possible. The prospect he foresaw gave him no pleasure. A generation later his successors thought otherwise. It has been a chief object of this study to argue that they did so irrationally.

Their irrationality was less in the assessment of policy than in the deductions they made from it. The policy of the United States might be judged hostile; it was not judged *naturally* hostile, the hostility did not conform to a larger pattern, it was not what one would have expected. This appeal to nature is implicit rather than explicit in writing about foreign policy in the late nineteenth century. The appeal to nature had slipped out of the language of political thought, and to reintroduce it is strictly an anachronism. Its use seems legitimate, however, to illuminate an attitude of

mind which was of great importance. The language of international Darwinism, with its reference to the race struggle, was,
after all, employing a 'natural' metaphor. But more than that,
even when 'natural' language has no footing in current political
discussion, some activities are apt to appeal to the emotions as
natural, and others as not. The extent to which these emotions are
rational ones may vary, but they are effective even when they are
extraordinarily difficult to justify.

Generalization from so limited a study must be tentative; but it
may be worth suggesting that although irrational emotions con-
fuse judgments of policy, they change, no less than does policy,
in response to changes of power. The changes of power may be
relative, between the two states concerned, or absolute, affecting
the place of both in a larger power structure. They modify
national attitudes far more than changes of policy do.

If there is any truth in this suggestion, the development of
Anglo-American relations may have been somewhat as follows.
The power relations between the two countries fall, broadly
speaking, into three periods. The first is that in which the United
States was both small and distant, something that could be ignored
in the consideration of power politics. The second is that in which
the two countries were roughly comparable in power. The third,
of course, is that in which the United States is very much more
powerful — though it is perhaps permissible to envisage a time
when the growth of other states will make power differences between Britain and the United States less dominant in the relations
between them.

The first period is that in which the dominant image of the
United States — in the rest of Europe as well as in Britain — was
that of the embodiment of a radical political theory. This role is
one that can be played inoffensively only by a small state, and
safely only by a state remote as well as small. A shift in power
beginning about the time of the Civil War — after which the
United States began to move towards the status of a Great Power
— made its impact on the British consciousness towards the end
of the century. It became less easy to think of the United States
as the harmless embodiment of a political theory when that
country was already outstripping Britain in population and indus-
try. The prevalence at that time of Darwinian theories of race

and the race struggle dominated the new image. Those theories themselves hardly survived for more than twenty years, but the image they had helped to induce survived rather longer. When it began to break down it did so because of a further growth in American power which made inappropriate an image developed in response to a situation of rough equality. To this latest shift we are still slowly adjusting, as we cling to our old power pretensions. The change may take another generation to complete.

Anglo-American relations in the late nineteenth century, then, display the elaboration of an unusually effective myth. (The word myth here indicates not an idea which is merely false, but one which, whatever its content of truth, is sufficiently persuasive to influence men's judgment of reality, and so their political behaviour.) In one respect, however, this myth is somewhat unusual. The normal function of a myth is the justification of larger claims than reality allows. It is essentially a moral weapon. Men try to defend old privileges in a changing society, or to justify the demand for new ones, by describing their role in society in terms which, bearing some relation to reality, do not conform to it. This myth is different in that, so far from justifying a sense of grievance, it minimized it, allowing a larger measure of concession than would have been possible without it.

The contradiction is a real one, but its resolution may lie in the peculiar nature and the extraordinary rigidity of the nation state. Myths concerned with the place of man in society are dealing with a fluid medium. Claims can be enlarged or diminished in an infinite series of small gradations. But the relations of nation states are well defined and closely interlocking. There can be no enlargement of the claims of one which does not strain the whole complex structure. Nor is this rigidity incidental. Debate about the moral nature of man and the proper structure of society is unending, and it frequently involves debate about the nature of the state. But such debates have almost always been internal to the state. It was in its international relations that the state earliest acquired rigid definition, as the protector and the collective voice of the people who composed it, a definition as yet effectively unchallenged, and certainly unchallenged at the end of last century.

When, in these circumstances, two nation states came into

conflict, the only possible use of a political myth was in minimizing the claims of one. That was its use in Anglo-American
relations; but to be effective the myth had to have larger reference
than the nation state, and had to appeal to the race. The concession of British interests was made in a context which could
represent it as the furtherance of Anglo-Saxon interests. The
climate of opinion which fostered imperialism, which strained
British resources and brought Britain and the United States into
conflict, also bred the theories of human progress and the sense of
kinship which prevented withdrawal from appearing defeat.

INDEX

Adams, Brooks, 157, 186

Adee, A. A., 102–3

Alaskan boundary dispute, 3, 182, 187, 189, 194, 207; and isthmian canal negotiations, 49, 50, 53, 64–5, 96, 97, 102, 105; contrasted with Venezuelan dispute, 89, 96, 97, 124; summary of, 89–91; *modus vivendi* in, 89–90, 92–5, 99, 102, 104, 106; Russo-British treaty of 1825, 90–1, 100, 104, 105, 117, 121 n; Canadian arguments, 90, 95–6, 98; attitude of British government, 99–100, 102–4, 105; arbitration proposals, 96–9, 104–105, 109–13; proposal for lease, 100–2; influence of Roosevelt on, 105–8, 111; discussions in London, 108–9; the arbitration tribunal, 113–16; its result, 117–18; British reaction to result, 118–24; Spanish-American War and, 155

Aldritch, Senator, 57

Alverstone, Lord (Lord Chief Justice), 114, 116, 117, 120, 123

American foreign policy, moral content of, 22–3, 25, 205–6; limits of, 125, 190–2, 206; British reaction to, 189–91, 192, 195–7, 206–8; tradition of independent action, 191–2; brusquerie of, 192–3; *The Times* on, 192–3; spontaneity of, 193–195; isolation and, 205–6; 'Jacksonian', 206

American-Canadian Joint High Commission, 49, 84, 91–2, 97, 98, 100, 104, 118, 126

American Civil War, and Spanish-American War, 148, 151

Anderson, Sir John, 109

Anglo-American concord, Russian view, 171; basis of in United States, 198–200, 204; myth as basis of, 210–11

Anglo-American conflicts, survey of, 3

Anglo-American relations, inter-pretations of, 4–5; British attitude towards, 9–10, 45, 196; and Venezuela, 45–6; contrast with Anglo-German, 9, 78; and Hay-Pauncefote Treaty, 79, 82, 83–4; *The Spectator* on, 79, 82; *The Times* on, 83–4; and Alaska, 118; American attitude towards, 198, 200, 204–5; and power changes, 209–10; social Darwinism and, 201–3, 204–5, 208–209; political myth in, 210–11

Anglo-Chinese agreement of 1897, 161

Anglo-Japanese Alliance, 8, 183

Anglo-Saxon race, in Far East, 181, 183, 185; British ideas of, 195–198; American ideas of, 199–200, 203–4; and Anglo-American relations, 210–11

arbitration, in Venezuela crisis, 12–13, 20–1, 26, 27–9, 38–9; general agreement on, 38–9, 40–41; in Alaskan boundary dispute, 96–9, 104–5, 109–13

Armenia, 147

Armour, J. D., 114

Ashmead-Bartlett, Sir Ellis, 37, 118

Asquith, H. H., 26

Austria-Hungary, 138, 141, 144, 145, 166

Aylesworth, A. B., 114 n

Balfour, Arthur, 37–8, 39, 73, 118, 143–4; 145, 166

Barclay, G., 136, 138, 139, 140

Bayard, T. F., 17, 19, 23, 26

Beresford, Lord Charles, 162, 170

Bertie, Francis, 15 n, 26

Boer War, and British policy, 8, 51, 55, 74, 102, 106, 207; Canada and, 51, 196; and Spanish-American War, 153; American attitude to, 203–4

Boxer rising, 55, 102, 158, 178; policy of Powers, 178–9, 181; Lord Salisbury and, 179; American policy and, 179–81; Anglo-American cooperation, 181–2; *see also* China

46–7, 196; and isthmian canal negotiations, 49–51, 53, 64, 71; and Alaskan boundary dispute, 100, 102, 103–4, 125; and Spanish-American War, 137, 138, 141, 143; and Far East, 167–8, 179, 183

Sanderson, Sir Thomas, 17

The Saturday Review, 43, 150–1

Schomburgk line, 13 and n, 20, 27, 29

Scott-Muraviev Convention, 174–175

sea power, limits of British, 29–31

Senate, and American policy, 77–8, 110, 199; and isthmian canal negotiations, 50, 53–9, 64, 77, 81, 83, 193; and Alaskan boundary dispute, 101, 106, 110–11, 112, 113, 118; and Cuba, 132, 143; and Far East, 184

Sherman, John, 169, 180

Sino-Japanese War, 157, 161, 163, 164

Skagway, 97, 98, 103, 105, 123

Smalley, G. W., 17, 18 n, 37

South Africa, in British policy, 27, 32 n, 34

South America, Germany in, 32–3, 36, 191; American hegemony over, 39, 44, 45

Spanish-American War, 33; and isthmian canal, 48, 54; the Powers and, 127–8, 133, 135–6, 137, 138, 140–6, 154; and Anglo-American relations, 127, 146, 153–4, 155, 187; Spain in Cuba, 128–9, 134–5, 138, 139–141, 147–8; Spanish policy, 127–8, 130–1, 133–4, 135–41; the *Maine* explosion, 131–4, 136, 139–40, 141; American policy, 129–31, 132, 134, 136–145 *passim*, 187–8, 189, 192; British policy, 133–4, 137, 138, 140–5, 154–5; British opinion on, 146–54, 197–8; and Alaskan boundary dispute, 155; and Far East, 169–70, 175; *see also* Cuba *and* Philippine Islands

The Spectator, 46, 79–80, 82, 122–123, 124, 152, 165, 173

'sphere of influence' policy, 158, 161–2, 175

Strachey, John, 80

Suez Canal, 52, 62

The Times. 7, 9, 20, 37, 78, 83–4, 102, 147, 174, 192–3

traders, in China, 159–63, 168–70, 177

trans-Siberian railway, 163, 165

Tribune (New York), 55

Turkey, and Spain, 147–8; and China, 147, 158

Turner, George, 114–6, 122

United States, image of in Britain, 9–10, 205, 206–8, 209–11; characteristics of policy, 186–9, 190–5, 199–200, 202–6

Venezuela crisis, 3, 189, 192, 193, 194, 207; summary of, 11–21; character of Cleveland and Olney, 21–4, 193; Salisbury's attitude, 24–7, 31, 35–6, 196; British concessions, 27–9; British and American strength compared, 29–31; the Powers and, 31–4, 35–6; British opinion and, 36–40, 41, 42–6, 195, 196; American opinion and, 14, 16, 40–2, 194, 203; U.S. negotiates for Venezuela, 27, 39, 44, 45; and Alaskan boundary dispute, 89, 96, 97, 98, 103–4, 123, 124

Venezuela, Anglo-German action in, 119–20

Villiers, Francis, 96, 98, 109, 113

Walker, J. G., 56

Weihaiwei, 164, 174, 194

Weyler, General, 134

White, Henry, 198; and Venezuela crisis, 19 n; and Hay-Pauncefote Treaty, 49, 50, 55, 64; and Alaskan boundary dispute, 97, 108, 111

Woodford, General, 130, 132, 136–137, 138, 139–40

Yangtze Valley, 162, 175, 179

Yukon, 89, 90, 91, 101–2. 103, 125